D1613528

TRADERS' SECRETS

Psychological
&
Technical Analyses

Real People
Becoming Successful Traders

Murray A. Ruggiero, Jr.
Adrienne Laris Toghraie

Foreword by Alpesh B. Patel – author of *Mind of a Trader*

100 Lavewood Lane
Cary, North Carolina 27511

A Division of Trading on Target

Ruggiero Press
18 Oregon Avenue
East Haven, CT 06512

A Division of Ruggiero Associates

First Published in the United States January 1999
Second Printing July 1999
Third Printing September 2007

© Trading on Target
© Ruggiero Associates

The right of Adrienne Laris Toghraie and Murray Ruggiero to be identified as
authors of this work has been asserted by them in accordance
with the Copyright, Design and Patents Act.

ISBN 978-0-9661837-3-3

All rights reserved: no part of this publication, unless
indicated may be reproduced, stored in a retrieval system, or
transmitted in any form or by any means, electronic, mechanical,
photocopying, recording, or otherwise without either the prior written
permission of the Publishers or a license permitting restricted
copying in the United States issued by the
Copyright Licensing Agency Ltd.

This book may not be lent, resold, hired out or otherwise disposed of by way
of trade in any form of binding or cover, without the prior consent of the
Publishers.

MURRAY A. RUGGIERO, JR., is president of Ruggiero Associates in East Haven, Conn., a firm which specializes in the development and testing of market timing applications using state-of-the-art computer technologies.

One of the world's foremost experts on using intermarket and trend analysis to locate and confirm developing price moves in the markets, Murray has been called "The Einstein of Wall Street" by those who know the value of his amazing work.

Some say Murray comes by his analytical abilities naturally, having been raised around the research laboratories of Yale University by a father who held 29 patents. Whether that tale is true or not, Murray is one of those rare individuals who loves dealing with statistics and mathematical data., and he thoroughly enjoys the challenge of using that data to help solve real-world trading problems.

Murray's personal and work history reflects his attraction to mathematics. In college, he earned his degree in Astrophysics – hardly a major for the mathematically challenged.

After college, Murray began working on neural net and Artificial Intelligence (AI) systems for applications in the investment arena.

As a result of that work, Murray's reputation as a system developer quickly grew, and it wasn't long before some of the most powerful names in the investment world came to him for help.

John J. Murphy, the "Father of Intermarket Analysis," noticed Murray's work early on, and on several occasions invited the young analyst to appear as a guest on his CNBC television show. Murphy remains one of Murray's staunch supporters, openly applauding the practical applications of his work.

Business Week magazine recently featured Murray as one of the nation's leading experts on using neural networks in finance and investing.

Dozens of high-profile traders and professional money managers seem to agree; they come to Murray for analysis and systems development work on a regular basis.

Unlike many in the ego-driven investment world, Murray has no desire to keep his research results only for himself. He has published more than 50 articles on Intermarket Analysis and other subjects over the years, in *Futures* magazine, *Omega* magazine and several other prestigious periodicals.

Murray's first book, *Cybernetic Trading*, revealed details of his market analysis and systems testing at a level seldom seen in the investment world. Reviewers were universal in their praise of the book, and it became a "best seller" among systems traders, analysts and money managers alike.

In addition to his other published works, Murray's own bi-monthly *Inside Advantage* newsletter includes not only the results of his analysis and system testing, but also the computer code that allows readers to input his systems into their own computers. Murray's willingness to openly share "proprietary" information is like a magnet to traders, attracting thousands of subscribers worldwide.

ADRIENNE LARIS TOGHRAIE, MNLP, MCH, is a trader's coach, an internationally recognized authority in the field of human development and a master practitioner of Neuro-Linguistic Programming (NLP) for the financial and business communities. She is the founder and president of *Trading on Target* and *Enriching Life Seminars,* two companies dedicated to helping traders, sales people, and other high achievers to dramatically increase profits and success in all areas of life. Using her 20 years of study in the science of Modeling Excellence, Neuro-Linguistic Programming (NLP) and numerous other forms of psychological development, Ms. Toghraie has helped her clients to push through their self-imposed limitations to extraordinary and documented new levels of success.

Over the past nine years, Adrienne Toghraie has interviewed and coached the most successful people around the world: What makes these great people unique? What makes them so successful? The answers to these and other questions are explored in her seminars, books, and tapes, which form the core of Ms. Toghraie's Modeling Excellence work with professionals who want to reach higher levels of success. Ms. Toghraie's public seminars and private counseling have achieved a wide level of recognition and popularity, as well as her television appearances on CNBC and keynote addresses at most of the major industry conferences.

Adrienne's articles and interviews have been featured in most of the major financial trade magazines and newspapers throughout the world. She has authored *Get A Life: Treasure Diary for Creating Wealth and Happiness*, *The Winning Edge 2: Traders' and Investors' Psychological Coach in a Book*, and *Dear Coach Potty Training for Traders, Brokers & Investors*. and co-authored *The Winning Edge: How to Use Your Personal Psychological Power in Trading and Investing* with Jake Bernstein.

Table of Contents

Dedicated to:

Our Clients

Acknowledgments to:

The team efforts of these extraordinary people made this book possible:

Roger Reimer
Chief Editor

Wendy Clouse
Coordinator

Antonia Weeks
Editor/Writer

James Geuder
Final Editor

and especially to the real traders in this book.

Foreword

Alpesh B Patel

author of

The Mind of a Trader: *Lessons in trading strategy from the world's leading traders (FT Pitman 1998)*
Trading Online: *A step-by step guide to cyberprofits (FT Pitman 1999)*

Traders' Secrets passes the two requirements for any book to become a classic - it combines crystal clarity with original, insightful detail. Each chapter describes the methods of its interviewee in precise detail. It further provides a psychological profile and context. Too often trading books provide minimal generalizations about trading strategies and systems, and worse, yet negligible detail about all important trading psychology. Consequently, *Traders' Secrets* is a fresh, original and valuable break from the norm in trading books.

The interviewees in this book have been tremendously helpful and generous in describing their methods, systems, backgrounds and years of research. They come from a variety of backgrounds - fundamentalists, intuitive, technical analysts, stock, futures, commodities traders. There is something for all traders in here. Modeling oneself on the success of others is probably the best way to success for oneself. Why wait to learn from your own mistakes when you can learn from the years of mistakes and successes of others?

A feature of the book I found particularly valuable was the interviewee profiles based on analysis and psychology. These ensure that no one should finish a chapter feeling they did not 'suck the marrow' from it and learn every single valuable lesson contained therein. This feature of the book also amplifies its clarity and means the reader can test the systems for themselves and see what suits their own personality. It's about time more trading books were written with a similar concern for the reader.

The subtitle *Real People Becoming Successful Traders* only modestly hints at a vital feature of the book, namely that these interviewees are 'real', 'normal' traders who have proved successful. They are traders with whom the reader can more readily relate than if they were the Soros's or Buffet's of the world. And this is very important yet novel. The traders in this book probably make far better trading models than the big institutional traders or fund managers who employ whole research departments and Nobel Laureates to form their systems. (Although, I understand that Nobel Laureates can be a distinct trading disadvantage.) The interviewees in this book, unlike some trading 'wizards' will not baffle the reader with fuzzy logic, artificial intelligence or undisclosed black box systems. The analysis used by these successful traders is open to all.

In researching my own books, probably the most important lesson I have learnt from meeting and interviewing some of the world's best traders is that there is no substitute for hard work, planning and self-discipline. Trading appears deceptively easy, especially in a world of Internet brokers where online accounts can readily be opened. If you want trading success, your path will be shorter and more direct if you read this book.

Introduction

Adrienne Laris Toghraie

A year ago, Murray called to say that he had a great idea for a book that he would like to write with me about people who came into trading from other professions and how they eventually made their living trading. Murray said that these traders would not necessarily be "market wizards" because he wanted the book to be about people to whom the average person could relate. While I thought the idea was an excellent one, initially I declined. I remembered a conversation with Jack Schwager, who wrote *Market Wizards,* in which he told me that an interview book was much harder to write than a book in your own words. Well, obviously, Murray talked me into it because he was right - it was an excellent idea.

And Jack Schwager was right too. The most difficult part of writing an interview book is turning conversational language into readable language while maintaining the individual flavor of each personality. After the first four editings, we sent the chapters to our traders for any additions or deletions they might want to make. Some were prolific writers and made dramatic changes, while others hardly changed a word. Because we wanted this book to be about the people we interviewed (and not about us), we did not attempt to impose a consistent structure on the book. Each individual we interviewed is unique. While we worked with an outline, we allowed each person to share his life and trading methods with you, the reader, as much he was willing to do. For that reason, some of the chapters are significantly longer than others, some chapters do not have charts, and some traders tell you precisely how they trade, while are unable to put their trading technique into precise words.

As Murray and I worked on this book, we realized that we could create a modeling study from the material on each trader. Again, we went beyond the original interview and asked each trader to make additions to the study. When we found that many of the same statements applied to each individual, we decided to include the most salient points, the qualities that we thought stood out, plus the qualities which our traders thought should be added.

Then Murray and I took the book one step further. We felt that our own unique backgrounds gave us each a perspective on our subjects, which we could also share with you, our readers. The result is the technical analysis provided by Murray and the psychological analysis provided by me. In my psychological analysis, I chose one quality of each person to model as most of the traders had most of the qualities.

Having worked with hundreds of rookie and veteran traders who wanted to become better, Murray and I knew about the invaluable trading knowledge that could be gained from the experiences of real people coming from a variety of professions to become traders. In the following pages, we are proud to offer real life trading experiences that can provide insight, inspiration, guidance, and possible solutions for all traders as they work to become "Masters of the Markets."

Note: We have included the interview dates because references were made to particular trades or specific time periods.

CHAPTER 1

Yousef Hashmi

The Canadian Don Quixote - How a successful broker, money manager and private trader used psychology to trade his account from $100 thousand to $3 million in 1998.

Tell us about your family and where you were born?
I was born April 16, 1961, in Canada in the small town of Moncton, New Brunswick. My father had grown up in Pakistan and immigrated to Canada in 1957, and then he met my mother. He worked as a civil engineer for the Canadian National Railway until 1985. I have one brother and one sister.

As a boy, I loved sports, mostly hockey and basketball. Later, in grade eleven and twelve, I began playing golf. Now I play golf competitively. The other activity that filled my free time was reading books about personal development, such as Anthony Robbins "Peak Performance Strategies and Modeling," and following the market. I started following the market when I was in grade nine or ten.

Did your Mom work?
Initially, she worked out of the home. But, basically, she was a stay-at-home mom. When I came home from school, she was always there. My childhood was spent in a very traditional type of setting, "Leave it to Beaver" type stuff.

Tell us about the time period of high school?
I was an average "C" student. I liked economics, psychology and history courses.

During the time that my Dad was an engineer, he bought a small corner store with gas pumps. A few years later, he bought a couple of motels. My Dad and Mom stayed at one motel while my brother and I operated the other while we were in high school. It was a neat experience to learn many different skills at such a young age. It was also very beneficial to be on my own because going off to the university was not such a big adjustment.

What university did you go to and what did you study?
I attended the University of Prince Edward Island in Charlottetown, Prince Edward Island in Canada, which is where I reside today. I started studying business, but I did not like accounting. So, I switched to economics and graduated in 1985 with a Bachelors Degree in Economics.

When you were attending the university, did you run the motel?
No. I worked odd jobs such as painting, and I worked at golf courses in the summer months. I liked to party, play golf, and socialize in my free time.

You got interested in the markets at a very young age. Would you tell us how that happened?
I became interested in the markets when I was in grade 10 because my father knew "absolutely zero" about the market. One of his colleagues gave him a "hot tip" to buy Brunswick Mining, which was a silver mining company.

When did this happen?
Somewhere in the 1975 to 1978 time frame, which was when the silver markets started moving. The silver and gold markets had big moves in 1980. The mining company stock peaked out at $44 per share. I started following it every day because my father owned a $1,000 worth of this stock. Curiosity increased my interest in the stock market, because I wanted to know why he did not make a profit when he could have.

In high school, I wrote a report on the market. From that time on, I knew that I wanted to become a stockbroker/trader. Through my father's little bit of exposure to the markets, my eyes were opened to the opportunities and away I went with it.

In what activities did you participate in college?
During college I began to play golf competitively. I refereed hockey games and also worked as a campus police officer, which made it easier to get into social events.

What did you do directly after college?
In the fall of 1985, I tried to get a job as a broker all the way from Toronto down the East Coast, but there were no openings for a beginner. So, I painted houses until I finally got a job on January 4, 1987, as a broker in Halifax, Nova Scotia. I stayed there until the summer of 1988. I went through the Crash in October 1987, and the brokerage firm went through restructuring, which put me out of work at the age of 25. Without being properly trained as a broker, I went with another firm selling tax shelters for nine months. This firm eventually went bankrupt. At that point in time, I started my own business distributing industrial lubricants to heavy equipment operators and contractors.

In 1992, I reentered the brokerage business when a friend told me that ScotiaMcLeod in Charlottetown needed someone, a brokerage where I had contacts! I have been with ScotiaMcLeod ever since.

Do you consider yourself a broker? A trader? A money manager? Or all of the above?
All of the above. My clients accept my advice on what to do with their investment decisions. Most brokers focus on selling product, but I view myself as managing people's money for them.

How much money do you manage now?
I manage over twenty million dollars, and growing.

Do you trade equities only?
Sixty percent of my business is options on U.S. stocks. The rest is stocks and bonds. I do trade OEX during the week of expiration for myself.

How did you do?
I started trading my own account very unsuccessfully with two thousand dollars in the summer of 1993.

What is your definition of unsuccessful?
Roller coaster syndrome would be a good description. I was not actively trading because I was building a client base as a broker at the same time. I really did not get into trading actively until March of 1995.

So the problem was that trading was not a priority in your life back then?
No, and since it was not a priority, I was not successful.

As a broker, I was looking at fundamental analysis, which did not pinpoint a way to make money. The manager of the office introduced me to technical analysis of the markets. I found technical analysis really worked because price action is more important than the fundamental analysis. While fundamental analysis was great reading, it did not make money.

What education led you to technical analysis?
The first book that I read on technical analysis was William O'Neil's book, *How to Make Money in Stocks*. His strategy is coined as CANSLIM.

So, are you a 'CANSLIM guy'?
Yes, I am a 'CANSLIM guy' with modifications. I do not like small cap stocks. It is not good for the options market either.

I combined both technical analysis and fundamental analysis, which works for me. I use CANSLIM, basic charting patterns, double tops and bottoms and trend lines. I consider myself a trend follower.

I also read Martin Pring's book, *Technical Analysis Explained*. After applying technical analysis, I was able to take $4,000 and build it the next three months to $15,000 by March of 1995. Then it up and dropped down to about $10,000. I continued to be on this yo-yo cycle.

With that small account you probably were not using what you would consider sane money management practices today?
No, because my minimal contract size was about 10. Based on my present money management skills, I was betting 25% to 30% of my equity on each trade. While I seemed to be getting technical analysis down, I did not know anything about money management. Back then I had a hard time finding any books on money management.

In 1995, there was a technical analysis seminar presented by the Canadian Society of Technical Analysts in Toronto. There were four speakers to be presented - Ralph Acampora, Ed Seykota, Mark Douglas, and one other speaker. After meeting Mark Douglas, I read his book *The Disciplined Trader*, and attended a two day seminar he was giving in Toronto. My account went to $25,000 in about one month, and kept on moving until it peaked at $75,000. Then, there was a drawdown to about $40,000. Now I was still yo-yoing the account, but at a higher level.

Were you trading other people's money, too?
In the options department, yes.

And how are you doing for them?
I have many accounts that were up 400% in a year, but the accounts were only $6,000 to $10,000 U.S. Now, I will not take an account of less than $50,000 U.S.

Why did the drawdowns get so high?
By this time, I was trading 100 to 200 contracts and making all kinds of money. Then the market started getting choppy and moved against me. I tend to trade more from the long side. I was buying too large of a position in volatile markets that were expiring worthless. If you buy 100 contracts at two dollars, which equals twenty thousand dollars, it does not take long for the equity to drawdown quickly.

Were you overtrading?
Absolutely. I was trading a minimum of 40 to 50 contracts and would not back down. That is why the equity levels would drop so rapidly.

Since the positions were too large, did you have a problem of holding on to a loser a little too long?
Yes, because once you start thinking about the capital involved, it becomes more difficult to take a loss. When you start hoping and wishing about a trade that the market will come back, you know you are done.

If you are long the market, you tend to focus on the uptick, as opposed to the downtick. You are not focusing on the information that the market is telling you at that moment. It took some time to learn that, but with the help of the Mark Douglas Program, I learned to interpret market information much better.

In the summer of 1997, I moved the account back up to $75,000 and made $200,000 in the months of June and July buying stock options on Micron Technology. I called it the 'Micron Effect' because I made $200,000 on trading one position. I kept pyramiding the position with the options. When I closed the position out, I had made about $250,000. The problem is that I felt so powerful, on top of the world. It was an exciting ride to make a windfall of that size by following the market and getting each tick. I was flowing with this stock. Something like this can be the worst thing that can happen to a trader because rules tend to be forgotten in a situation like this. My contract size went up to 300 contracts because I was pyramiding the position up. The market can humble a trader quickly.

Do you think about reducing risk by cutting down size and actually risking 5% of capital?
That started happening after the 'Micron Effect.' After that trade, I went to Las Vegas and met Adrienne at the Dow-Jones Telerate Conference and went to her presentation. Now, I am conscious about what I do, and how I do it. If I am not flowing with the markets, I reduce the contract size of my position and will buy in five or ten lots. Before I thought trading lots under 50 to 100 contracts was a waste of time.

Tell us about how much you have made since I saw you?
My capital had gone from $250,000 down to $100,000, which represents a 60% drawdown. Since I worked with you, in this last year my trading capital has gone up to 2.7 million.

So, you have made about twenty five times the amount you started with since you began working with Adrienne?
Yes. And this has been accomplished in fairly difficult markets for what I trade. In the month of July, August, and September, my account was down only 10% when the S & P was down 20%. If I had not been to see Adrienne, the account would have fallen. I would have had at least a 50% drawdown during the same period. Filling out Adrienne's *Business Plan for Trader's* helped me to clarify how to improve my profits and not take as much risk.

Did you have goals as to what type of return you were looking for?
No, I did not have goals on a specific rate of return, but I have a figure for ultimate trading capital that I want to have.

Does your perception of returns have some effect on the amount of risk that you are willing to accept? I am asking this question

because it has a big effect on your risk level. We have had interviews with traders who risk a very small percentage of their capital while other traders claim that you are not risking enough to make money unless you have 40% drawdowns.

The standard rule-of-thumb about taking drawdowns is a trader who takes a 10% drawdown while averaging 30% per year return is regarded as extremely good. If a trader is taking 35% to 40% drawdowns and is making 200% plus on his money and is comfortable with that drawdown characteristic, I say it is okay to trade that way. The only problem with that much drawdown is that clients cannot handle the drawdown psychologically.

5% on $100,000 is only $5,000. 40% on $1,000,000 is a lot more. As you get more trading capital, your drawdown percentage-wise must become smaller.

Does it also depend upon how you view the money, whether it is your money or the house's money? If you are up 100% for the year, you must be more willing to take a 40% drawdown?

To some degree that may be true, but it is still your money even though you are taking it out of the market. If you are up 100% for the year and factor in a drawdown of 40%, you still finish the year up 60%, which I would consider to be a good year. If you lose 10% or 15% from the highs, I would consider that a pretty good year. I look at the peak of capital as opposed to starting capital, which is the classic definition of drawdown. At one time, I was comfortable taking 30% to 40% drawdown; now I am not comfortable with that level because my trading capital base is larger. Now that I have more trading capital, I take less risk as a percentage.

But, on the other hand, if you took $5,000 to start an account, you must be willing to let that account go down until they tell you that you cannot trade?

If someone gave me $5,000 and told me to build the account up again, I would go back to the original plan. I would trade in small amounts and take a little bit out of the market at a time.

Even with a $5,000 account?
In order to take a $5,000 account and build it up to $100,000 or $1,000,000, there are certain basic fundamentals that must be adhered to. Suppose there is a contest and someone gives you $5,000 to trade. You have to stick to the strategy and enjoy the process so you can stay in the game. I am not going to put $5,000 on one trade because I will get blown out of the water. I am going to take that $5,000 and try for small gains and losses. That way you are able, over a function of time, to grow the account. It has to. So, I still believe that in order to build from $5,000 to $1,000,000, you must have the basic fundamentals intact.

Talk about the caution sign that I gave to you.
It works really well for me. The caution sign came about when Adrienne and I got together because of the 'Micron effect.' We found that there was a very consistent pattern I had with "yo-yoing" my account. Right after a large win in the market, I would start losing capital. Adrienne said to me, "After huge wins, take out your caution flag, look at it, and then reduce your contract size."

How do you determine when you want to put a trade on?
I give a percentage probability to each type of chart pattern.

How do you calculate that probability? Did you actually use statistics or is it discretionary?
Some statistical work is involved, but the process also has discretionary elements. I find that certain patterns have a higher probability of success than other patterns.

Do you print the charts and segregate them on the floor: this is pattern one, this is pattern two, etc.?
Yes. For example, the chart pattern that has a smile at you or a gap. I have found that gaps in price continue to move in the same direction,

93% of the time. I did a statistical study on this observation and found 90% to 93% continuation of the move on the gap in that direction. By using seven or eight patterns, I have placed a probability percentage to each pattern.

Since this is not stock trading, do you require the real open of the stock in order to do your gap analysis?
I look mostly at daily charts, but sometimes I look at weekly charts. From there, I run a tick chart of the day. The tick charts are only used in intraday analysis that I do on the S&P 500 and the stocks that I might have options on. I follow the S&P on a tick chart and what I like to see is that my positions have a higher relative strength than the markets. If you are following a stock, of course, you would like the S&P to be on your side. When I decide I am going to buy an option on a particular stock, I want to see that the daily chart looks good. The chart that looks better will have a larger position.

Do you give a rating to charts?
I just know in my mind that this chart looks better than another one. What I look for are the basic patterns of technical analysis, nothing fancy. I see the chart unfolding and look for the momentum building to the upside before I put on a number of contracts. The size of the position is based on the energy or velocity of that market.

Are you defining the rating based upon how much risk you think is in the trade? Do you have your risk defined so that you are wrong if the stock goes below a certain price level?
Yes, I have defined my risk to a point. Actually, I have come up with a new rule because I got banged up recently on one trade. On the downside, if the stock price takes out the low of the previous day, I am out.

What does "velocity" mean to you?
Energy. If you get into a trade and the stock is acting anemically, you get out of it. The trade is not going in your direction.

Will you re-enter a trade if you get stopped out?

Absolutely, I am not married to anything. I do not have any emotional attachment. I have lost money in Intel and a certain number of other stocks. But that does not prevent me from re-entering the trade if the market reverses and if the chart looks good. I do not have a problem if it reverses and goes north; I am going with it. I know that with certain patterns I have a higher consistency of making money and certain stocks, too. If you look at a listing of my trades, some stocks will have a success rate of 50% and other stocks will have a success rate in excess of 90%.

What stocks are the ones in excess of 90%?

Bank of America, Microsoft, and Dell. If you look at a corn chart or any commodity chart, there are times when the markets get very active or volatile. Think of the individual type of personalities that are trading those markets as opposed to someone who is buying Microsoft. You have different personality types for different markets. For example, trading the Internet stocks, such as Yahoo or Amazon, can be very volatile. There are different types of traders who are trading Yahoo as opposed to Microsoft. I have noticed the difference in certain stocks and in certain markets. That is why I stay away from currency markets and stuff like that. What I look for is energy and velocity in a particular market. That is extremely beneficial to me when looking at a successful trade. If I see a lot of velocity in a stock, there is a higher probability of a success in that trade.

What does that 90% really mean? Do these scores equate to probability or do they equate to something else?

90% means that based on history or past movement, that markets keep going in your direction. These scores equate to probability of a chart pattern having a higher probability of winning than other chart patterns.

So, you actually believe in some ways in seasonality?

To some degree, depending upon which market or market sector that is being looked at. An example of seasonality would be technology stocks that tend to do well in the fourth quarter.

Something that really made a difference in your trading was your money management. Would you tell us about that?
When I was working with Adrienne, she found that there was a consistent pattern of huge winners followed by periods where I would give the profits back because I did not vary my contract size. One rule that has made a big difference in my trading is that three losses in a row serve as a signal to reduce my position size down to five or ten contracts. I was trading 500 at a time; but now, my position size is way down because of the volatility in the market. This is one of the ways that Adrienne has helped me with my trading. And, of course, the yellow caution flag after big wins. Last month, I had a big winner, took out the caution flag, and did not get chopped up in the markets, as I would have in the past. She has also convinced me to reduce my core equity at risk.

Another thing that I have found through working with Adrienne is that handling your emotional issues and taking the emotion out of trading makes it become very easy. In the month of April, I made $150,000 in one day. When I closed out the trade, it was not a big deal. It would not have mattered if it were $5,000 or $150,000.

You try to keep your emotions even, even if you get beaten up?
Yes, absolutely. That is the key because you are focusing on what the market is telling you instead of what you are trying to tell the market.

Could you provide us with a few charts and go through a couple of trade sequences? Maybe a couple of trades that worked out and one that blew up on you and how you got out of it without getting hurt?
Yes, sure. The best trade that I have ever seen is back in April with Citicorp.

What we are looking for is an example of your methodology and what type of analysis you are doing. Then we can include some of your charts in the book.
I am fairly discretionary in my trading.

I am not as mechanical as I used to be either. Adrienne will tell you that.
I enjoy sitting in front of a screen. I always enjoyed watching TV as a kid. I think that is an attribute for being a trader who is not an emotional type of individual.

It sounds like you are aware of the statistics for indicators that you are looking at on the charts.
Oh, absolutely.

So, it is not like you are really discretionary. You do not trade because you get a warm feeling in your chest.
Actually, Adrienne and I went through that in our work together. If I get a real good-looking trade, I get the feeling in my head. If a trade is going against me, or I should be out of it, I feel pain in my chest. I do listen to that.

Do you use statistics?
I cannot get into the mathematical side of trading. I do not use a lot of statistical work. If a chart looks good, I go with it. If the chart looks ugly, I stay away from it.

Shall we go back to the personal side of your life? Did you get married? Do you have children?
Yes. This is my second marriage. I was separated in October 1992, when I was a broker moving from one province to another. I found that my first wife was having an affair. I say this because it was an extreme learning experience for me. I learned that there is a bigger picture and that this experience is not the end of the world. No matter what happens, I am responsible for me and my actions. My belief is

that you as a person are more important than anything.

So, even though she made the choice, you took responsibility for it as something that was not entirely her fault?
I was somewhat responsible for it because she felt alone as I did not come home enough for her. However, she is responsible for her actions, not me. Leading up to that choice, I am sure that I was not the proper husband in her mind.

Were you working a lot?
Working a lot in that I was moving out of province so that I was not getting home as much. I was trying to build my clientele.

So, then you got married again?
Yes, four years later, I remarried. Julie is quieter and more compatible for me than my first wife. My wife was working out of the home, but is now staying at home because we just had our first child July 1st, a little girl named Kayla.

Where do you want to go from here with regard to your life, your trading?
We would like to have one more child. I would like to continue to do what I am doing. I would do this job for nothing. All I have to do is to watch the screen, make some trades, and make some money. It is a fairly simple business. The markets are just a collective thought and when you allow yourself to be part of that collective thought you make money. In terms of my trading equity, my ultimate goal is 100 million dollars.

What is your number one tool for doing your analysis?
I look at *Investor's Business Daily* where I see the daily charts and fundamental information, such as earnings, growth, etc.

Do you think someone could make money just buying *Investor's Business Daily* and following CANSLIM?

14

Yes, absolutely. The only difficulty has been in the last three years. The small cap market, which his strategy really focuses on, has been brutal. I do not think any of those guys are making money. What I have done is to use CANSLIM with some modifications because when I first started using CANSLIM, I did not make any money with his strategy because of the high stop-out rate. I would rather be stopped-out the least amount of time. I find that small cap funds have liquidity problems. You may have one or two huge winners for the year. So, I took CANSLIM and modified it to look for more liquid names and stocks that had options. I buy breakouts and high probability patterns.

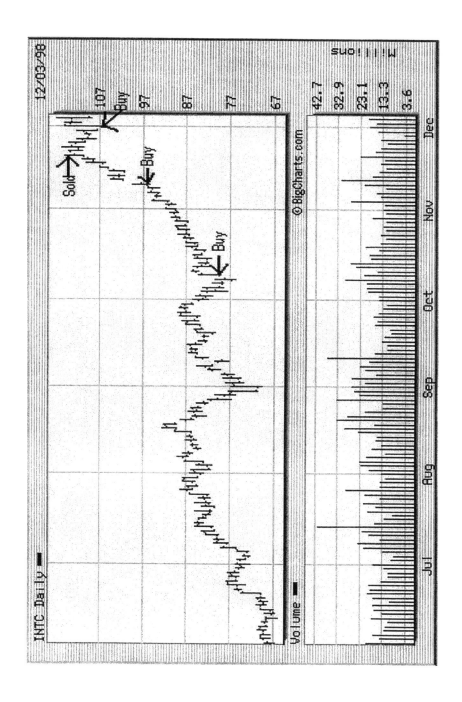

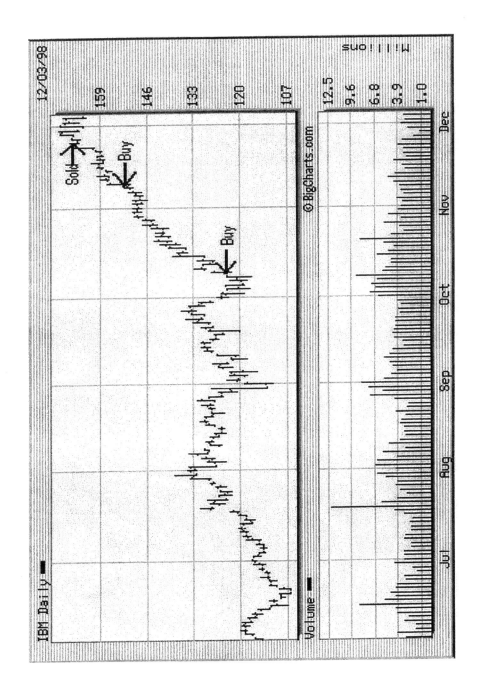

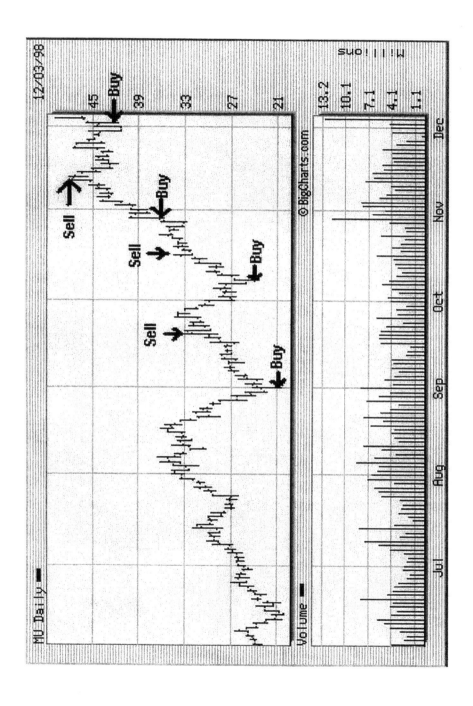

MODELING STUDY

CHILDHOOD FAMILY STATUS
- Yousef experienced growing up in a middle class family in a small town of New Brunswick, Canada

MENTORING - INFLUENCES
- Father entrepreneurial
- Tony Robbins material
- *The Disciplined Trader* by Mark Douglas
- The Islanders

ENVIRONMENT
- Stable home environment
- Supportive wife

EDUCATION
- Bachelor of Arts Degree in Economics and a minor in Psychology

INTERESTS -Skills - Abilities -Honors
Childhood
- Hockey
- Basketball
- Read non-fiction
- 9-10 years old followed markets
- Economics history and human behavior

Adult
- Competitive golf
- Reads everything on trading

QUALITIES
- Pragmatic

- Is always willing to do what it takes to improve his ability
- Does not have emotional attachment to positions
- Loves trading
- Loves to watch screen
- Participator
- Competitive
- Analytical

BUSINESS EXPERIENCE
- Managed motel for his father while in high school
- Painted houses
- Beginning stock broker
- Sold tax shelters
- Owned business selling industrial lubricants

PHILOSOPHY
- There is a bigger picture out there. I take responsibility for everything that happens.
- You as a person are more important than anything
- Do not let ego get in the way of your progress

TRADING EXPERIENCE
- Money Manager
- Stocks and Options
- Technical base with intuitive action

RECOMMENDATIONS
- *How to Make Money in Stocks* by William O'Neil
- *The Disciplined Trader* by Mark Douglas
- *The Business Plan for Traders* - Adrienne Toghraie
- *Investors Business Daily*
- Technical Analysis Program of Ralph Acampora, CMT

TRADER CONTRIBUTIONS
- Makes money for clients

FUTURE PLANS
- One more child, $100 million dollars and improve my golf score

TRADER GEMS - Fundamental - Intuitive - Psychological
- When you start hoping and wishing a trade will come back, you know you are done
- If you are long, you tend to focus on the up-tick and not on what the market is telling you
- When you feel too powerful because of a windfall, you tend to forget about rules
- As you get more trading capital, your drawdowns must become smaller as a percentage
- Uses a caution flag to reduce contract size when after a huge win
- Assigns a rating to charts based on the probability of their chances of winning
- When you keep your emotional issues out of the market you are focusing on what the market is telling you and not what you are telling the market
- Certain personality types trade specific markets and create high energy (high velocity) which is useful in making money when you use it

TRADER GEMS - Mechanical - Analytical - Technical
- Yousef is a CANSLIM stock trader with certain modifications to suit his personal trading style. The CANSLIM methodology for trading was developed by William O'Neil, publisher of *Investors' Business Daily*. Yousef got his start in using these methods by reading his book *How to Make Money In Stocks*. We will explain the basics of this method in the analysis section.
- Yousef combines CANSLIM chart patterns, double tops and trend lines.
- Yousef pyramids into his positions as he develops profits.

This aggressive method of money management is how he has produced his amazing returns as a trend follower.

- Drawdowns should be based on a percentage of your expected returns.

    40% returns with a 5% drawdown is good, but 35% to 40% drawdown with a 200%+ returns is also good.

- When you trade with a large sum of money you should cut risk as a percentage
- Yousef studies chart patterns using a combination of discretion and statistics. He printed charts, hand-sorted them, and then performed the statistical analysis based on the human expert selected categories

Murray's Analytical Modeling Study

Trade Methodology Analysis
Mechanical--Objective: Use of CANSLIM charting methodology

Mechanical--Automatic: Charting of indicators and stocks plus use of information from *Investors' Business Daily*

Discretionary: Combines these items into the analysis of a portfolio of stocks

Analysis of Yousef's Methodology
This is a quick overview of the CANSLIM methodology. William O'Neil's stock picking method is outlined in *Market Wizards* by Jack Schwager from pages 219 to 235 and in *How to Make Money in Stocks* by William O'Neil from pages 2 to78.

CANSLIM means:
C= Current quarterly earning per share--Up at least 18%
A= Annual Earning per share--Good for at least five years
N= New product, management, industry conditions, or new stock price highs
S= Supply and Demand--Small number of shares outstanding-- Volume increases with price
L= Leader--Buy only market leaders
I = Institutional sponsorship--Stock is owned by a few funds with good track records
M= General Market Conditions

When these elements all set up, Yousef likes to see the stock break out of a basing pattern. Some of the common names of these patterns are "cup with a handle," "saucer with a handle," "double bottoms," and "flat bases."

In addition to this, *Investors' Business Daily* publishes a set of indicators for stocks every day. These are detailed in the box above the stock listing in the paper.

Earning Per Share--1 low to 99 high percentile
Relative Price Strength--1 low to 99 high percentile
Industry Group--"A" high to "E" low
Sales+Profit Margins+ ROE--"A" high to "E" low
Accumulation/ Distribution--"A" high to "E" low

O'Neil claims to have computer backtested this methodology over the last 100 years and uses an 8% stop loss on any given trade.

Adrienne's Psychological Modeling Study

The Achievement Model

Yousef Hashmi approaches trading like a golfer approaches improving his handicap, by always thinking about how he can improve his score. Yousef is the consummate achiever. While he enjoys the comforts of money and the acknowledgment of success, the achievement of getting to each new level of success is his ultimate reward. He identifies areas and obstacles as welcome challenges, because he sees them as opportunities to improve his handicap, i.e., opportunities to achieve and he does this by seeking out new mentors.

Yousef's father was his first mentor model. Yousef watched his father's development from a civil engineer to an entrepreneur. The question for many people who want to be an entrepreneur is "How can you become successful in a business?" For Yousef that was a given. His question was "How do I improve the business?"

Yousef is drawn to motivational mentors to help him recognize the barriers and overcome them. First, Anthony Robbins led him to become a more successful person and businessman. Mark Douglas identified some of his disciplinary problems and was responsible for helping him to improve his handicap as a trader/broker. I was able to assist him in money management by overcoming psychological issues, which eliminated more barriers.

Although Yousef is probably not aware of it consciously, one of the important influences in developing his Achievement Model was his competitive golf play in college. Because golf is not a team sport, the emphasis in competitive play is on improving individual achievement. In this environment, small and achievable goals are set and met on a continuing basis, or you are out of the sport. This environment is a very good breeding ground for the Achievement Model to grow.

On the way toward his achievements, Yousef believed that no job was too small or too big; it was all part of being an achiever - from taking out the garbage in a motel to being a house painter while waiting for his opportunity as a broker and trader. His stint painting houses is another place for individual achievement to take root. In many careers, your progress toward a goal is difficult to trace. However, the monotony of painting a house is made bearable, even unfelt, if you concentrate on the very visible progress you are making toward the achievement of your goal. Brokers are also very achievement directed. Every month they bring home only what they earned that month. This monthly feedback is reinforced by constant motivational efforts with a focus on your results.

One of Yousef's strengths is that he does not let his ego get in the way of progress. He takes responsibility for everything that happens to him. Yousef is one of the few brokers who approaches being a broker as being a money manager, and, therefore, consistently makes money for his clients.

As a result of Yousef's Achievement Model, he wanted to break the barrier that had prevented him from reaching his trading goals and sought me out as a mentor. When we discovered the pattern that was responsible for his giving back his earnings to the market, Yousef applied himself to breaking through his barrier, without ego, without excuses, and with stunning results.

CHAPTER 2

Glen Ring

A jack of all traders - How a highly regarded analyst, teacher, writer and mentor to farmers overcame great adversity to maintain himself as a trader over a long career.

Tell us about your upbringing?
I was born to a poor farm family in Murdo, South Dakota, in 1955. I got off to an interesting start because I was born in an inn. There was a measles outbreak in the area and the hospital was quarantined. For that reason, the top floor of a local hotel was turned into a maternity ward. I was delivered for a $25 bill.

Did you have brothers and sisters?
I was the youngest of three children. I have a brother who is eight years older, and a sister who is four years older than I am. Our family lived in a farming region that was next to the Badlands in South Dakota. It was quite a desolate and rough area where people had to be survivors. It did not take "The Great Depression" to cause tough times in this area; there were always tough times.

I bet you learned to be resourceful.
You had to learn resourcefulness out there because it was 80 miles to the nearest town. If you had something break down, it was not easy to run to town to pick up parts.

What did your father farm and were you able to make ends meet?
We farmed primarily wheat with some cattle and hogs.

My father was sick with juvenile diabetes for 26 years, which put a strain on our family. We were far from poverty stricken, because I believe that is a state of mind, but economically we were "tight to

27

the vest." My mother worked as a teacher, and my dad took care of us during the school year when I was young which made us very close.

The care of diabetes during that time was no where near the science that it is today. When my dad died at the age of 51, the autopsy on him reported that he had the body of a 75-year old.

My father was very respected in the community. Our house had the coffeepot on to welcome visitors at all times. Dad had gone to a special high school in the late 1930's in conjunction with the South Dakota College of Agriculture. That was enough "higher education" to make him respected as an authority in the community.

Would you tell us about your school days?
I went to a country school where all eight grades were taught in one room. As a country school, ours was considered large with 20 kids. In my grade, there were 3 kids and we competed with each other. This helped in pushing us well ahead of the curriculum.

What were the activities that you enjoyed growing up?
I enjoyed spending time with my dad and helping with the farm work. The first time I drove a truck was when I was four. My dad was feeding cows off the back of a flatbed truck, and he needed the truck to move along in the pasture as he fed the cows. All I had to do was let the clutch out slowly, but I let it out all at once. I still remember the image of him, the hay, and the pitchfork all flying in the air as we unloaded the truck in one spot. Needless to say, it was at least two years before I drove again.

My grandfather and I would make a game of guessing weights of livestock and calculating their value in dollars per head at the winter auctions. One of my father's favorite stories is the time I asked him why he did not raise his hand like the other guys. Of course, they were bidding on the cattle, but he apparently did not give me a satisfactory answer because later I raised his hand for him. He ended up buying the cattle even though he had not wanted to bid. As it turned out, he said it was one of the best buys that he ever made.

My brother and I loved to build things together. We once built a canoe out of 55-gallon drums, which sank, of course.

When I got older, I played baseball. I did not really consider myself a good athlete, although I ended up doing quite well in athletics. It was not because of my physical ability, but because of my thinking ability.

What position did you play in baseball?
I pitched all three years that I played in the league. Playing in the league taught me an important memory lesson for later in life. I read an article in *Sports Illustrated* by Ted Williams, who was the last person to bat .400 in the major leagues, about the science of hitting. He explained in the article that the actual hitting was the art of the application of the science. I raised my batting average by .160 the next season after applying what I had read in that article and led the league in hitting. The application of that lesson made me appreciate both the science and the art of doing things and made me realize that they can be different, but they can also be very compatible.

How many acres was your farm?
Just short of 1500 acres, which may seem large to some people, but it was a relatively small farm for that area. A farm double that size would have been sizable.

I spent a lot of time learning to do things by myself. You could walk to parts of the farm and never know whether the year was 1997 or 1797, because you could not see anything modern. There was total isolation and you could really get in touch with your senses.

What were you like in high school?
High school did not leave me fond memories because I became such a loner. My parents had very strong values and my high school was very bad in terms of alcohol use. During those years, I really respected authority and the high school situation made it uncomfortable. Nevertheless, I made some good friends in high school. At that age, I was having a lot of internal struggle.

As a boy of seven or eight, I remember being unable to sleep at night because of the internal dialogue that would never stop.

What was that dialogue like?
I remember focusing on my inadequacies and on the mistakes that I made. I had aunts and uncles who lived in the area that were very critical of people. The voices did not quit and they haunted me for many years. They actually prevented my accomplishing many things at that time. I am not sure when I became a fighter and survivor, but when I plan things now, I get them done.

Tell us about college?
I went to South Dakota State and earned degrees in Animal Science and Agronomy. Agriculture was what I really loved.

Did you play any sports in college?
I played hockey in college. A lesson I learned in playing hockey was that repetition has a lot of value when you want to master something. I had practiced shooting backhand until it became automatic. There was one goalie that we played against that I could never beat. On one occasion, I had a breakaway opportunity against him. He came out of the net to challenge me and was not expecting my backhand shot. I scored a goal, and we went on to win the game, and the championship. I use the lesson of repetition today in my trading and analysis. If you want to learn to follow a rule, you practice it the same way over, and over, and over again.

Did you return to farming?

My father died when I was 19 and a sophomore in college. I remember my mother asking me if I could run the farm. I told her that I was going to finish college, but that I could run it. I hired my brother, who had no interest in farming, to care for the livestock, and I arranged my schedule at college so that I had Friday or Monday off. I would drive the 300 miles home after class on Thursday, get on a tractor, and farm all night. I would farm for a 3-day weekend, get 6 or 8 hours of sleep, and drive back to school in time for class on Monday morning. For two years, this was how I got the crops in during spring and harvested them in fall. We also planted wheat in the fall.

When did you decide to leave the farm?

We had the explosion in grain prices in the early 1970's. By the late 1970's, the expenses involved in farming had risen dramatically while prices had fallen to much lower levels. It was very hard to make farming work by that time.

When did you start learning about the markets?

I learned about markets while I was in high school. We were raising hogs and I remember reading an article in *Successful Farming* about something called a "hog cycle." After I read it, I realized there was something to the article because every time prices were low, we had a lot of hogs and every time they were high, we did not have very many.

What lessons did you learn?

It was 1980, and I was standing in a grain elevator buying feed for the hogs that we were raising. As I stood there waiting, 3 or 4 farmers came in asking what the price of wheat was. It was $3.96 and each farmer said the same thing as they came through, "When it gets to $4.00, call me and I'll sell you some." I had not sold my wheat either, and it finally clicked in my head, $3.96, and we are all waiting for $4.00. I sold my wheat on the spot and it never reached $4.00 at that elevator. I had been studying cycles through the

1970's, but that was the first time I really started appreciating the behavior of the masses.

Tell us about the transition from working on the farm to not working on the farm?
I met my wife in college, a Minnesota gal, and brought her out to what some call "God Forsaken" country. She worked in a 12-bed hospital and commuted 54 miles each way. Sometimes, she would work double-shifts because of the drive. When we got married, I promised her that she would only have to put up with this for five years. As fate turned out, when the five years were up, I was ready to move on.

In 1980, while observing the parabolic shaped rallies in the gold and silver markets, I decided that the formations in the agricultural sector fit the description of a multi-generational cycle peak. I recognized that if farming does not work when prices are at their peak, things would be terrible when the peak was behind us. Armed with this observation, I spent the next two years preparing to get out of farming.

Another reason I moved from the farm is that I was in love with the markets and wanted to be an analyst. That is really what started the transition from the farm. As I began winding the farm down, I watched livestock cycles and was able to liquidate our livestock at fairly good prices. After finishing the 1982 season, I walked away from the farm with nothing, which was better than ending up in bankruptcy like so many others at that time.

How did you start in business?
I started as a commodities broker. I moved to Watertown, South Dakota, which is from one corner of the state to the other, and opened a branch office for a firm. I was the office owner and manager for one year. Not many months later, the bull market of 1983 imprinted on me how easily things could go up. I spent many years looking for that next grain bull market. That was how I got

my start and where I learned about sleeping like a baby. You sleep for an hour, you wake up and cry for an hour, and by morning the bed is wet. That was how I felt.

Why?
The stress bothered me. Coming from an impoverished region, the money that we were getting into trading accounts was not that big, but it was bigger than I was used to dealing with. Having it disappear into the markets really bothered me.

It sounds like you were personally involved with your clients?
I cared so much and took their losing money personally. The voices I had at night as a kid were back in full force, and I became shell-shocked. Because of that, I could not make market calls. I believed that if I was not always right, I was a failure.

Were you trading the grain markets?
The grain markets, silver, bonds, and the meats. I became fairly proficient in my early years with the hog market.

I closed my office and moved to the main office in Aberdeen, South Dakota until 1984. I was doing some seminars at the time, and I really loved teaching about the markets.

Did your economic situation improve?
No. By this time, we had two children. I had to walk away from the commodities markets in early 1984. I felt like a failure.

What did you do then?
I sold insurance. Talk about jumping from the frying pan into the fire when self-esteem and self-worth are an issue. But, the insurance company offered a $1200 per month draw.

Were you successful in getting customers?
It was said that I probably had the most unique insurance marketing strategy ever. After selling insurance for six months with little

success, I started holding commodities seminars for farmers. Afterwards, I would prospect them for insurance. My meetings were free, and I was sincere and believed in what I was doing. I was fairly successful at selling insurance this way. Later, when I started charging for the seminars, more people came to them. They actually started paying me to prospect them for insurance. My general agent came one day to hear my presentation and told me I did not belong in insurance sales; I needed to be in the markets. I quit selling insurance in 1985, and made the recommitment to the markets.

What do you believe about the markets?
I believe that the markets are living, breathing organisms and have personalities. They are reflections of behavior and have an anatomy, a physiology, a structure, and a life cycle.

Did you have what was necessary to make it in the markets?
No. I was not properly capitalized to trade and I did not know the first thing about trading. I knew a great deal about markets, but trading is an entirely different business than analysis. They can be complementary, but they can also be competitive and counter productive.

Were you still struggling? What did you do then?
Boy, were we ever. One day in August of 1985, my wife asked how we could buy groceries. We were expecting our third child, and I had taken our last $25 to buy a roll of stamps. On credit, I rented a meeting room and printed 100 invitations to a free meeting. At that meeting, I announced that I was beginning the publication of a market newsletter in October. Of the 20 people in attendance, I got a 100% response. The $1100 that I collected that day looked like a fortune to people with no groceries.

Over the years, I have leveraged that $1100 into where I am today.

Where did you go next?
I kept doing meetings. I started offering three and five night seminars. The first evening was free and the next meeting they paid. I would return to the same town weekly for the next three or five weeks. I kept raising the price, and the crowds kept getting bigger. In 1985 and 1986, I did over 150 presentations. I learned to be an entertaining speaker on what some people would consider a boring subject. I got over the hump when 44 people came and I made $4,000 from one meeting. Suddenly, things started mushrooming and I was running meetings five nights per week.

From there, I started a service helping farmers market their production. I picked up a partner to handle the bookkeeping and detail part of the business. We would meet with the farmers, make out marketing plans, and charge a per unit fee for our service.

Sounds like you were pushing yourself to the limit.
Yes, that is true. I was driving up to 200 miles to do these evening meetings. Phone calls would often start at 5 A.M., and would continue until 1 A.M. It also turned out that I was doing these meetings on a broken foot that the doctor said must have been at least three months old from the amount of healing.

At this time were you making it financially?
In 1986, after our son was born, things were going fairly well. The marketing business was making money, and I had leveraged the initial $1100. One afternoon, my wife took our ten-month old son to a neurosurgeon and found that he needed surgery to correct a fluid buildup on his brain. I had no insurance, so we were cleaned out. The concern was that he might be impacted mentally, but that we would not know for several years.

Fortunately, he is as sharp as a tack, but he did end up with some physical challenges. Until he was 12, we did not know if he would survive or not.

What effect did that situation have on you?
Security suddenly had an entirely different meaning to me. While I was building a good business, I told my partner that I could not take the risk. My family needed insurance coverage because of my son's condition. Since then, he has had seven more surgeries.

In 1987, I made the decision to get a job. That is when I got the job with the company that owned *Futures Magazine* and *Pro Farmer.*

How did you manage to do that?
When I was a broker, I met a floor commentator that I had kept in touch with as I studied the markets.

I called him to see if he knew of any job openings for an analyst. He called me back three weeks later and asked if I was willing to relocate. A position had opened at Oster Communications. This was no accident. There was divine intervention that directed the opening for me.

In August 1987, I joined the staff of Oster Communications at Cedar Falls, Iowa. My new job was to write the *Commodity Closeup* newsletter. I was also given the title "Chief Technical Advisor" to *ProFarmer.*

Do you believe you have had other spiritual or clairvoyant experiences?
My wife would constantly tell me that I was uncovering things that I should not know as I would tell her things in premonitions. One night I was pacing the floor saying something big was going to happen. The next morning as I was on the phone to a customer, she told me to turn on the television, something big had happened. The space shuttle Challenger had blown up.

I do not know if markets and life have a destiny to them, but I feel there is a tremendous unity of life force out there. I believed that you could predict markets.

Do you still believe it?
Yes, but at the same time I have learned which beliefs are useful. It does not mean that you are going to predict them all, but analytically, markets have degrees of predictability.

From a trading standpoint, it is not useful to believe that you can predict markets. I think that 99.9 % of the people that go down the road of trying to predict markets find that it is a dead end for them because they want to trade their predictions.

I have learned to separate myself from my predictions. Now, I deal in what the evidence says and develop scenarios. If the market gives me a trading buy signal and my scenario is contrary to that signal, I will buy the market.

Give us an example?
Lately, we have been in major downtrends in the grain markets. Recently, I picked a buy signal on wheat and I bought it. It did not go very far, but I made four or five cents. Then came a sell signal, and I was able to reverse out and get back on the short side of the market, which agreed with my initial scenario.

When did you start to learn to be a trader?
I went to do a seminar called *Futures Magazine's Best Tools and Trades* in December of 1987, in Chicago. I did not know if I had value to give to the audience when compared to the other speakers. I still remember 5 of the people from that first seminar. There was Dr. Gill, Jake Bernstein, Joe Granville, Jeff Elliott, and me. I realized that this was <u>The</u> Jake Bernstein who was known throughout farm country because of the seasonal work he had done. I was the first speaker. So, I went out in my naïve way, and gave my predictions. After speaking to this crowd of 400 people, everyone was crowding around me like I knew something. When I finished listening to the rest of the speakers, I realized that I did know something and gave value.

How do you make some of your predictions?
Sometimes, I cannot explain it and other times it is because of a preponderance of evidence. Some of the predictions that I make are based on knowing that certain times of the year are critical to certain markets. Ultimately, I view the marketplace to be like a big jigsaw puzzle. Each market has its place and I just have to fit them together.

Can you walk through how you would analyze soybeans?
The first thing I look for is the bullish opportunities. In studying years of soybean charts, I have found that soybeans typically bottom in August or October. If they are going into a bullish phase, they almost invariably bottom in August. If not, the bottom occurs in October. At a major bottom, the only other time in history that soybeans have bottomed is February, which is an alternative time.

The all-time low for soybeans was posted in 1939 on August 15th. I started studying history and found August 15th and the previous week to be a historical time for turns. Then, I go back and start looking at what date projected into the future is important. I would project from a Gann 30-day count, a 60-day count, and a 90-day count from a previous high.

How do you pick the high?
My methodology is taking my life's experience and combining it. I am not just a Gann person. I also work with Elliott Wave. I just know this beast I call "A Market." I do not know how I know.

Just take any time when there was a major prediction. Go back to the time before you made that major prediction. What were you looking at? What were you listening to? What was going on at the time?
Okay, a major prediction was made the week after November 15th, 1987. I made the statement in a *ProFarmer* weekly meeting that soybeans had entered the second greatest bull market in history. I really got my ears pinned back.

38

You said you looked at the markets and saw something. What did you see?
At that point, I saw a gap on a weekly chart, which told me that we were starting to enter an Elliott Third Wave. This was in conjunction with the major cycle timing having turned bullish in early 1987 for at least a one - to two-year period. (refer to chart on page 50)

So, you saw something, and then you heard something. What did you hear?
Having studied market after market, Adrienne, markets talk to me all the time. It was the market that was talking to me. The market told me, "I am starting into a Third Wave."

So you saw something. The markets talked to you and said this is what I am going to do, and then what happened?
I also felt it. I get this feeling in the lower rib cage area.

And how specifically do you feel it? Is it a tingling sensation?
It is warmth. It is a combination of the senses coming together. I will go through looking at a market thinking I know what is going to happen and then, all of the senses will click.

Your strategy so far is you see a signal, recognize it as familiar, hear a voice, which tells you this is what the market is going to do. You feel warmth in your chest. Now is it time to trade?
There is one other sensation that you might find interesting. I can smell it. It comes out of my mouth almost automatically.

What does it smell like?
Burnt sienna that was in the Crayola box when I was a kid. It is what I would imagine burnt sienna would smell like.

So, this is your intuitive indicator?
It is for the best trades. There are many of them that I see, but never smell. When all of those senses come together, I know it is my best indicator.

What is one of the biggest mistakes traders make?
They try to be too perfect.

A doctor can run a computer diagnosis and hit 80%.
A doctor uses the process of elimination. He gathers all of the evidence that he can, but he is not going to walk in and tell you that he absolutely knows what is wrong with you. He is going to tell you that based upon the evidence, it is likely that this is what is wrong, this is the likely course it is going to take, and based upon experience, this is the conclusion.

Do you think you can pick tops and bottoms?
I do not know if you can always pick them, but I have picked quite a few in my time.

Did you consider yourself to be a good analyst?
At that point, I was probably one of the best analysts in the business, but I was not a great trader. I can help people understand markets better than they already do, which is my biggest asset.

What was your next step?
I started looking internally. A big influence to that understanding was a seminar I attended given by Van Tharp and Adrienne.

I started reading books, going to seminars, getting tapes, anything I could do to work not just on self-improvement, but self-under-standing. Even though I was successful, my expectations were preventing me from accomplishing a lot more.

Any other big influences?
Yes, I read the book *Learned Optimism*. I learned that optimism or pessimism is a learned behavior. While I did not become an optimist overnight, I did over a period of time.

How did this affect your trading?

It changed my perspective. It made me realize that I was involved in a business where being right or wrong was an issue. The analyst may be able to predict market direction, but the only thing the analyst has riding on his prediction is being right or wrong. He has no money riding on the prediction. So, his vested interest is to try to prove that he is right, to find more evidence that he is right even if the market is saying something different.

Whereas, the trader's issue is not right or wrong in that sense, but rather to effectively make more money when he is right than he loses when he is wrong.

What did your studies do for the rest of your life?

Through this process of self-discovery, I found a richness of happiness and internal peace. This is more precious to me than anything that the market is ever going to give me.

From there, what was the process that you used to become a trader from a technical standpoint?

Today, I do not consider myself a technician. The analytical capabilities that I have fulfill one step of the process, which is to help me identify opportunities. Then, I take a step-by-step approach that changes an opportunity into a trade. That is where the technical understanding of the market came in for me.

Do you still predict the markets?

I consider scenarios. If the market is consistent with a major scenario, I look for trading opportunities. The moment an opportunity becomes a trade it becomes a methodical, structured approach. That is the key. The moment I put on a trade, my scenario is a guideline, but I also have to realize that I am talking about a probability. When the market quits doing what it is supposed to do within my scenario, I respect that. There is a big difference between being the analyst and the trader.

41

How do you define opportunity as far as entry is concerned?
I use patterns in the market. First of all, the opportunity is defined with my major scenario. I run long-term cycles, but I only use cycles in maybe a third of the markets that are out there. I am not satisfied that my cycles adequately describe the rest of the markets

Cycles that you are measuring from peak to peak, or valley to valley, instead of spectral analysis?
A narrow definition of a cycle for me is a low to low pattern or a high to high pattern. I also use timing points in the market that can be low to high, high to low, or low to an acceleration point. I have four different things that can occur at a point in time. As I said earlier, I have a belief that the entire marketplace is like one big jigsaw puzzle. I do a lot of monthly degree intermarket analysis, so I start having certain markets become lead indicators. The CRB Index tends to be a lead indicator for grains and other markets. The dollar tends to be a lead indicator for the CRB index. Many times I will have long lead times.

The CRB index will tend to parallel or lead corn and the grain markets by as much as 2 or 3 months

How do you analyze the dollar relationship?
The dollar will lead the physical commodity prices typically by 10 to 18 months on a monthly degree, and that is in terms of pressures.

What are your money management rules?
The main rule is 3% risk of the entire account. Along the way, I have risked more to help my account grow. When there is a breakout pattern that gives me two different entry signals, I will put half of a position or 1.5% risk on the initial entry. If it gives me a second signal, then I will go to another 1.5% risk.

These percentages of risk have one big problem. Sometimes the fiscal risk of a trade based on the market does not fit your profile. Let's say that you have $100,000 dollars in your account

42

and you are trading the S&P. You have an opportunity for the moon shot, the 300-point rally, but you have to risk 6% of your account to make the trade?

I pass the trade if it does not keep me within the 3% parameter. Where the stop goes is established by what I call market-generated information. There will always be another trade.

What is trading to you?

I have a metaphor for what trading is to me. When people ask what type of animal or creature the marketplace would be, you often get responses like tigers, lions, or things that are vicious. The implication is if you turn your back you might get eaten or killed. For me, the marketplace is a milk cow. In general, the milk cow is a relatively docile, domestic creature that provides you with a benefit without your having to kill her.

She gives milk, but really you have to take it. The whole concept of a milk cow is something you care for and get a benefit from. You do not get to milk her just anytime of the day; that cow must be milked on her schedule when she is ready to be milked. When it is time to milk her, you do not just milk a cup; you have to milk her for all she is worth. If you continue to milk her after she is done giving milk, she will get cantankerous and kick you.

I am looking for cows that are ready to be milked. When the market says it is time, I have to milk the market on its own time; not when I decide. There are three, four, or five of those markets every year.

You talked a bit about monthly degree that is pretty reliable in terms of lags and leaps. What do you use for the bond markets?

The CRB Index tends to parallel or lead the bond market by about three months, but there are times when it will lead by as much as eight months. It just gives me a general bias. I also use congestion pattern analysis and go with the breakout. Very clearly, the bond market is one where I may walk in with a useful bias based upon my scenario, but I am consciously aware that I have to be willing to change courses in a flash.

The bond market runs a couple of technical indicators fairly well. I use a fourteen-period weekly stochastic oscillator and I filter that with a MACD. Once the bond market gets into a trending move, I will use an ADX to determine whether or not the trending movement is still going. The bond market is a great market for the very simplistic pattern of an uptrend making higher highs and higher lows and a downtrend making lower highs and lower lows. Once I see the market starting to establish these patterns, it becomes my dominant indicator.

In late 1994, why did you believe that we were still seeing all time highs in T-Bonds?
The market was forming a pattern. Overall, it had been making a pattern of higher monthly highs and higher monthly lows. You cannot arbitrarily look at highs and lows, you need a definition of what constitutes a low or a high. When we came down on the break in the bond market in late 1994, my last true reaction low was 97-09. The market actually held that area on a monthly closing basis. We traded down to 96-01, but the lowest monthly close was 98-11. That reaction low was never taken out on a closing basis. The integrity of my higher monthly highs and higher monthly lows, which had begun in 1984, was not violated.

Where did that target come from?
It came from the previous monthly reaction low. That is the point where the long-term bull pattern would have actually been violated. Since it was not, the uptrending undercurrent was still intact. The old idea that the trend is your friend is very important to me, and the market held an area where it was supposed to hold. We went up into 1995 and early 1996, and the market effectively double-topped the 1993 high. Many were screaming that we had seen the major top in the bond market. Keep in mind that I was also using my long-term

analysis on the CRB Index, but I still believed that was not the case.

What made you believe that?
Cycles. My timing work all pulled together and synthesized.

How do you analyze the CRB Index when it began trading in 1987?
There is cash data available on the CRB Index that goes back decades, or you could recalculate what the cash index would have been. I use the cash CRB data.

What about the T-Bond market in 1997?
The Bond market rallied into 1996 and double-topped. We retraced and stopped on the break in the 106-00 area. That area was important because prior to 1992, the all-time futures high in the T-Bond market had been at 105-15. It is very common for markets to stabilize on old resistance after they break out. When we came down in 1996, the market held support on the old resistance area the way it should. I maintained my bullish bias and the market rolled up and back down in early 1997 and took off again. The market continued to make equal or higher lows even though we had only nominally gone to a new high at that point in time, but it was consistent with my bullish bias. (refer to chart on page 24)

When you are in an uptrend or have a bullish bias because of evidence, it is very important to watch the lows of the move. I watch for higher highs, but my dominant key on a monthly chart, even with flat tops, is the market will likely resolve itself to the upside until the higher lows have been violated.

Remember, one of the things I like to use in T-Bonds is congestion patterns on daily, on weekly, and on monthly data. The monthly Bond market after the 1986 high made a wedge or triangle for six years. One of my best trades was in 1992, when I thought Bonds were on their way to 121 and they went to 122.

Did you measure the size of the triangle?
That is one of the things I do. I measure the size of the triangle and project it and I use the minimum projection. I also go back to the idea of squared numbers. Eleven squared is 121.

I have never heard of anyone using that.
A number that is important in one market is more than likely going to be important in another market. Just the fact that the numbers work is all that I need to know. I think the market follows mathematical templates.

Do you take all of the squared numbers?
I watch all of the squared numbers. 12 squared being 144 is an obvious one, the Fibonacci number. I do not necessarily mean for the bond market. I mean for any market. A current example that jumps to mind is the oat market and its play recently in the 144.00 area. If you check the British pound, I bet you will find a lot of support around 144.00 throughout history. Try the British pound in the 169.00 area, which is 13 squared. This is one of my tricks of the trade.

A little more about the Bond market. As we stand to date, I am still long-term bullish on Bonds because there have been no violation of the bullish patterns. The Bond market would have to fall below 106-00 for me to discard my long-term bullish scenario. In the meantime, I observe congestion formations. For the past four years, the Bond market has been forming an ascending wedge. It is congestion, and if we rally through the highs that were made in early 1998, this Bond market has another major leap to the upside.

Where do you think the stock market is going to go now?
Up or down. I made one major projection just this week and I have a target at 9300. I have a target at 10460 that was made public two years ago. I took a parabolic shaped pattern, pointed out the acceleration point, and projected my top side targets at 7200, 8100, 8900 and, oh yes, my wildest dreams of 10460. The projection

comes basically from taking an acceleration point and doubling the market.

There are times when I do not have scenarios on markets and that is okay. But the trend is up, and I know that we are in an extraordinary position in this stock market now. We are in a parabolic rise. This market has been trending since 1974 and we are 24 years into a parabolic bull market. I think that this bull market could go down in history as being a major mania along with the tulip trade of the 1600's.

For me to project where this market is going to stop is ludicrous. When a market is making new all-time highs, I have a very simple rule, "Do Not Sell It." But when it quits . . .

When did you start becoming profitable in your trading?
I was profitable off and on over the years, but I had to work so hard at it. Trading became much more effortless in the early 1990's when I understood the steps of the process. I consider myself to be an average successful trader today.

A challenge I have as a discretionary trader is to make sure that I do not see too many opportunities and overtrade. Each year, I get better at not overtrading.

When did you make the transition to go out on your own?
When God gave me a signal.

How do you measure God's signals?
I believe we are given choices along the way and that God lays out the choices for me. If I make an inappropriate choice, I will struggle. One thing that is very important to me in life is the Biblical teaching of the need to surrender. I surrendered myself to God and things got so easy. That may be viewed as my way of abdicating responsibility, but I know that as long as I do things with

a positive intent and follow my religious beliefs that things are going to go well.

I can now assume more risk because my son has turned 12 and is through with surgeries. In the fall of 1997, I received an answer that was as clear as a bell. It took me three weeks to arrive at the conclusion that I needed to go into business for myself.

When it came time for me to make that change, I had choices. I could have quit the public arena and become a full-time trader, but I would not have been using the talents that God had given me. He gave me the market understanding, and He gave me the ability to communicate and empathize with people. My greatest success is being a "Player Coach."

Do you trade your retirement money?
Yes, I do long-term scenario work and that has helped with my retirement planning and positions in the market.

Some of my most successful position trading has been with my retirement money. I was in the stock market and I moved 100% into bonds in 1997 with the attitude that the bond market was going to make a major move. It has treated me really well.

When I do my long-term analysis, I will usually do scenarios out years ahead. For example, I already know what I want to do in the corn market as a general bias. My scenario is bearish to the corn market into the late part of 1998. I want to buy corn in 1998 for a rally into 1999. I want to roll back down in late 1999, and buy it again. In the year 2000, I am looking for another bull market. I already have these scenarios laid out in advance.

I believe that we are near the end of what I call a three-generation cycle of perceived value. This is a socio-economic cycle, which is unlike price cycles because it combines social trends and markets. The real bottom line is that the cycle tends to end when paper assets are held in high esteem. The next cycle will begin before this cycle ends and smart money will start moving toward mankind's basic needs of food, fiber, shelter, and religion. I expect to see a religious upswing in this country in the next one to three decades. I also expect to see mankind's basic needs come to the forefront. We have seen that start to happen in the 1990's when lumber almost doubled in price, cotton went to a moderate all-time high while not quite eclipsing the Civil War highs. Wheat and corn also made new all-time highs. Yes, the markets have fallen back, but I think those are the initial shots in a multi-decade move toward food, fiber, and shelter.

Your prediction work is valuable. Would it be more valuable to someone who is trading mutual funds that are metal based or commodity based?
I do not know if I would say more valuable, but maybe especially valuable. I have people that use my information for their business investments in locating where they need to focus. I work with about 60 area farmers and I really enjoy the connection to agriculture. I do not tell them what to do, but I hold their hands. The farmers do not need me when they have a normal seasonal market. They know that grain prices tend to be high in April, May, and June and low in the fall of the year. It is when we get into these major cycles and when we are at the cycle extremes that they need the help.

What are you going to do to improve your trading?
I continually re-evaluate each area of my trading. I use five steps in my process and try to find which step is the weakest at the present time. I also evaluate my strategies and my applications. I am continuing to study money management aspects to further leverage the capital that I do trade with. I am doing more work on understanding state of mind because I am firmly convinced that the difference between achievers and non-achievers in this world boils down to the differences in state of mind.

What other plans do you have?

I want to be able to give to my community. I enjoy working with kids and coaching sports. I want the freedom to do that, which is something that I have gotten.

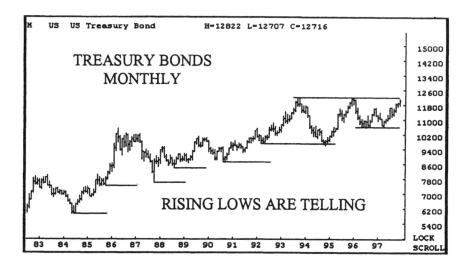

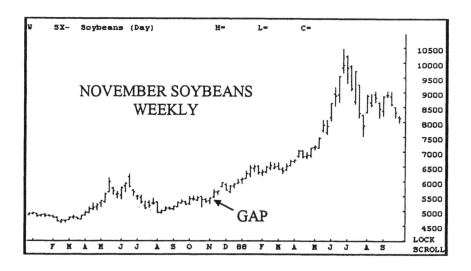

MODELING STUDY

CHILDHOOD FAMILY STATUS
- Glen grew up in a relatively poor farm family in South Dakota

MENTORING - INFLUENCES
- Close relationship with father
- *Futures Magazine* - Best Tools for Trades
- Gann and Elliott Wave
- Monte Woodford - instilled passion for technical analysis
- Van Tharp and Adrienne Toghraie for internal understanding
- Book - *Learned Optimism* by Martin E.P. Seligman

ENVIRONMENT
- Youngest of three children
- Born in desolate, rough area where he learned to be a survivor
- Father was chronically ill, so he had to take on many responsibilities around the farm
- Passersby were welcomed visitors at his home
- Rough kids in school made him a loner
- Internal struggles as teenager
- Supportive wife and three children

EDUCATION
- One room school house
- Bachelor Degrees in Animal Science and Agronomy

INTERESTS -Skills - Abilities -Honors
Childhood
- Drove truck while adolescent
- Loved to build things
- Baseball
- Hockey

Adult
- Athletics
- Religion
- Books on self-discovery
- Gardening

QUALITIES
- Resourcefulness
- Tenacity
- Survivor
- Principle driven

BUSINESS EXPERIENCE
- Ran farm while completing college
- Commodities broker
- Insurance agent

PHILOSOPHY - SUCCESS BELIEFS
- Science and art complement each other to enhance abilities
- If you want to learn to follow a rule, you practice it over and over
- God lays out my choices for me, I just have to listen and surrender
- Driven by the need to help others help themselves
- Accomplishment results from having structure in your life

PROSPERITY CONSCIOUSNESS
- Tithes to church
- Local school activities - coach
- Helps farmers and community with time and energy

TRADING EXPERIENCE
- Market analyst
- Commodities broker

- Technical base with intuitive indicator

RECOMMENDATIONS
- Anthony Robbin's material
- *Learned Optimism* by Martin E.P. Seligman
- Ray Kelly's presentations
- *Market Wizards* by Jack Schwager
- *The Magic of Thinking Big* by David Schwartz
- The Four Gospels from The Bible
- Adrienne Toghraie's products and services
- Van Tharp's products and services

TRADER CONTRIBUTIONS
- Trading coach, teacher, and lecturer
- Chief Technical Advisor to *ProFarmer*
- Writes column for *Futures Magazine*
- Publishes newsletter called "View of Futures"

FUTURE PLANS
- Continue to build my own company
- Continue to develop myself as a trader and a good human being
- Give to my community by coaching youth sports

TRADER GEMS - Fundamental - Intuitive - Psychological
- The biggest mistake that traders make is trying to be too perfect
- Milk the markets the way you would milk a cow - when the cow is ready to be milked
- When the market is making an all time high do not sell it
- The difference between achievers and non-achievers boils down to having a positive state of mind

TRADER GEMS - Mechanical - Analytical - Technical

- When you enter a trade, you need to develop scenario guidelines. When the market does not follow a given scenario you need to respect that
- The first step in Glen Ring's analysis is to view long term cycles measured from low to low or high to high. (note long term cycles only hold for about 1/3 of the commodities)
- Glen uses intermarket analysis on a monthly timeframe. For example, the CRB Index tends to lead the grain markets by as much as 2-3 months
- Never risk more than 3% of your account
- Do not take a trade with too much risk based on a market defined stop
- The CRB Index will lead T-Bonds by about 3 months (Note: the markets are negatively correlated)
- Another good indicator for the bonds is the fourteen-period weekly stochastic filtered with MACD
- The simple concept of higher highs and lows for an uptrend and lower highs and lows for a downtrend works very well in T-Bonds
- It is very common for markets to stabilize at old resistance levels during a downtrend
- The size of the triangle can be used as the minimum price projection for a breakout move from the triangle
- Prices naturally gravitate to square numbers for example, T-Bonds old high was 122 and 11 squared is 121
- When a market goes parabolic prices will often double from the point were it goes parabolic
- We are approaching a new commodity boom in the next one to three to decades

Murray's Analytical Modeling Study

Trading Methodology Analysis

Mechanical--Objective: Looks at long-term cycles objectively. Uses Elliott wave analysis in addition to intermarket analysis. He also uses Gann analysis.

Mechanical--Automatic: Charts indicators used in Analysis. Looks at statistical analysis of market turns.

Discretionary: Combines many different technical methods, both mechanical and subjective into a single forecasting model.

Glen's forecasts have been amazing. For example, he called for the Dow to hit 8000 by July 4, 1997. He came within 3 points of being correct on a forecast made in January 1997.   The problem with forecasts is that they are not tradable. He uses short-term methods, which let the market tell him what to trade based on market activity.

Analysis of Glen's Methodology

Glen Ring is an artist. His analysis is a combination of many different methodologies. Let's walk though Glen's method for analysis of a market. In our interview, he looked at the soybean market as an example. Glen would start analyzing a chart and try to identify when the market would normally bottom. Believe it or not, many markets from grains to T-Bonds have seasonal times in which tops and bottoms form. In soybeans, bottoms typically form in August or October. If they are in a bullish phase, the bottom will form in August. If we sort a seasonal pattern based on price action up to a given period, we create something called seasonal analogs. These are very powerful predictive tools, which can produce huge profits.

Next, he will study long-term charts and find all-time lows and highs. The all-time low in soybeans is August 15, 1939. A study of price history shows that major turns in soybeans often occur around August 15.

Next, we can use Gann analysis and project important dates from a previous high. After that, he adds a little Elliott wave analysis and other methodologies such as intermarket analysis to analyze this beast called a market.

One example of this analysis is his November 15, 1987, prediction for a multi-year bull market in soybeans. This forecast was made based on market conditions, October would have signaled a bottom, and the market was at a multi-year major cycle timing bottom. This told us to look for a start of a bull move. Once the market chart pattern began to show an Elliott wave 1,2,3 sequence confirmed by a gap on a weekly chart to the upside, we knew we had a wave 3 and the beginning of a bull market

My work shows that Glen is right. Market turns do happen over and over again at predictable times. For example in the S&P500, tops often occur in February and August. If looking for a shorting opportunity, this timeframe would be the best time to look for the technical setup to produce a downtrend. Glen also looks at the longer- term view. For example, on a monthly basis he will look for higher highs and higher lows to define a bull market, and lower highs and lower lows to define a bear market. Learning how to combine simple tools can produce amazing results as part of the art of discretionary trading.

Intermarket Analysis is a Powerful Tool
Glen also uses intermarket analysis on a weekly or monthly basis to detect future market turns. His research shows that the CRB Index leads the corn market by as much as 2 to 3 months. The dollar leads these markets by 10 to 18 months on a monthly basis. The CRB Index also leads the bond market. Corn is positively correlated to the CRB Index and both the dollar and T-Bonds have an inverse correlation to it.

I have done a lot of intermarket analysis, and my work shows its value in predicting market turns. This is why one of the most powerful trading signals is an intermarket divergence between markets. For example, if both the CRB Index and T-Bonds are rallying, odds are that Bonds will soon put in a top. This topic received detailed coverage in my book, *Cybernetic Trading Strategies*, which was published by John Wiley and Sons, 1997.

The heart of Glen's work is fitting together technical pieces and seeing how they can be combined to develop forecasts and trading scenarios. One important point to remember is that forecasting is not trading. You trade based on what the market is doing, not based on a forecast. The longer view will only help when it agrees with short-term reality. This is an important point which cannot be over-looked.

Adrienne's Psychological Modeling Study

The Tenacity Model

Glen was forced to become tenacious at a very early age. The only other choice was to drown. By his difficult beginnings in South Dakota, Glen was met with a series of challenges. From meeting and overcoming these challenges, his tenacity was made even stronger. He took on the responsibilities of a man as a child with the limited resources of a poor farm. He learned not only how to make do with the resources that he had, but to use each little success as a step to greater heights.

Glen did not allow limited funds to keep him from getting a college education, nor did he allow the farm to chain him to a meager existence. Glen plodded and plowed his way to becoming one of the most recognized names in the futures industry. Because farming is one of the riskiest businesses in the world, Glen turned his resource of handling risk to developing a road show for teaching farmers how to hedge their crops. The long hours and the grueling pace of the road, traveling from city to city, prevented Glen from giving in to illness or personal family challenges that would deter his momentum. Once again, Glen relied upon his Tenacity Model to get him through difficult situations.

In addition, Glen worked as an insurance agent. Anyone who has ever successfully sold insurance knows that tenacity is a vital key to success. If you do not come into insurance sales with the Tenacity Model, you will have to develop it if you stay in that business for any significant time. As an agent, you cannot let the dozens of rejections deter you from finding the one customer who will say "Yes." When Glen was an agent, he worked with broken bones and fevers, often traveling hundreds of miles a day.

Glen's tenacity led him to being recognized as an analyst with keen foresight for the direction of the markets. The futures industry grabbed him up to use his tenacity in developing the futures conferences. Glen believes that his strength is built on a foundation of the Rock of Ages. His driving force is a belief in God and the faith that, no matter how hard the challenge, he can meet it with the certainty of success. Now, Glen is back on his own, trading as he says, like "an average trader." But to sustain average in the business of trading is an incredible feat, and Glen demonstrates that tenacity is one of the key elements in realizing success in the business of trading.

Another piece of the puzzle for Glen is that he is driven to help others help themselves. The most important person in his life was his father. Glen provided arms and legs for his father whose debilitating illness limited his physical strength and activity. Through this experience, Glen learned the importance of helping others, which is what he loves to do most, and has provided one of the driving forces for his tenacity as an adult.

Two final influences supporting Glen's Tenacity Model are the Neuro-Linguistic Programming writer and counselor, Tony Robbins, and the book, *Learned Optimism* by Martin Seligman. Tony Robbins is a model of tenacity himself. He rose from poverty to great success and then lost nearly everything through the misdeeds of a partner. He later rebuilt his career to even greater heights. In the book, *Learned Optimism*, the reader learns how to translate pessimistic thoughts into optimistic ones. By definition, optimism is not just the notion that everything will turn out rosy, but the belief that one setback or defeat does not equal the rest of your life. Optimism and the belief in the limited impact of a negative experience are essential to the Tenacity Model. Glen knows that if he perseveres, he will thrive.

CHAPTER 3

Herb Drechsler

Never too old - How a late-bloomer, ex-mining executive and college professor on his third career became a successful full-time money manager and trader.

Tell us about your early years and family?

I was born in Chicago and lived there for 10 years before my family moved to Boston. Eventually, I returned to Chicago and went to high school there. My mother and father both worked, so I helped care for the household. To earn spending money, I worked after school on a paper route.

My father started working as an apprentice tailor when he was fourteen, and my mother formed her own seamstress business when she was sixteen. My father lived to 99 and my mother to 101. He was still working at 98.

Were they supportive?

My mother was supportive of my efforts, but my father and I had very different ideas about my future. He was very much against my going away to the university. Then, when I decided to go into the mining business, both my parents thought the idea was crazy. They much preferred that I become a pharmacist or a lawyer or something with which they were familiar.

There was tension between my father and me because of the differences in our thinking. I was very fortunate to have had the opportunity to make peace with him before he died because most people never take that opportunity.

Did you find it necessary to make peace?
I believe that all children have something to resolve in their relationship with their parents - it is just in the nature of growing up. It was good that we could arrive at the understanding that my father did the best he could with the resources available to him. Sometimes things worked well for him, and sometimes they did not. It is a deep, profound experience when you discuss subjects of importance like that with your parents.

What is the best personal quality your parents instilled in you?
Persistence. I have always tried to do the best I could with what I have, just like my father, even though sometimes it did not work.

Did you eventually have a family of your own?
Yes. My first wife and I started our life together by eloping because we came from different religions. We went on to have four children. My eldest is 43 years old and my youngest is 37. Our life together ended tragically when my wife died of lung cancer from smoking in 1985.

I started dating again and met my second wife, who is a teacher. Two years ago, after 10 years together, we thought it was a good idea to get married.

What does your wife think about your involvement in the markets?
She does take an interest in what I do. It amazes her that I can put up with the amounts of money it is possible to lose in a day because teachers are very much security oriented. At first, she thought I was very rich, but now she knows better. However, I believe that anyone who makes more than twenty-five thousand dollars a year in this world is rich. So, by my definition, I am rich.

Are there particular activities that you enjoy?
I like a variety of activities, but three of my main joys are travel, reading, and skiing.

What is your favorite part of traveling?
I like exploring the place I am visiting and experiencing what it has to offer.

Do you have favorite subjects that you prefer to read?
I enjoy studying Spanish, modern science, cosmology, and religious books. One book that I highly recommend is *What the Bible Really Says,* by James Kugel. I also enjoy reading cooking magazines, because I love to cook and do our cooking. However, I do not like to do the shopping, so I leave that to my wife. Cooking is very relaxing for me. I cook like I trade. I take a recipe, and then I'm creative around it.

Do you take the opportunity to ski often?
I ski almost every weekend in winter. I have a respect for the danger of the slopes, just like I do for the markets. I am one of the few people you will see on the hill with a helmet.

Do you wear a helmet when you trade?
No, but I wear suspenders, so I won't lose my pants.

Could you relate wearing a helmet to using stops?
When I put in an order, I always put in my stop. I never take a naked market position without entering a stop. The exception is if I enter the market with a limit order.

What is your approach to attaining a new skill?
I believe that before you can take on any new skill you should go to someone who has the necessary expertise and learn to do things correctly. Many skills can be learned much more quickly and effectively if you have a teacher to help you. I did this very thing with skiing, motorcycle riding, and becoming a professional trader. At this time, I have given up motorcycle riding because I find it too dangerous.

What similarities do you find in being a good athlete and being a good trader?

Focus. If you are skiing and lose your focus, a fall is likely with the possible consequences being personal injury. If you lose your focus in trading, you are going to suffer similar consequences with the resulting injury being financial in nature.

What is your educational background?

I went to college in Butte, Montana to study mining. At night, I worked in the copper, lead, zinc, gold and manganese mines in the area. I was an average student because I put time into my many other interests, one of which was being on the football team.

After college, I started working as a miner and eventually became an executive in several mining companies. I worked for a company called American Metal Climax in New York City in the building which was called Radio City Music Hall. I was in charge of the overseas mining investments. This position required traveling around the world once a month, which created a tremendous amount of stress for my family. The kind of intensity the position demanded conflicted with my family life. I could not raise a family, be gone six months of the year, and be successful at both.

My family's welfare was more important to me, so I decided to change careers and become an educator. The key problem was that I had to go back to school, and get a new union card, which was represented by a Ph.D. in the university teaching system. At the time, I did not have a Masters degree, but found that at Columbia University I could get a Ph.D. in four years without having to get a Masters degree. My Ph.D. was in international business and group psychology.

When did you start your teaching career?

I taught mineral economics, general economics, finance, and accounting from 1968 to 1975 at Columbia University. From there

I continued teaching at the University of British Columbia in Vancouver.

Why did you start investing in the markets?
Investing for me was about making money. In the 1960's, I decided it would be a good idea to invest money in the stock market rather than work only as an engineer for a salary. I started learning at first by winning on some trades and then losing on some, too.

When did you start your trading career?
While I was at the University of British Columbia, I began trading the markets. I also set up an economics consulting business with a partner, which did consulting for anti-trust and litigation purposes. At one point, we had one of the largest businesses of its type in North America with over 100 employees. Because of its size, that business became really crazy to manage, so we got rid of it. This all occurred at about the time that I became a full-time trader. In 1992, I started to do more and more trading and less investing, except in the stock market, where I invested in mutual funds.

After the partnership ended, I established a trading business with a new partner. We now work in a pleasant, serene atmosphere looking out over the Vancouver harbor while we buy and sell.

Are there any books on trading that have influenced you?
Lefevre's book, *Reminiscences of a Stock Operator,* (John Wiley and Sons) is one that I highly recommend. Another good book is Stan Weinstein's *Secrets of Profiting in Bull and Bear Markets,* (Dow Jones Irwin, 1988). I also liked some early Bruce Babcock work. My partner and I have probably the largest investment libraries around here and there are many books that I could recommend. I guess that comes from my academic research background.

Are there mentors whom you have had?
I never had any investing mentors, but there are people like you, Adrienne, and Van Tharp, who have helped me significantly. Also,

Chuck Lebeau has been very influential in offering advice about practical and realistic trading strategies.

What markets were you trading at that time besides mutual funds?

I was trading in copper, gold, oil, corn, cocoa, wheat, D-Marks, Canadian dollars, T-Notes, and Eurodollars.

When you first started trading, did you have good results?

When I first started trading, I was at Columbia University and I was using the investment advice I got in school from my professors. Using this advice in the time period from 1968 to 1975, I proceeded to lose a lot of money. My way of trading is probably shorter term than the ideas of most professors.

Did you feel that what they were teaching did not work?

It did not work well for me. I was trying to forecast the future with Gramm and Dodd analysis. I switched from that to technical systems using harmonics and cycles. There was a book written at that time by Hurst, *The Profit Magic of Stock Market Timing,* (Prentice-Hall, 1970) that influenced my market studies. He had this idea that stocks cycled up and down and his theory was that you could buy at the bottom and sell at the top. One of the strategies I used was to draw pictures with plastic instruments and I would count the number of bars and develop cycles. At that point, the stock market was not good and I was trying to go long into a down market and the results were not the best.

How did your expertise and knowledge of mining contribute to your trading in this area?

I created all kinds of personal biases, which took me about 15 years to throw away. For instance, mining prices are cyclic, but when I took a longer-term view and started looking at long-term cycles in mining, I did not do well. Gold had started down in 1982, and copper prices were going up and down and I had the idea that I could buy at the bottom on the longer-term view. This was a strategy that turned out to be a poor idea for me. Everything considered, my most comfortable investing horizon is rather short term, 2 to 10 days.

What is your methodology?
I just look for momentum changes and support and resistance levels. I use Stochastics, RSI, momentum changes from MACD's, trend lines and trading patterns. I try to simplify my trading life and have as few tools and indicators as possible. Over the years, I have become very aggressive in cutting my losses. If I were to tell you the secret of my success, it would be from being aggressive in cutting my losses which start at the peak or trough of a move or from where I entered a trade.

What hurdles did you have to overcome early in your trading?
Initially, my setbacks came out of trying to find a trading system that would work for me. As I developed my knowledge base, too many indicators, and confidence problems were the next hurdles I had to overcome. I also had to deal with the emotional problems of fear of cutting my losses and then cutting my losses too soon, which was really a mistake. Looking back over all of the hurdles I had to overcome, I would say that the biggest problems I had were my psychological problems, which   still occur occasionally.

What were those psychological problems?
Pulling the trigger on entry and exit, fear of losing or not making money, losing focus, just normal kind of stuff.

What happened when you wanted to pull the trigger?
I started to talk to myself and tried to forecast the future. My biggest successes have come when I stop trying to forecast and just take things as they come.

Before a trade, I write:
    1. What do I believe about this trade?
    2. What do I fear about this trade?

3. Is my belief greater then my fear?

Suddenly, I had this insight that I did not believe or fear anything about this trade. I had no idea whether the position I took was going to go up or down. When I stopped worrying whether it was going to go up or down, I started having the insight that when you get a signal to take, you do it.

I am not 100 percent mechanical. If the risk of a trade is too high, I will walk away from it even though I know it is a good trade. I am quite tough on the money management part of the trade.

Is your trading mechanical or is it basically subjective?
Initially, it was mostly a combination of subjective and mechanical, but as time has gone on, it has become more mechanical.

Do you have any other rules to break your rules?
My rules come out of risk avoidance, and following my rules.

If any part of your methodology is not working, how quickly do you change your rules?
Very slowly. It may take me a month or two to change a rule that is not working as it should. My rule changes are mostly strategic changes rather than rule changes. I don't change my rules, only my strategy.

Do you think there is anything unique about the way you trade?
Ninety five percent is not unique and five percent is unique.

Have you defined your protective exits and reentry strategies and what rules can you share with our readers?
The rules are very simple. For example, now, I am watching Cocoa, Canadian Dollars, Crude Oil, German D-Marks, Eurodollars, Gold, Copper, Soybeans, Sugar, and Wheat and those are all just numbers on the screen. I watch very simply the momentum changes on a 17/9/5 day MACD and the direction of a five day stochastic

smoothed with a three-day moving average. The other indicators I use are the direction of a 9 and 3-day RSI. If all three of these indicators are moving in the same direction, i.e., if the momentum is going up and the stochastic and RSI also turn up, that is my signal to trade for the longer term. Just prior to picking up the telephone and placing my order, I measure my risk exposure. If the trade is going to risk more than 2 1/2% of my trading capital, or the stop is greater than two times the average true range, I do not take the trade. I have more than one system that depends on the time horizon or way the market is moving.

Another thing that I am willing to share is that trends in the markets have become shorter over time. I think this is because of the use of computers and more sophisticated analysis. For this reason, I now exit using a target profit on my trend-following trades. That target is based on a percentage of the three-day average true range.

One of the most important things in trading is to limit risk exposure. I will often not take trades that I believe could be very profitable if too much of my trading capital is to be at risk.

How do you define the risk of a trade?
My definition of initial risk is the difference between where I put my stop and where I am going to get in. My stop is placed one tick away from the previous three day low or high.

Have you actually tested what you do?
We have tested everything we do over time. We are always experimenting with something here.

So, you have not used testing tools like TradeStation or Excel?
No, sometimes it takes 6 to 8 months to test an idea.

Your system is tested on real trading over a relatively short period of time while many systems are tested over 20 years using system testing software and a long-term database.

Yes, but you are taking 20 years of price history and testing on the computer very quickly while my six months takes six months. We have found that you can adapt a system more quickly when you are testing it real-time short-term. You begin to get a feeling about which trades will work and which ones will not. When trading a system I have not tested very long, I will reduce my risk exposure below my standard limit. If the system is working well, I will increase my positions. If the pattern goes into a bad period, I will continue to trade it, but in a very small way. This is the money management side.

What personal strong points do each of you, as partners, bring to the table?
My strengths are persistence, confidence that I can solve a problem, tenacity, and the ability to follow my rules. There are dozens of little pieces of papers with rules all around my trading area. Another strength is the ability to look at the big picture. My partner's main area of strength is his extreme attention to the details of running the business.

What one primary element makes your partnership work?
We trust each other. If we were climbing a mountain, I would trust that he would not let go of the rope.

What prompted your decision to become a money manager?
Originally, it was for ego reasons. It was a statement to the world saying, "Look at how smart I am! I can show you!" Some part of that comes from my background as a teacher. It is not so important now, but I still have a ways to go with that. The main reason now for trading is to increase the capital base available and to make money.

Is there anything unique about your service as a money manager?
I tend to keep people out of the commodities markets and put them into the stock market in mutual funds. My objective in the funds is

to beat the S & P Index by about 5 % annually. That means buying and selling funds, not daily but over time, following the trend of the market. In a down market, I spend a lot of time in money market funds. I don't like to be in a fund if it is going down.

Do you use similar trading techniques in trading the funds?
No, on the funds it is even simpler. We get the fund closing prices every day and plot it on a graph with the direction of the close. From the chart, you can measure and get the change, and as long as the sun is going up, that is good. If it is going up faster then the S&P, that is even better. And if it is not going up faster than the S&P, then we switch to a fund that is. All I am looking for is a rate of change. As long as the funds I am in are going up faster then the S&P, then it makes sense for me to be there. When stocks are doing badly, it is time to get out. In addition, I also filter using the direction of RSI and trend lines. I do not use RSI as a classical overbought or oversold indicator; instead, I use it as a momentum indicator to get into short-term trends.

How do you exit your commodities?
The exit is an art form. Almost anybody can tell how to get in - that is the easy part. Getting out of a market position is the complicated part because it becomes much more subjective. What I have found over the last 18 months is that the volatility has been increasing and that the sustainability of the trends has been decreasing. I do not believe there is much profit in the trends, so, what I have got to do is take profits when they are available. If it hits my limit order, I get out and stick to my low risk strategy. What I have done, depending on the commodity, is measure off the average true range and establish a profit target. When I reach that profit objective, I get on the phone and exit the trade, put the money in the bank, and go on to the next trade.

What makes you sure the trends are not following through?
I watch the charts and look at them every day and in commodity after commodity, there is no follow through on trends.

Do you find published commercial charts more useful than generating them yourself on the computer?

No, but they do give me a 2-3 year perspective, which is useful.

Have you ever tried charting by hand?

Yes, years ago, and I have found that charting on the computer is the same as charting by hand, but the results are instantaneous. You do not have hours and hours tied up in piles of charts.

Did you ever come close to blowing out before you started to make money consistently?

Yes, I came very close to blowing out. My drawdowns have been between 50% and 70%, but then it would crawl back up again.

Do you care about fundamentals?

I avoid information like the fundamentals. If I let what is happening in the news and reports affect my thinking, I start the self-talk and that tends to really screw me up. Typically, my longest position in the market is 4 to 5 days. I am a short-term trend trader and fundamentals do not have a great effect on this short timeframe, in my opinion, other than for market shocks.

Do you use filters determined by the direction of a longer-term trend?

I used to, but I do not anymore. From my experience, I have found it works better by not using this type of filter.

I carry short-term and long-term trading systems with the longer-term trading system being somewhat technical. I take a 7-day plus and minus directional index, a trend line and the MACD. When they line up in the same direction, that gives me an indication that perhaps I should add to my position, hold my position a little longer, or change my 3-5 day system to a slightly longer outlook, and start following a trend line. If I am going to follow a trend line which is in a long-term system, I'm going to take it back 3 days and follow it on up until I decide it is time to get out. This description is the art form of trading.

What thoughts go through your head at this point in a trade?
I look at the fact that the market has gone on very rapidly and perhaps there are beginning to be gaps in the chart. Gaps are only partially good because when they occur during a trend it means that it is nearly at the end of the trade. Gaps that are counter to the trend and do not fill are very good and can lead to explosive moves. What it also means is that people are starting to jump into the market like crazy, and now is the time for me to look for a place to jump out. I do not look for big moves, I merely look for the next trade. Trying to get the big move is one of my measurements of greed, and one of my personal struggles is to avoid greed.

Can you tell us how much of your own money you have in the markets?
I currently have about four hundred thousand dollars in the markets with part of it in the commodity market and part of it in mutual funds.

How much outside money do you currently manage in the markets and what results have you been having?
We are currently managing about five hundred thousand dollars. Last year, our results were better than the S & P 500 Index, but it was a real struggle because the market stopped doing anything after September.

Where do you want to go from here?
At some point in time, I will want to retire from working in an office. Retirement for me will be trading from my home and spending time discovering more about myself and the world around me.

- On 11/4 long term signal, i.e., ± 7 day DI, trendline and 17/9/5 MACD, gives a buy signal, but the risk to 805-758 is too high for the volatility.
- On 11/9 buy at 788 with stop at 783

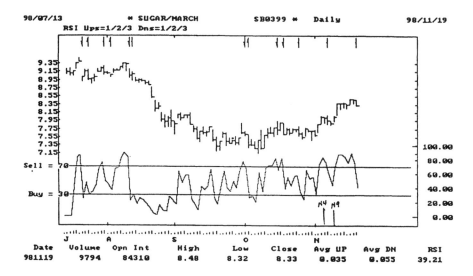

- On 11/19 long term and short term signals are weak. While placing an order to move my stop, I get a mental message, "Don't move the stop just get out." So I immediately change the order to sell at Market and get out.

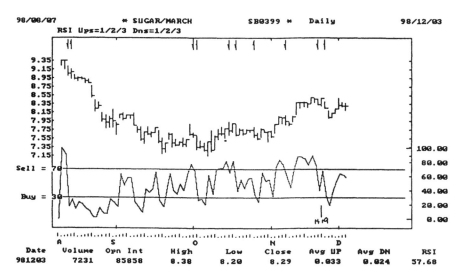

MODELING STUDY

CHILDHOOD FAMILY STATUS
- Herb experienced poor to middle class while growing up in Chicago

MENTORING - INFLUENCE
- Physical endurance/good genetic background
- Parents both were entrepreneurs
- Parents instilled persistence
- Early Bruce Babcock books
- Adrienne Toghraie as trader's coach
- Van Tharp on trader's psychology
- Chuck Lebeau on trading strategies

ENVIRONMENT
- Very supportive mother
- Supportive wife and four children as an adult

EDUCATION
- Studied mining
- Ph.D. in International Business and Group Psychology

INTERESTS - Skills - Abilities -Honors
Childhood
- Ball sports

Adult
- Culinary skills
- Skiing
- Traveling
- Motor cycling
- Reading modern science, cosmology, religion and Spanish

QUALITIES
- Tenacity
- Self-reliance
- Persistence
- Ability to trust
- Optimistic
- Sense of humor
- Team player
- Iconoclastic

BUSINESS EXPERIENCE
- Entrepreneur at early age
- Mining
- Executive position with international responsibilities
- College professor-mineral economics, finance and accounting
- Economics consulting

PHILOSOPHY - SUCCESS BELIEFS
- Confidence in problem solving abilities
- Persistence--keep going, never give up

PROSPERITY CONSCIOUSNESS
- Supports general charities

TRADING EXPERIENCE
- Stock and commodities trader
- Money manager
- Technical base with some discretion

RECOMMENDATIONS
- *What the Bible Really Says* by James Kugel
- *Reminiscences of a Stock Operator* by Edwin Lefevre
- *Secrets for Profiting in Bull and Bear Markets* by Stan Weinstein

- *The Profit Magic of Stock Transaction Timing* by J.M. Hurst
- *The Futures Game* by Teweles & Jones

TRADER CONTRIBUTIONS
- Makes money for his clients

FUTURE PLANS
- Work out of home
- Continue to travel
- Study the markets and myself

TRADER GEMS - Fundamental - Intuitive - Psychological
- Keep your focus
- Hire mentors as teachers
- Do the best you can with what you have
- Learn to avoid greed
- Cut losses aggressively
- Overcome emotional hurdles
- Take trading signals without question
- See the big picture as well as the small picture
- Create a stress-free working environment
- The art of trading is the exit because it is more subjective

TRADER GEMS - Mechanical - Analytical - Technical
- Avoid forecasting the markets, let the market tell you what to do
- Before entering a trade write
    1. What do I believe about this trade
    2. What do I fear about this trade
    3. When you realize that you have nothing to fear about a trade, then you can follow the system
- Combines mechanical trading methodology with subjective analysis allowing him to adapt to market conditions
- Since trends have become shorter, uses target profits based on a percentage of three-day average true range

- Gaps in the direction of the trend often occur near the end of the trend or prior to a correction
- Counter-trend gaps that are not filled often lead to explosive moves

Murray's Analytical Modeling Study

Trade Methodology Analysis

Mechanical--Objective: Looks for simple patterns in indicators; for example, all of the indicators moving in the same direction. His methodology is trend following with strict money management rules.

Mechanical--Automatic: Charts indicators used in Analysis. Does not backtest any methodology, they are tested in real time.

Discretionary: Uses judgment to develop a feeling for pattern setups and considers exiting a trade an art form.

Analysis of Herb's Methodology

Herb shared his long-term trading method for commodities. Here is a step-by-step discussion of the simple mechanical type entry that he uses.

Herb's requirements for a long entry are as follows:

1. 17/9/5 Moving Average Convergence Divergence rising
2. Five day SlowK rising
3. Both a 9 day and 3 day RSI rising

When all of these requirements are met, he has a long entry, but he uses discretion to judge the quality of a trade setup before accepting or rejecting a trade.

Let's look at the short side entry parameters, which is the mirror image.

1. 17/9/5 Moving Average Convergence Divergence falling
2. Five day SlowK falling
3. Both a 9 day and 3 day RSI falling

This is the setup for a short trade, but once again he filters the setup of a trade using discretion.

Herb limits his risk to 2.5 percent of his account based upon the technical protective stop he needs to use. If the risk is too great in a trade, he does not take it. He defines his initial risk as the three-day low -1 tick on long trades, and the three day high + 1 tick for short trades.

Exits on trades are part of the art form. He uses a target price based on the three-day average true range. This is a relatively new feature in his trading and is the result of the markets not trending as well as they have in the past.

Mutual Fund Trading Analysis
Herb also trades mutual funds using a very simple method. His method for trading mutual funds is as follows:

1. Buy funds which are advancing faster than the S&P500
2. Filter trades by requiring the momentum of RSI to be up

The first rule is the heart of most of mutual fund switching methodologies used by professional traders, and is normally described as selecting funds with a higher relative strength than the S&P500. One model based on this methodology of sector analysis is the work of Pankin, published in the January 1996, through April 1996, editions of *Formula Research* (Volume 5, Numbers 5 through 8), a newsletter written by Nelson Freeberg. Herb filters his fund selection by requiring the RSI to be rising. This element prevents him from buying a fund during a downtrend. This approach will give better risk-adjusted returns than the S&P500 when money market rates are included in the calculation and volatility is reduced.

Theories on Gap Analysis
Herb also discussed his theories on gaps. First, gaps in the direction of the trend often occur near the end of a trend or shortly before a

correction. This is because the moves are often blow-off moves at the end of a trend. The correction could be small and either be a gap fill or it could be part of a larger correction especially during an Elliott wave 5. Counter-trend gaps, which do not fill, often occur because of changes in fundamental elements; for example, a frost that kills the coffee crop. These gaps often become runaway gaps and lead to a major move. Another time that runaway gaps occur is at the beginning of an Elliott wave 3 when it takes out the high of wave 1.

Gap analysis is a powerful tool in trading and can be an effective filter for many different trading methods based upon where you are in a current market cycle.

Herb's trading style is an art, and he has done well for his clients. But, his base methodology does not backtest well. He adapts his methodology in real time as the markets change. He might filter out entries under given conditions because he has seen that they have failed over the past few months and then will continue to filter them until they work again. Linda Bradford Raschke said, when interviewed for *Inside Advantage* in 1996, that a great trader is able to adapt to changing market conditions; Herb is a master at that.

Adrienne's Psychological Modeling Study

The Self-Reliance Model

From early childhood, Herb Drechsler learned self-reliance by helping with the housework while both parents worked. Then he took on a paper route to earn his pocket money. When a child goes against his parents' wishes for his future, he must take on more responsibility in order to succeed. When Herb chose to become a mining engineer and married a woman from a different faith, he went against his parents' wishes. As a result, he lost their support and was forced to rely upon his own resources. His Self-Reliance Model, which had already been established in childhood, allowed him to create a successful life on his terms.

While Herb has enjoyed team activities, his avid love for reading, motor biking, skiing and cooking are solo activities requiring self-reliance in motivation and action.

Midway through Herb's career, while supporting a family of four, he decided to change direction and teach at the university level. A teacher must create lessons and, basically, put on a one-man show all day. Part of Herb's discovery about self-reliance was realizing that to learn a new skill quickly, you could enlist the help of all of the available resources - other teachers, books, as well as seminars or private coaching. In the process of making these changes in his life, Herb discovered that self-reliance does not mean that others cannot help you along the way. This realization expanded and improved his Self-Reliance Model for future use.

Investing and going into business became Herb's way of going beyond a salary to develop entrepreneurial financial possibilities. Self-reliant people do not want a cap on their earning potential. In fact, they do not want to be limited in any part of their lives. They see every part of their lives as an opportunity for expansion and development. While pursuing his economic potential through trading, Herb came to the realization that expanding his understanding of himself while overcoming his foibles was the most important key to self-reliance.

Herb's risk averse approach to trading comes from the fact that he appreciates the value of the efforts that it took to earn his investing capital. He knew that he was the one responsible for his results. Working from his Self-Reliance Model in trading, Herb has been in the markets for a very long time and has consistently produced a good living from them. This model prevents him from falling into the self-sabotaging traps that eliminate so many traders from the business: fear, helplessness, greed, and lack of inner discipline. His self-reliance allows him to trade from a sense of self-confidence and optimism. He knows that he can solve problems and that if he perseveres, he will come through any situation. Finally, if there were ever a signal that a man was determined to rely on his own wit and resources to keep him going, the sight of a seventy-something man flying down a snowy slope on skis, wearing a crash helmet, would be it. Herb also knows that while he might not need a crash helmet for his trading, he always remembers to wear suspenders so he does not lose his pants.

CHAPTER 4

Sheldon Knight

A knight in technical armor - How an ex-physicist used his
scientific training to increase $75,000 to 1.2 million 6 months before
Larry Williams made his reputation for a similar feat.

**Tell us about your beginnings. What was it like to grow up in
your household?**
I was born in a small farming town of about 7,000 people in
northern Missouri. My father had studied at the University of
Missouri for two years and then transferred to MIT. He went there
for three years with a double major in mechanical and electrical
engineering. After the third year, his health broke down and he had
to return to the small town where we lived.

My mother had an Associates Degree from Stevens College in
Columbia, Missouri, and she was a teacher.

My parents were married in 1925, and I was born in 1933. I was
their only child.

Did you grow up on a farm or in a farming area?
We had a farm, but we lived in town. The town was the county seat
of an agriculturally-oriented area. We left there when I was in the 6th
grade.

What were school days like?
The school was located next to the county library, and I spent a great
deal of time there. I took music and piano lessons. I have never
been interested in sports.

What was your father doing during this time?
My father was manager of the local electric cooperative during this

time. When I was in the 6th grade, we moved to St. Louis where my father had taken a job with the Rural Electrification Administration of the U. S. government. During World War II, many government offices were moved out of Washington, D. C. to the Midwest because there was fear that the Nazis would bomb Washington, D.C. from submarines. The Rural Electrification Administration was moved to St. Louis, so that is where we moved.

What happened from there?
He was transferred to Arkansas after a short time. I went through 7th and 8th grade in the little town of Conway, Arkansas, which is about 30 miles north of Little Rock. Then, my dad took a job with a much larger electric company in Cedar Rapids, Iowa. I always enjoyed going to different schools. There was a big disadvantage, of course, in that I did not really make many long lasting friendships, but I always had a pretty good time.

What were you like in high school?
In high school, the courses I took were analytical or language oriented. I took Latin, French and a lot of math courses. I loved music, and was awarded an organ scholarship at the local college.

I have to honestly say that if someone had asked me what marijuana was while I was in high school, I would not have known. I probably would have started looking at the map to see if it was some country in Africa. Drug use was unknown even among the worst kids in town. It was a very straight, small town existence, but it was big enough that quite a bit was going on.

At this point, did you even know what trading was?
No, I had absolutely no idea. Except for the one year in St. Louis, I grew up in small towns and was not exposed to trading or the markets.

Tell us about college?
I went to Iowa State in Ames, Iowa, and majored in Physics for 3

years. Meanwhile, my father had retired and my parents had moved to California. When I was preparing to register for my 4th year at Iowa State, I discovered to my dismay that I was considered an out-of-state resident, which meant that my tuition was going to be outrageous.

Being in somewhat of a jam, I applied to Cal at Berkeley. One evening in conversation, my father suggested that I really should go to Stanford. It was July, and the freshman admissions list had been completed almost a year earlier, but because Stanford was a private school, I thought that perhaps they might bend the rules. The fact that I was taking 27 units, had a 3.7 grade average, and was working 40 hours per week impressed the man in charge of admissions.

Where were you working?
I was working as an engineer for a radio station, and doing background organ music for the local television station. For the majority of the 40 hours, I was a transmitter operator, which meant watching the dials and taking readings every half-hour. So, 30 out of the 40 hours could be used for studying.

Were you admitted to Stanford?
Yes, conditionally. The only thing they could not waive was the college-board examination.

Where did you go from there?
When I graduated from Stanford in 1955, I received a commission as a Second Lieutenant in the Air Force. I was in ROTC at Iowa State and Stanford. The Air Force liked Stanford graduates since it was difficult to get them interested in the military at that time. A colonel called to ask if I might have an interest in an award called the Distinguished Military Graduate. The prize for winning the award was a regular commission in the Air Force instead of a reserve commission. I had nothing to lose because I could always resign a regular commission. In 1957, I was accepted into pilot training which took a little over one year. After that I was assigned

to McGuire Air Force Base at Wrightstown, NJ. and flew transports between the United States and Europe for the next 3 ½ years. In 1960, I resigned my commission, went to work for an aerospace company in Mt. View, CA and went back to school part time to get a Masters Degree in Electrical Engineering.

Where did you go?
I returned to Stanford and completed my Masters Degree in 1962, with specialization in a very arcane subject called Statistical Communication Theory. The subject matter related the mathematics involved in detecting very weak intelligent signals in the presence of large amounts of random noise. Basically, it was the study of calling home from Jupiter on a cellular telephone. At the time, it was a brand new area of study, and much of the impetus for it developed from the space program, which was just in its embryonic stage. Everyone realized that it was going to be necessary to transmit pictures and data from deep space with very little power, since power is at a premium on spacecraft. The whole field dealt with how to code information and then decode it, while obtaining the highest signal to noise ratio using current knowledge about the signals.

Did you know about trading by this time?
Yes, by this time I knew about trading, but I had not traded yet. My father was a small investor in stocks and, through my conversations with him, I learned that there was such a thing as trading. I understood the rules of the game, but how to make things happen was another matter. I knew nothing about the futures market.

When I went to work for the aerospace company, I had access to a large-scale computer. Since a database was neither available nor affordable, I keypunched all of the stocks that began with the letter "A" in *The Wall Street Journal* every day. This was my beginning database and I found that I could not apply the statistical techniques that are based on stationary, normal statistics to the markets because the markets are not normal and stationary. Studies like multiple

88

linear regression and many other studies of that type that can be used in a physical situation just will not work with markets.

Playing with the markets on and off for the next ten years kept my interest, and as a result I got a little feeling for how stocks moved.

In 1974, I started my own company, K-Data, Inc.

What did K-Data do?
Our claim to fame was very sophisticated project management software. While at the aerospace company, I was Vice President of Engineering and I was responsible for management of all of the projects. I quickly found that the project management software we had was hopelessly inadequate. In the dark of night, I figured out how the accounting system worked and programmed my own project management software. Other companies with the same problem became aware of my development and were interested in it. I was getting tired of government contracting and decided to see if I could market this as a separate product. K-Data began with this project management software, and we were very successful for quite a few years.

How many people were involved in K-Data?
At the peak, I had four people. We would go into a company's accounting department and design a customized, integrated system for their accounting and project management. At the time, integrated systems were not very common. Generally, you first entered data in a payroll system, and then entered the data separately into another system, that produced the general ledger. From there, the data was entered once again into whatever program you had for project management or labor distribution. The process was labor intensive and the chance for error increased with every re-entry. I came up with a totally integrated system that was transaction oriented. A person had to learn how to enter a time sheet and the system distributed the data to all of the various reports and subsystems as needed.

Another aspect of K-Data was that we offered to operate the integrated system for the clients. With only one exception, our clients took us up on the offer and we actually ran the system on our computer. We would give the customer data entry software to create the input for us in their facility and they would transmit the data to us by modem. This process helped us to recognize idiosyncrasies to streamline each client's operation.

In the early1980's, I decided I wanted to get serious about trading, so I started going to seminars and buying books.

What was available back then?
Remember when Jake Bernstein and Larry Williams had their dog and pony show called Futures International Symposiums (FIS)? They would have lots of speakers and workshops. Also, at that time the Technical Analysis Group conferences were starting. I went to several of those conferences and read many books.

Were any of the books useful?
Perhaps one or two. Bruce Babcock wrote a book called *The Dow Jones Guide to Systems*, which had some good ideas in it. Larry Williams' early books had some good ideas in them, too. One of them was *How I Made a Million Dollars Trading Last Year*. Wells Wilder's book was also very interesting.

Missouri is called the "Show-Me-State." Being from Missouri, that was my attitude. I did not believe anything that I read until I actually programmed it to see whether people knew what they were talking about. Of course, I quickly found that at least 90% of the information out there was total nonsense.

I was fortunate that I had the computer capacity and the ability to program long before TradeStation. At that time, you could just begin to get data. Mike Marriott of MJK Associates had been producing data in machine-readable format since the late 1960's and is almost a neighbor. I bought his entire database.

Tell us about your family.

During my training as a pilot, I went to New Orleans. The lady I eventually married was on a riverboat cruise that I took while I was there. She was watching some stevedores on the dock who had stopped to eat lunch. I turned to her and said, "Look at that, the people watch the monkeys and the monkeys watch the people." It turned out that she was from Germany and did not know the word "monkey." She asked what I meant in broken English, and since I spoke fairly good German, I talked to her in German and asked her out to dinner. We were married in 1960 and have been happily married ever since. We now have three grown children and four grandchildren.

What about your children, what do they do?

My oldest daughter is a partner in a large Southern California law firm. My younger daughter was Director of Corporate Communication for a large electronic company and has now just started her own company called Tanis Communications. My son, who is the youngest, was a floor trader on the Chicago Mercantile Exchange. He traded the Goldman Sachs Commodity Index contract (GSCI) and was very successful. Now, he is trading interest rate products on Project A over at the Chicago Board of Trade. He thinks that electronic trading is the wave of the future.

Let's get back to your trading?

I was collecting ideas from Jake Bernstein and Larry Williams and testing them on the computer. Larry introduced me to the "Volatility Adjusted Breakout Concept." The basic idea is that you establish an upper and a lower breakout level by adding and subtracting some volatility measurement to some significant market point. For example, you can take the average range of the last five days, add and subtract this measurement to yesterday's close to get an upper and lower level for today. If the market moves through the upper level you go long and if it moves through the lower level you go short. This is a very simple implementation of the concept. You can apply it to previous highs or lows or pivot points. The basic concept is that you use some type of distance measurement off some significant market point to establish a breakout level. There are a 1,001 ways you can modify this and make it better, which I did. I have yet to find any basic trading philosophy that works as well as the "Volatility Adjusted Breakout Concept."

What about the "Donchian Channel Breakout?"

The Donchian channel breakout system, also known as the "four-week rule," is a breakout concept without the volatility adjustment. The use of some kind of volatility adjustment on market breakout studies will make it much better. The use of volatility with my system has been the most powerful enhancement.

Whose idea was it?

The idea of volatility breakout was introduced to me by Larry Williams, but I found that Wells Wilder had talked about this idea back in his book, *New Concepts of Technical Trading.*

Where did you take it from there?

With this idea, I realized that short-term trading is more profitable than long-term trading. You make less money on each trade, but you have so many more trades that you end up with more money at the end of the year. It was also evident that in developing a short-term trading system, you must have tick data. Short-term trading in this case means trades of no more than two or three days, and, in many cases, intra-day trading.

You were using volatility breakout on intra-day data?

Yes. The first question was data. I found that you could buy data directly from the Chicago exchanges. To this day, you cannot get machine-readable time and sales data from the New York exchanges, but both the Chicago Mercantile and Chicago Board of Trade will sell time and sales data on magnetic tape. The data was fairly expensive, but I bought it for the S&P and for T-Bonds going back to the beginning of trading. This was late 1985.

Did you have the computer capability to handle this type of data?

Yes. It was on the half-inch industry standard magnetic tape that was used then. I transferred all of the data to disk after compressing it. I wrote routines to read the tapes and put them into my tick data format. I could get a reasonable amount of data on the disks that we had. From this information, I developed a system based on a very short-term volatility breakout.

What type of filters did you use?

In the initial incarnation, I took all of the signals. The average trade was about $350 per trade on the S&P and something over $200 on the T-Bonds. The average holding period was just a little over a day. The system was either long or short and was always in the market. That is something that I still believe to this day, and I never use stops on these trading systems. If you should not be long the market, then you ought to be short. Seems pretty obvious to me.

When did you know to get in and out of the market?

You have entry rules. The entry rule for the short-position is the exit rule for the long-position and vice versa. So, you are constantly flipping back and forth between long and short.

I found very little serial correlation between trades. That is, the profit of one trade had almost nothing to do with what happened on the next trade. Going even further, I looked at the next trade in the same direction. For example, if you have a long trade that is a loser what does that mean for the next long trade that you take? I found almost no correlation.

Did you use indicators like Average Directional Index (ADX)?

No. I use none of the standard technical indicators.

Did you use trend filters?

No. Nothing. It was simply volatility breakout. I had my own method for computing volatility, which differed from what other

93

people had done.

So that was your proprietary claim to fame?
Yes, basically that was it. Later on, I did embellish the system with some day of the week studies. I found that the system tended to lose money at certain times of the month and certain days of the week. Performance results could be improved substantially by not taking trades based on the seasonals.

We are getting toward 1986?
Yes, I still had not actually done any real trading, but in June of 1986, I decided I was ready to trade. On June 1, 1986, I opened two trading accounts. One was opened in K-Data's name with $45,000, and another one was opened with a different broker with $30,000 in my name. Within one year, the two accounts were $1.2 million.

So, this is the man who on his first set of trades, who had never traded before, took $75K in accounts to $1.2 million before Larry Williams did it?
I had about a six-month head start on Larry. It was calendar 1987, when Larry did it.

And you only traded S&P and T-Bonds?
Yes. Exclusively.

Now was there anything particular about that year that made it different than trading now?
Absolutely. The 1986-1987 period was unique in many respects. I have often speculated on what made the short-term trends so powerful in the financial futures during that time. In the case of the T-Bonds, it was the time when Savings & Loan institutions were losing their shirts. Most of the S&L's had discovered the T-Bond futures market, and they were trading heavily, but they did not know what they were doing. Good short-term systems were making money at that time.

How many trades a week were you making?
On the average, I was trading 4 to 5 times per week. I was strictly playing very short-term trends that would last a few hours up to a day or two.

What was your time frame?
I was watching it during the day. I had a real-time feed at that time from CQG. I was looking primarily at five-minute bars. I took 100% of the signals mechanically. I never elected to override the system and I can think of two times that I used discretion, if you can really call it discretion when I decided not to trade.

When was that?
The first time was actually shear stupidity on my part and I still kick myself for this. There was a stock trader named Ivan Boesky involved with insider trading. The government caught him and sentenced him to prison. He worked out a plea bargain for a certain amount of prison time. He had to divest himself of approximately 100 million dollars worth of stocks. The news of this came out one Friday afternoon while I was in Atlanta attending one of Robert Prechter's Elliott Wave seminars. We were standing around at the cocktail party and someone asked whether this was going to have an impact on the market. Bob's answer was, "Boy, you better believe it. This guy is going to be selling 100 million dollars worth of stock next week, and I sure would not want to be long."

I was long 25 contracts in the S&P at that moment, and worried about it until about 15 minutes before the market opened on Monday morning. I called my broker and asked, "What's the call on the S&P?" He said, "Down 200," which was two full points.

That was about ¾ of a daily range and would be about 10 points now?
Yes, exactly. I put an order in to sell out the position on the open. It opened down about 200 points just like they had called it and that was the low for the day. Then, the rest of the day it continued to

climb and it actually closed higher for the day. I sat there kicking myself all day and thought I would never do that again.

With good money management you might have made $1.6 million?
That's right. As a matter of fact, just for drill, I sat down the other day and looked over that year and tried to figure out where I would have been if I had just completely followed the money management system. It turns out, instead of the $1.2 million, it would have been a little over $4 million. What hurt me was not this moment of insanity when I decided to close out the trade, but that I was taking money out of the account. At one point, I took 50% of the account out because the account got up to half a million dollars. I had never seen so much money in one place in my life. I just could not sit there and wait.

So, that one point something million you are giving us is with the money that you took out?
Yes, that includes the money I took out. I took $250,000 out of the account when it got up to $500,000. So, that $250,000 was no longer available for trading in the account.

When was the second time you overrode the system?
The Crash in 1987 and that I would do again, by the way. I was long 30 or 40 T-Bonds at the time, and during the day, while the world was falling apart on stocks and stock indexes, the T-Bond market was gradually drifting lower. I was underwater by quite a bit on the position already. I had gone long the day before and the bonds were drifting lower on October 19th. When they actually closed the day, I had a $35,000 to $40,000 open loss on the position. The market did not go far enough to hit the lower breakout point, so I was still long at the end of the day. This all happened during the time that the T-Bond market was trading the night session. I called the broker shortly before the night session opened and asked for an opening call. He told me the call was up three. When the T-Bonds opened, they were not up three tics - they were limit up at three full

points. I not only made up the open position loss, but was well into the black with a large position. The question was, what should I do? The bonds were sitting limit up and I was long. The world had just ceased to exist as we knew it for stocks.

How can you predict this sort of thing in back testing?
All of the back testing in the world is useless in a situation like this. A situation like this had never occurred before, and as far as I knew the bonds could be from limit up to limit down in ten minutes, because there was not much liquidity in the market. Everyone was in a state of shock. I made someone very happy. I put an order in to sell my position at limit up and closed it out. I did not trade for almost a month. Things were so different from any previous historical period that it was probably wise to not rely on any of the historical trading models.

Did volatility breakout systems stop working?
No. If I had gone on trading, it would have been great; but in retrospect, I still think that I did the right thing because I did not know.

What did you do with all of the money?
My oldest daughter got married and that took care of quite a bit of it. No, I am only joking. Actually, I saved it. As I mentioned, I had two accounts: one in my name personally and one in the company's name. The company had a profit sharing and retirement plan. By talking to a good tax person, I found a way to put quite a bit into that plan, which I subsequently closed out and rolled it over into my IRA.

Did things change after that?
One thing that changed significantly was the performance of the system. During the time that I had this great run, the success was largely in the T-Bond market. I started out trading both the S&P and T-Bonds, but the slippage got so bad on the S&P that for about the last 6 months, I was trading only T-Bonds. I stopped trading the

S&P. About this time, the opening time for the T-Bonds was changed from 8:00 A.M. Chicago time to 7:20 A.M.

What difference would that make?
It makes a difference because government reports are released at 7:30 A.M., Chicago time. Under the old opening time, when the Bonds opened at 8:00 A.M., all of the emotionalism was released during the opening range when everybody had 30 minutes to think about it before they could trade it. I am convinced that this was a large component of the good performance that systems of this type could turn in back then.

Could you stay out the first forty minutes of trading?
No, because the emotion has already leveled out by that time. Of course, you cannot get filled during the time that the announcement comes out. For example, if you have a stop order in the market when unemployment comes out, you might be filled 16 points away from your stop. So, you cannot trade on stops through the reports.

You cannot take advantage of the overshoot from the irrational behavior that builds as a result of worrying thirty minutes before actual trading started. The change did make a significant difference, and the system has never worked as well since.

What did you do then?
In 1989, I got itchy to trade again, so I opened another $100,000 account, and I traded for 3 months. The account was doubled to $200,000 at the end of the three months. I was trading in the S&P market. At that point, I stopped trading again.

In 1990, I was just playing around with a small account. I would take a few trades, but I really did not do very well. I just broke even.

Then in 1991, I decided I could use a little more money, so I went back to the trough to do the volatility breakout game again in the T-Bonds. Meanwhile, I had done some more research and thought I

98

had greatly improved the day of the week filtering. I also thought that I had improved the algorithms I was using for the volatility breakout. At the time, I opened a $120,000 account. All of the back testing I did indicated that I should get a drawdown of no more than 50 to 55%, which is the typical drawdown that you get with this type of trading.

What do you mean 50-55%?
Well, the maximum drawdown that I should have experienced with the system should have been in the neighborhood of 55% of the previous equity peak. For example, if the account got up to $200,000, I should expect a $110,000 drawdown.

Does that mean that you traded multiple contracts?
Yes. You always trade multiple contracts. The money management is an integral part of the system. Depending upon your money management system, one method of entries and exits might be better than another method on multiple contracts, but not perform up to the first on single contract trading. The money management system that you use will affect what system is optimum.

Take us through those years.
To paint the black side of this, in 1991, I opened a $120,000 account expecting that I could have·maximum of 55% drawdown. Well, I got a 65% drawdown, and stopped trading because this was·outside of the parameters that I was expecting.

Why do you think that happened?
Mostly market conditions, because markets are random variables. When you have a random situation like that in principle, anything can happen. It is like the classic case in a physics course I took. There is a calculable probability that all of the air molecules will move out and away from your nose and mouth and you will suffocate, because they are all in random motion. You can calculate this probability. It is so small that I am not going to worry about it, but in principle it could happen. The entire world is basically

stochastic. It is basically random and markets are like that, too. During this time, the way the markets moved was such that this particular kind of volatility breakout system lost a heck of a lot of money.

What happened in 1992?
I stopped trading. I did not even look at the markets very much during that time. I was still working with K-Data and I started writing some articles for *Futures Magazine* and taking part in some of the conferences. Since 1991, I have traded a little on and off, but not in an intensive way.

I have also been winding the K-Data business down. I figure it is about time to do some of the things that I really want to do.

What is that?
One of them is more intensive market research, which I have been doing. All of this seasonal stuff is new, and I have spent quite a bit of time on that.

Where did you get the idea to look at the day, week, and month activity?
It was actually sparked by the trading experience back in 1986-1987, when I noticed that trades that were taken on certain days, particularly triple witching days, almost always lost money. Also, the third Friday of almost any month is a bad day for trading a breakout system because of random motion that is created by the evening out of option positions. The intra-day statistics on these days are quite different than they are on other days. With further observation, I found that there were more differences in the deliverable futures. The period around first notice day is different because people are rolling from the expiring contract to the next contract out. Periods around holidays are also different. I think this is probably a psychological effect because many active traders do not like to carry positions over a holiday. There is some different activity that takes place there.

Do you think that money can still be made at the rate that you made it with systems?
Oh no, absolutely not. At least I do not know how to do it.

What could you realistically do if you were trading now?
If I went back at it with the focus that I had in 1986 and 1987, and really wanted to devote full time to it, I think I could rather easily double the money every year, 100% a year.

So, if you were trading at a return of 100% per year out of a SEPP, which is protected from taxes, you could retire from the world in 15 to 20 years?
Well, not quite. As accounts get larger, trade execution gets more difficult. This problem limits the long term return. Also, 100% a year average, does not mean that you are going to make 100% every year. But yes, if you were trading out of a tax protected SEPP and not paying tax on it you could do very well indeed.

Do you think volatility breakout still works?
Yes, I do.

Why does it work?
It is very logical in a way. The whole breakout concept, whether it is the Donchian four-week rule, short-term breakouts, or breakouts based on averages of the highs and lows is a way of following trends. The volatility adjustment helps adapt to current market conditions by measuring noise. This avoids excessive loses due to false breakouts.

Have you noticed trends being shorter lately?
It depends on the market. If you look at the Japanese Yen, it has shown very long-term trends both upward and downward. No, I think there are short-term trends and long-term trends in markets. Any breakout system exploits this fact. Now, the problem, of course, with breakout systems is random noise. The markets will spike and will take you through a breakout point that really does not represent

the beginning of a trend. With some kind of measurement of how much noise is in the market, you can move those breakout points further apart or closer together to adjust for that noise.

What do you mean by noise?

People who work with markets usually call it volatility, but to me it is noise or meaningless motion. It is motion that does not go anywhere and some way to measure it is needed. You move your breakout points further apart or closer together depending upon how much noise is present. This strikes a balance between a breakout point that is close enough to pick up a true trend and not so close that the random noise is going to flip you one way, then the other, chopping you to pieces.

If you can calculate that right, then you can exploit short-term trends?

That is right. I am still convinced in the financial futures, which tend to be very liquid and have large ranges in dollar terms that these short-term trends will make more money over a long period of time than the longer-term trends. I still believe in stop and reverse trading because the markets are almost symmetrical, but not quite.

What is the difference?

Well, generally the financial futures fall faster than they rise. Your method of setting the breakout points on the upside and on the downside is not necessarily going to be symmetrical. Now, I cannot speak for other markets. Maybe all the markets have this characteristic, I do not know.

You are going to count on more noise on the downside?

Yes, there generally will be more noise on the downside especially in the recent S&P trading. You will get these very short spikes that last an hour or two, and then the market comes back.

Do you get these things like "oops" and classic gaps?
Oh, yes, as a matter of fact, "oops" was a part of the system that I was trading back in 1986 and 1987.

Getting back to money management, what is good money management?
In my opinion, you need at least $50,000 to effectively start trading because any kind of acceptable money management system is going to begin trading with multiple contracts. If you have losses right away, you can peel contracts off as your equity goes down. Philosophically, the correct money management approach will add contracts as the equity goes up and reduce the number of contracts that you take on each signal as the equity draws down. You have to start with enough equity to put on a minimum of three contracts. If you have a string of losses right away, you can go from three contracts, to two, to one and you do not run out of contracts right away.

The problem with a lesser amount is a loss right away will put you to the point where you have zero contracts.

Could you keep trading one contract until "Mr. Margin" tells you that you are dead?
No, because at some point, one contract is too many for your equity according to your money management rules. These are rules that you have researched and checked out. After losing half of your equity on one contract, you do not have enough for any contracts. You will have enough margin for one contract, but you will go broke in a hurry if you try to max out the contracts based on margin. That is why you should have enough equity to start out trading a minimum of three contracts. If margin is a factor in your trading, you are overtrading and are almost sure to lose.

Otherwise, what you are doing is sheer luck?
Yes. Exactly. Maybe you would be lucky like I was in 1986 and get the equity run up first before the initial drawdown. I should also add

that during that big run up there were times when I did have a 50% drawdown. Any good system is going to have 50% to 55% drawdowns.

Would you rescale your money management if you were professionally managing money?
Absolutely. As a matter of fact, I have been doing some consulting for a CTA and he asked me to come up with the proper money management system for a portfolio, which is managing public funds. The name of the game in that situation is not to make all of the money you can make, but to avoid losing it. You are trying to establish a maximum drawdown or maximum equity retracement and then, consistent with that drawdown, maximize your return on investment. So, that is what we did. We developed a brand new concept in money management. Of course the returns are nowhere near what the private trader who can accept 50% drawdowns might make.

What ideas could you give our readers from what you learned in the 80's?
One idea is a variation of the fixed fractional money management idea where you have so many thousands of dollars of equity for each contract put on. The way to set that parameter is based on statistical analysis using "Monte Carlo Simulation." This is a standard statistical technique that is used when the mathematics of the analysis is too complex to handle. Imagine taking a basketful of ping-pong balls, and matching each ball with a trade that a system has generated historically. You write the profit or loss of each trade on one of the ping-pong balls. Then, you throw all of the balls into a blower like they use in Las Vegas for the Keno game.

You randomly select balls with each one representing a real trade profit or loss from the historical back test. You put together a new synthetic series of trades based on this random sampling from all of the trades that have been created in the past. Assume that each series of tests are actual trades that have been made. From each series of trades, you calculate and plot the curve of drawdown versus return on investment as leverage changes. That is, as you change the amount of equity that is required to trade one contract and it creates a graph, which rises at first, comes to a peak, and then falls off as you over trade - it is too high a leverage factor.

Did you do the same thing back then?
I was doing twenty "Monte Carlo" tests, that is twenty random series of trades. I took the worst test and looked at the equity curve that resulted from it. I picked the leverage factor that was just a little bit to the left of the peak. According to the tests, there was less than a 5% chance that a drawdown greater than 50% was going to occur. The 50% drawdown came from the worst of the twenty curves that were created from the "Monte Carlo Simulation." I have forgotten what the predicted return on investment was, but the actual return on investment was pretty close to what was predicted.

Now, in the experiment in 1991, I did the same thing, but instead of 50% drawdown, the first thing that happened was I got a drawdown of 65%, which was beyond my parameters.

What would happen if you had run 1,000 Monte Carlo simulations?
Then, you would be finding worst case parameters that should only happen with a probability of 0.1%. I think this is being too conservative. The results would be so bad you would probably just put your money in T-bills, crawl under the bed and wait to die.

Would you have come up with the 65% drawdown if you had run more Monte Carlos?
Well, sure you would. The more tests you run, the worse the result is going to be.

How do you know when a mechanical system is not doing what it is supposed to do?
The situation that I described in 1991 is a perfect example of that

situation. I had done all of the analysis and had predicted that there was less than a 5% chance that I was going to have more than a 50% drawdown. In other words, there was less than a 5% chance that I was going to lose half the account at any point in time from the maximum peak.

When I started trading, the first thing that happened was I lost 65% of the account. To me, that was far enough beyond what reasonably would be expected that something was not working.

Did you see what happened after that?
As a matter of fact, the drawdown continued to get worse. It peaked out at around 75%. Then, it turned around and would have made the losses back and would have been profitable in about two years. That does not bother me. I followed the rules and it got to the point that things were not working in the way that I had predicted, so I quit. And that is what I would do again.

What have you found to be the most exciting part of this whole path of trading?
I would say it is a tie between the research and trading. I have always loved research activity, whether it is in the physical sciences, engineering, the markets, or mathematics. Almost equally, I like to see the money.

What would you say is the reason that you have been able to be so disciplined? Has there ever been a time when you have questioned your discipline?
No, I never questioned my discipline except the one ill-fated adventure with Ivan Boesky. I have grown up with engineering and mathematics, and have total faith in it. From the time I was a little kid, my father was an engineer and he spent time talking to me. I loved mathematics and could see how things worked. I had a ham radio station when I was in high school, so I put together radio equipment to see how it worked. All of my life, I have worked in areas where math, engineering and science have led to predictable

results. I am totally convinced that discipline is the only way that predictable results can be obtained over a long period of time.

What do you want to do with your trading and your life from here on?
I will probably trade again on and off. Kicking and screaming, I got back into the project management thing here again about six months ago. A guy that became my largest client back 15 years ago sold his company and got millions of dollars out of the sale. He decided he was going to play golf for the rest of his life, but after about 4 years, was bored silly. He started another company, which he wanted me to help him set up. After a very long lunch and several martinis, he convinced me to help him. This project will keep me busy for quite a while.

Once I get that completed, I would like to do some more market research and will probably trade again.

wanted me to help him set up. After a very long lunch and several martinis, he convinced me to help him. This project will keep me busy for quite a while.

Once I get that completed, I would like to do some more market research and will probably trade again.

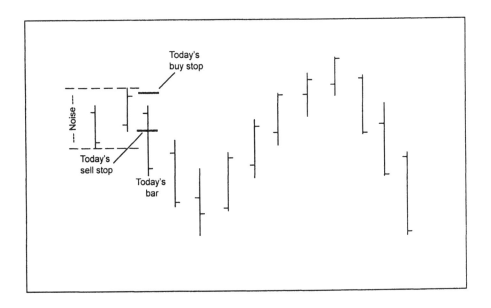

Basic Volatility Adjusted Breakout System

1.   Measure the current market "noise" level (volatility). Example: Take the difference between the highest high and the lowest low of the past two days, including today's open

2.   Compute some function of the noise and add the result to a significant market point to find today's buy stop; subtract a function of the noise from some significant market point to find today's sell stop. Example: Take 30% of the noise, limit the result to no less than 8 ticks or more than 35 ticks. Add this result to today's open to get today's buy stop. Subtract the result from today's open to get today's sell stop.

3.   The system is always in the market. If you are long, reverse to short if today's sell stop is hit. If short, reverse to long if today's buy stop is hit.

4.   There are countless variations of this basic idea. You might limit the number of allowable reversals in one day. You could use yesterday's close instead of today's open as a reference point. You could use recent standard deviation of price as a noise measurement. You could use different noise calculations for the buy stop and the sell stop, etc.

©1998 K-Data, Inc. Sunnyvale, CA

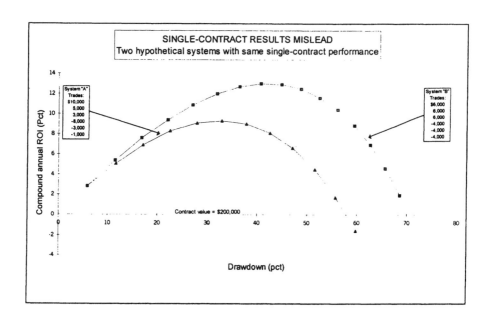

Money Management is a Critical Part of System Design

Optimum money management rules increase the number of contracts traded as equity rises and reduce the number of contracts as drawdowns occur. Selecting correct parameters lets you trade for a combination of return and drawdown you are comfortable with.

But your system design and testing must include the money management rules. Single contract results alone can mislead you. Here are two hypothetical systems with the same single contract profit ($6,000) and drawdown ($12,000) Looking only at single contract results you might say that they are equally good. However, with optimum money mangement System B returns 14% per year while system A only returns 11.5%.

©1998 K-Data, Inc. Sunnyvale, CA

110

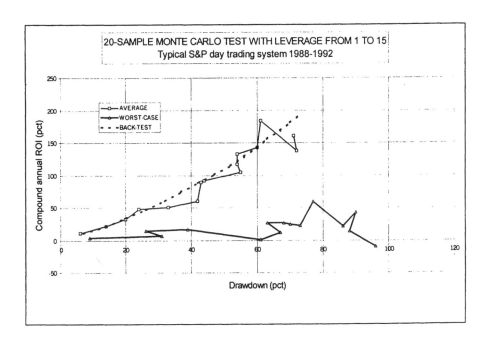

Monte Carlo Testing can provide useful worst-case estimates

The chart above compares actual backtested performance of this system with the worst performance from 20 random Monte Carlo tests. The results indicate that you can choose money management parameters that are 95% certain to yield 25% annual return with no more than 70% drawdown. Of course there are no guarantees. Trading is a random process and unlikely disasters can and do occur. Even the Las Vegas casinos, with an obvious statistical edge, occasionally pay out million dollar jackpots.

©1998 K-Data, Inc. Sunnyvale, CA

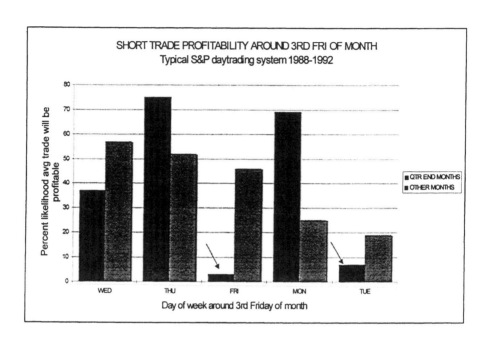

SHORT TRADE PROFITABILITY AROUND 3RD FRI OF MONTH
Typical S&P daytrading system 1988-1992

System Design Should Consider Day-of-week and Week-of-Month Effect

The chart above shows the effect of "triple witching day" (the third Friday of quarter-end months) on short trade performance of a typical S&P day trading sytem. Long trades show a similar pattern. Arrows indicate days when trades should be skipped. Likelihood of a profitable trade is computed from the student's t-test.

©1998 K-Data, Inc. Sunnyvale, CA

MODELING STUDY

CHILDHOOD FAMILY STATUS
- Sheldon experienced middle-class living in various small towns in Midwest

MENTORING - INFLUENCES
- Well-educated family
- Father was a small investor in stocks
- Futures International Symposiums - Jake Bernstein & Larry Williams

ENVIRONMENT
- Only child
- Small Midwest farming town
- Moved a great deal as a child because of his father's work
- Enjoyed a fun childhood
- Supportive wife and three children

EDUCATION
- Top student in Physics
- Master Degree in Electrical Engineering

INTERESTS -Skills - Abilities -Honors
Childhood
- Avid reading
- Music
- Awarded scholarship for playing the organ
- Loved analytical and language studies

Adult
- Received a regular commission in the Air Force through ROTC award program
- Highly developed research skills

QUALITIES
- Initiative
- Self-discipline
- Rational thinking
- Scientific

BUSINESS EXPERIENCE
- Engineer for radio station
- Background organ music for TV station
- Transmitter operator at radio station
- ROTC while in college
- Pilot in Air Force
- Vice President of engineering for aerospace company
- Established K-Data, a company that designs integrated management software

PHILOSOPHY - SUCCESS BELIEFS
- I do not believe anything I read until I program and test it
- Discipline is the only way that predictable results can be obtained over a long period of time

TRADING EXPERIENCE
- S&P Index and T-Bonds
- Technical trader
- Took $75K to $1.2M within one year
- Consultant for CTA

RECOMMENDATIONS
- *Dow Jones Irwin Guide to Trading Systems* by Bruce Babcock
- *How I Made a Million Dollars Trading Last Year* by Larry Williams
- *New Concepts of Technical Trading* by Wells Wilder
- Larry William's seminars

114

TRADER CONTRIBUTIONS
- Writer of articles for financial magazines
- Speaker at trading conferences

FUTURE PLANS
- Market research
- Helping set up project management systems for a new company

TRADER GEMS - Fundamental - Intuitive - Psychological
- Short-term trading of 2 to 3 days is more profitable than long-term trading - each trade makes less money, but you have many more trades and end up with more money at the end of the year
- Trading on 'triple-witching' days almost always loses money
- The third Friday of almost any month is bad for trading a break-out system because of random motion that is created by the evening out of option positions
- Money management is more important to successful trading than entry and exit points
- You need at least $50K to effectively start trading, because any kind of acceptable money management system is going to begin trading with multiple contracts
- Any good system is going to have 50-55% drawdown

TRADER GEMS - Mechanical - Analytical - Technical
- Volatility adjusted breakout analysis is one of the most powerful concepts in trading. A long position is taken at some level based on volatility above the close or open on a stop, and a short position at some level below the close or open on a stop. For example, you can use the five-day average range and add or subtract a percentage of that range to different levels
- Adjusting any type of breakout for volatility will improve results, this includes channel breakout

- Short-term trading over time combined with sound money management will be more profitable than long term trading
- Sheldon believes that a system should always be in the market long or short. This is also called a stop and reverse system
- Day of week and day of month analysis can greatly improve the reliability of a given breakout system. The effects are often caused by changes in short-term volatility caused by report days and/or holidays
- The key to developing a breakout system is striking a balance between placing the breakout points as tightly as possible while not getting fooled by market noise
- A sampling method called "Monte Carlo Simulation" can be used to predict the future drawdown characteristic of a system
- To implement proper money management strategies, you need at least $50,000 to begin trading. This amount will enable you to start trading multiple contracts and survive an initial drawdown without overtrading.

Murray's Analytical Modeling Study

Trading Methodology Analysis
Mechanical--Objective: None

Mechanical--Automatic: Mechanical trading system based on volatility breakout combined with money management strategies

Discretionary--In case of disaster only

Analysis of Sheldon's Methodology
Sheldon's main trading methodology is using volatility-adjusted breakouts. This is one of the most powerful concepts in trading. You buy at some level, based on volatility, above the close or open on a stop, and sell, at some level, below the close or open on a stop. For example, you can use the five-day average range and add or subtract a percentage of that range to different levels. The concept of volatility adjusted breakout was invented by Larry Williams and still works today.

One of the most common examples of this concept is the opening range breakout where you use volatility adjusted breakout pricing based upon where the market opens. When setting your breakout level, it is important that you recognize the difference between a real breakout and noise. In some of my research, I have used a percentage of the three-day average true range, or the difference between the close and low for an upside breakout and the high and close for downside breakouts or a variety of other measures.

Sheldon used his own formula for a measure in 1986 and 1987 to make over $1,000,000 in trading. His system was a stop and reversal system that was always in the market either long or short. The results of his system during this time period were amazing partly because of his discipline, and partly because of the times that he was trading.

In 1986 and 1987, he traded T-Bonds with this concept, which opened at 8:00 A.M. Central time and the major financial reports were released at 7:30 A.M. This created the effect that market moves off of the open as a result of the reports were continued and reliable. This changed when the opening of the bond market was moved to 7:20 A.M., which is ten minutes before the release of the reports. This hurt the performance of the system, but it is still a tradable method today although not as stellar as the wonder years of 1986 and 1987. You can experiment with this concept and develop your own measures and trading systems.

Volatility Adjusted Channel Breakout
Sheldon believes that any breakout system can be improved by adding a volatility term. Let's see if that is true by adding a volatility term to a simple channel breakout system. Our rules for this example are as follows:

Buy at Highest(High,N)+VolX*Average(TrueRange,3) + 1 point stop;
Sell at Lowest(Low,N)-VolX*Average(TrueRange,3) - 1 point stop;

We tested this system in several different trending markets and found that, in general, using a volatility adjusted channel breakout does improve the performance.

As an example, let's look at the coffee market. We will start with the standard channel breakout with a breakout period of five days for the coffee market over the period 1/1/80 to 9/14/98. Our results with no deduction for slippage and commission are as follows:

Coffee N=5 VolX=0 Standard Channel Breakout

Net Profit	$290,995.00
Trades	513
Win%	43 %
Ave Trade	567.24

118

Profit Factor	1.74
Drawdown	$ 26,900.25

We tested this basic system at differing levels of volatility adjusted breakout, in addition to variable channel length. We found that 50% of the three-day average true range was a good value to select based upon our optimizations. Our results were as follows over the same period with no deduction for slippage or commission:

Coffee N=5,VolX=.50 period 1/1/80 to 9/14/98

Net Profit	$357,360.00
Trades	298
Win%	42 %
Ave Trade	1149.01
Profit Factor	2.48
Drawdown	$23,039.25

Our overall results are better using the volatility adjustment in the channel breakout. In general, this is true in other markets, too, such as the currencies and crude oil. With the addition of the volatility term to the breakout, many false or small breakouts are filtered out of the trade mix. We can see this in the coffee example because we make more money overall, and we also have a higher average trade using the VolX term. This effect carried over in all of the markets we tested except heating oil, where the results of using a volatility adjusted breakout were not significantly better than using a classic breakout.

Day of week and day of month analysis can greatly improve the reliability of a given breakout system. The effects are often caused by changes in short-term volatility caused by report days and holidays. This is very true in the T-Bond market. For example, the average daily range is as much as 14 ticks greater on a major report day, such as PPI or Unemployment, than it is on an average day, which greatly affects trading.

There are also other patterns based on day of week in a given month, which can be observed. As an example in the S&P500, Mondays have a strong upward bias, having rallied about 290 points from 1/3/83 to 9/14/98 on Mondays on open to close basis. This represents about 40% of the total open to close bias in the S&P500. Tuesday and Wednesday are also up days with combined gains of about 40 points more than Monday alone. Thursday and Friday actually have a downward bias. Another example is that most of the upward bias on Mondays is found on the first two Mondays of the month. The study of day of week, month and report day effects as filters to a trading system is a very fruitful area of research, which I have covered in many of my articles and courses.

Predicting Future Drawdown of a Trading System
As mentioned in the Traders' Gem section, part of Sheldon's methodology involves the use of a testing procedure called "Monte Carlo Simulation," which can be used to predict future drawdown of a system. To use "Monte Carlo Simulation" testing:

1. randomly reorder the trades generated by a system
2. calculate the drawdown of this new order of trades
3. repeat this process multiple times
4. develop bins for the drawdown levels and calculate the probability of a given drawdown
5. runs will give you a good estimate of future drawdown

Bill Brower provided a copy of the results of a "Monte Carlo Simulation" called Advanced MCS. The tabular results of the simulation with an explanation are shown below.

Example of Advanced MCS Output
The first column indicates the various levels of drawdown. In this case, we incremented by $1,000, but this value is controlled by the user. Next is a column identifying the count that appeared in that drawdown increment. The last column identifies the probability that

the future drawdown will exceed the level of the increment. This column header also shows the window size, which in this case was 21 days. For instance, there is a 54.6% chance that the drawdown will exceed $2,000 in any 21 day period. Also, there is a 5% chance that the drawdown will exceed $6,000. These probabilities are all for the 21 day period. If the period were increased to 63 days, the probabilities of higher drawdown would increase. The period length is user controlled.

Since the tool uses a random number generator to perform the simulation, you will get slightly different results every time you run it. However, it will always be about the same as before.

Drawdown	Count	Probability of Greater Drawdown in 21 days
0	4	99.60
1000	163	83.30
2000	287	54.60
3000	231	31.50
4000	133	18.20
5000	87	9.50
6000	15	5.00
7000	26	2.40
8000	11	1.30
9000	8	0.50
10000	2	0.30
11000	0	0.30
12000	1	0.20
13000	1	0.10
14000	0	0.10
15000	1	0.00
16000	0	0.00

Monte Carlo Simulation of Drawdown Based on Daily Changes in Equity

121

Adrienne's Psychological Modeling Study

The Opportunity Model

The amazing thing about Sheldon Knight is that he learned at an early age to see everything as an opportunity. His unconscious model of life is that everything presented to him, regardless of how others perceive it, is a chance to do something new or better. I have worked with countless adults whose lives have developed serious, sabotaging patterns based upon the fact that they were forced to move many times in their childhood. The result for them was a feeling of isolation, unresolved relationships, painful losses, etc. That is not the case for Sheldon. He loved going to different schools and had a "pretty good time." Yes, he recognized the disadvantage of not making lasting relationships, but that did not prevent him from having a thirty-eight year marriage and children.

This ability to turn lemons into lemonade is not the result of a lack of intelligence, since Sheldon is a highly-trained electrical engineer with a degree from Stanford University. This model has allowed him to take what comes his way and use it to his advantage without forcing him to carry a lot of emotional baggage as a result. For example, instead of dropping out of Iowa State when the out-of-state tuition became too steep, he leveraged his education into a degree from Stanford University. He turned his 40-hour a week job during college into an opportunity to study 30 hours a week while being paid. He turned his ROTC experience into pilot training in the Air Force, which became an opportunity to pay for more schooling and a career in the aerospace industry.

This model made certain that Sheldon never sat in one place and stagnated for very long. It became his impetus for continual growth. One thing always led him to another opportunity and another world to conquer. In addition, by viewing the world as feeding him opportunities, Sheldon has steered clear of many of the negative thought patterns which would turn him into a pessimistic or victimized person. It has also allowed him to trade mechanically with impressive results, and not become caught very often in the emotional traps of the market. On the two occasions that he traded by discretion, he was badly hurt and, of course, saw these as lessons that he continues to review. In fact, Sheldon has viewed large gains as well as large losses as opportunities to do something else.

Now, as he gears up to start a new cycle of trading, he has realistically based it upon the current trading scene. He is not afraid to make mistakes or fail because he takes from each experience something valuable. He is optimistic about his opportunities in these markets based upon what he sees happening. This model does not guarantee that Sheldon will always make money, because he has lost in the past. And Sheldon does like to have action in his life, which is something that traders are particularly vulnerable to. Nevertheless, his ability to view events as opportunities has put him in the right place at the right time, so that his natural abilities can provide him with rewards.

CHAPTER 5

Stelios Christakos

A gifted Greek - How a computer wizard overcame his technologically limited environment to become a successful money manager and teacher.

Where did you grow up?
I was born and raised in Amfithea, Athens, which was a small, friendly neighborhood where everyone knew each other. My youth was very joyful because we had many places to play outdoors. I lived with my family in that same town until I became an adult. We were a middle class family. My father worked for the telephone company.

What did you like to play as a child?
In those early years, we were inventive with our surroundings and played games like "hide-and-go-seek" and football. Later, when we had bicycles, a whole new dimension was added to our play.

Were you a good student? What were your interests?
I was a lazy student. When I was in primary school, my main interest was how I could demolish my bicycle and build it up again. Finally, I had demolished it so many times that it could not be rebuilt. So, I just threw it away.

When you were in school, were there any special teachers?
In the fifth and sixth grades, I had very enjoyable teachers because they knew how to make learning fun by playing with us as we learned.

What were the biggest lessons you learned from your family?
The two most important virtues I picked up from my family were honesty and persistence.

From there, where did you go with your education?
There was a big change in my life between the sixth grade and the next level of education. I took the entry exams for two expensive private schools, Athens College, in Greece, and Lycee Leonin, a French School.

I passed the exams, which no one considered to be a possibility, and entered Athens College. The shift that took place was very pronounced. I moved from living in the style of a middle class suburban school with limited resources to a school with swimming pools and athletic installations.

How did that change you?
The first year was tough because I was a stranger among people who had known each other for several years. After the first three months, a few of the boys warmed up to me and school became more fun.

Did you know the direction that you wanted your future to go at that time?
No, not at that time. When I was 15, I told my mother that I would like to stop going to school and start my own business. Thank God, she did not let me do it.

So you were entrepreneurial from a young age?
Yes. I was working on weekends in order to earn money because my allowance did not allow for my expensive tastes. I did not want to feel limited in being generous with others and myself.

What type of work did you do at the time?
Any work that would pay, but mostly jobs that required muscles. The job that I liked the most was loading and preparing stones that were used for washing jeans. We dug the stones and loaded 50 kilos of them onto our backs and into a container. The reason I liked that job was that it paid well. We were getting full-time pay for part time work.

The four years at Athens College were preparatory for the university entry examinations. In Greece, to attend the university, you must pass certain exams and be selected. If you are admitted to the university, you pay nothing. The selection process is very competitive with about 150,000 people taking the exams and only 30,000 to 40,000 being admitted into the university.

What were your interests in school?
At first, my primary interests were mathematics and chemical mechanics. In my sophomore year at Athens College, I found that I was not enjoying my classes. So, two years before taking the university examinations, I changed my major and went into law school. I took an exam on ancient Greek basic vocabulary and learned an important lesson. I made 99 mistakes, which amazed the professor because he had never seen anyone make that many mistakes. I read many books to catch up with the people who already had two years of experience. The next year was easier. One of the reasons that I went to law school was that it wasn't mandatory to attend classes, which gave me enough free time to do whatever I liked.

What did you do with the time?
I had time to support my motorcycling and other hobbies. I loved nightlife and going to discos. The rest of my time was spent studying. Shortly after I entered law school, I began attending computer school in the evening from 5:00 P.M. until 10:00 P.M. So, I worked hard in the morning and evening, and whatever time I had left over was for having fun.

At what point in time was there a switch?
The major switch occurred when I started attending a two-year computer course. Before I started computer classes, I purchased computer magazines that were just becoming available. The new language of computers amazed me. I did not understand any of it, and I wanted to learn more. I loved the challenge of trying to understand the magazines. So, each month, I would buy new ones and understand

more until my interest was piqued enough to attend classes. After two or three months, I decided I wanted to do this for a living. I finished as one of the top students in the school.

When I finished school, I started working in the computer industry. Within a couple of years, I started my own business.

Tell us about your business?
My computer company is called Analysis SA. We develop software and the networking solutions necessary for a company to operate its business. Our responsibilities generally include assembling and networking computers, and organizing telecommunication equipment necessary for running software. Businesses depend upon us to keep their operations running smoothly. My company has done well since it began in 1990 and now employs seventeen people and is still growing.

Did you get married during this time?
During this time I was dating my wife, Despina. We met while going to school, became engaged in 1989, and married in 1992. Shortly after we married, I went away to fulfill my military obligation. In Greece, it is compulsory for able-bodied Greek men to serve for one year. Despina and I have been married for 7 years and have two children.

When did you begin to have an interest in the financial world?
This is a very funny story because maybe it was a message from heaven, but it seems that I did not get it. In 1987, a friend of mine introduced me to American stocks and options. I was intrigued by what I read. I asked him for as much information as he could get. He gave me a pamphlet and some information on the exchanges, which was all that he had. I began reading everything that was available. In Greece, investing was not a business at the time. Information was hard to get because there was no Internet in the late 1980's.

I began buying *The Wall Street Journal* and worked at trying to figure out the markets. All that summer, I studied the prices. I placed my first bet by buying options in late September of 1987, with $2,000 that I borrowed from a friend. That was a lot of money to me, because I was only working part-time while I completed my studies. This was the end of September in 1987, and as you know the 19th of October was the American Market Crash. So, the money was gone.

What was of interest to me was that I had bought options for a few months away and the markets started to go up. Near the expiration date of the options, they were worth something like $4,000 and it was a winning trade after all, although I sold early and I had to put up money to pay back the loan. This first encounter with the markets made me enjoy them more. I requested more information from several people by fax and continued to study the markets. I studied the stock market and options market until 1992, when I started to invest again.

At this point did you think that you wanted to go into the markets as a career?
No, I mainly thought of it as a hobby.

Who were the people that influenced you as far as the direction that you wanted to go in trading options and stocks?
I was influenced by classic trading books like Jessie Livermore's *Reminiscences of a Stock Operator*, *How to Make Money in Stocks* by William O'Neil, *Technical Analysis of Stock Trends* by Edwards and Magee, and the *Market Wizards* books by Jack Schwager. I also subscribed to many newsletters and magazines.

I found that magazines are helpful because they are filled with new ideas that can be added to your methodology. The advertisements are informative because you can find out about new products that are available, such as software. You must keep updated on new things in the market to have an edge. I find the information in magazines useful.

As far as newspapers are concerned, their usefulness depends upon the kind of trading that you are doing. I subscribed to two or three newspapers for two years, but information overload caused me to quit reading them. For me, the information was not that useful.

Are you currently subscribing to any newspapers or newsletters that are useful to you?
No, I don't subscribe to newspapers, and I have been very disappointed with most of the newsletters. Being a computer person, I analyzed the newsletter recommendations and kept track of them on my computer. Very often, writers that said they were up 20% were actually down 20%. It was hard to understand how they could have the nerve to make such claims.

There was one particular newsletter that I had paid $1,000 to receive. I sent a letter outlining my complaints about their false claims with charts to prove my point. The person writing the newsletter had said that over the past year the published recommendations had made 100% with a 30% drawdown. This claim simply was not true because I had tracked all of the trades.

For options, there are two or three newsletters that are very good about telling you where to place a trade, why to place a trade, and the strategies for the trade.

What are those newsletters?
Newsletters that impressed me were *The Option Advisor* by Bernie Shaeffer and David Caplan's *Opportunities in Options*. One of the problems of subscribing to a newsletter is the junk mail sent from people who purchase mailing lists. The one good outcome of going through all of the junk mail was that I read about a person who later became my mentor.

Where did you go from there as far as trading is concerned?
In 1992, I traded mostly stocks and options. In 1993, I continued doing the same thing.

What method were you using?

I was using the "do-whatever-you-think-is-best, and-pray-to-the-Lord-that-you-make-a-lot-of-money" method.

And how did you do with that method?

Not very well. I was well read, but needed experience. You have to feel it in your pocket in order to understand it. I used stops and had good money management rules, but did not make any money, because I lacked discipline. I would place very successful trades that would give me $4,000 to $5,000 in profits, but because I thought I knew that the trade was going to give me $10,000, I would end up with zero dollars. I was going after big trades. At that time, I failed to understand that trading was not a 100-meter race. You must think of trading as a marathon, meaning that you must have staying power to endure over the long haul.

I thought trading was about finding a few good trades and making big bucks, and that was all. The formula was that out of ten trades you would get three or four that were very big. I thought it would be very easy. I believed promotional statements of people in business. This gives an indication of how naïve I was at that time.

What money management did you use at that time?

My money management methodology was very simple. I usually risked 2% of my capital.

From 1992 to 1994, I was trading mostly stocks and options while reading as much about the markets as time would allow. In addition, I was also reading for law school and for my job. What free time I had was devoted to trading. I was hooked. Since I was a computer programmer, I programmed the computer to run various tests on the market data.

I was getting fundamental data on companies published by Value Line. With ASCII file data, I put together my own software enabling me to make comparisons between companies and sectors, etc. This process required three to four hours every week. I spent many hours reading reports generated from this information. From the recommendations, I would decide what to buy or sell.

Eventually, I came to the conclusion that nobody knew where a stock was going and that trading was mostly a game of luck. I had actual numbers from the past, forecasts from major analysts for future earnings and information on the growth of companies. I spent hundreds of hours studying these numbers and found that they did not work. You could not make money on the projections unless you were a long-term investor, which was not my trading style. I was 27 years old, and could not think ten or twenty years in the future.

I also found that there was a lot of volatility in the market. An analyst might say that a stock at $20 was going to $30. However, it would often go through $10 on its way to $30. I was looking at fundamental analysis and technical analysis, and both did not work.

In 1994, I had a big loss in the futures market. After this big loss, one loss followed another because I was trying to recapture my losses. I was after big trades, and the account was down 70%. In late 1994, I decided that I was doing something wrong, which was pretty clever of me. At that time, I bought a system and traded trying to make up for the losses and ended up with only 10% of my account.

In February 1994, I found the mentor that I was telling you about. I also started to re-evaluate everything that I knew about the markets and returned to stage one. I was missing a good model for the markets. In other words, I had a house with no foundation.

This mentor gave me the solid ground that I needed to build a system. I began re-evaluating everything that I knew and applied it to this model. Now I had a model, and I could compare it to other classic models like moving averages, etc. I spent most of 1995 in this evaluation and testing process. If my work concluded that I could not make money in the market, I was not going to trade again.

During 1995, I made a few conservative trades. After backtesting a number of commodities, I concluded that money could be made in the markets. I was now in the futures market and this became my main interest. I started trading again in late 1995.

Things turned because I had constructed both foundation and structure. Of course, then there were psychological mistakes that had nothing to do with the system or trading methodology. The result of all of my work and study is that I became a discretionary trader.

To be a good discretionary trader, you must feel good about yourself, resulting in stability and discipline. If you can handle your own psychological pitfalls, you can adapt to the situations that the market presents to you and trade according to your methodology. I began to start handling this part of the process in 1996. My account was up 60% from 1996 to 1997.

Please tell us about your actual system.
I use a model that evaluates the major trend of the market. It is the classic theory. There is a major long-term trend and a short-term trend. I use position trading in the direction of a major long-term trend at entry points that are high probability points in intermediate or short-term trend.

How do you describe a probability?
A good probability trade is a setup with historical probability between 65% and 85% and a risk/reward ratio of more than 1:2.5. If I do everything correctly and analyze the markets correctly, then the probability moves toward 85%. If I do a few things wrong and ignore a few signs or market information, then the probability goes toward 65% and less. But what I look for is to never go below 50% profitable trades.

What time frame do you use for trading?
The smallest time frame that I currently use is the daily range. I do

not trade intra-day, real-time. I position trade in the daily time frame and hold trades for weeks or months.

What particular signals do you use besides trends?
I am applying several different studies that occur at points where price has to react. For example, when I see a point of possible reaction, then I start watching the market closely. I evaluate the behavior and the character of the market. When I see that the market is supported at a certain level, I look for the best possible point to enter the market. For long trades, I have an existing order with my broker to buy above the market and place a stop below the point of entry.

What actually makes you decide to trade? At what point do you decide that this is a trade that you want to take?
If there are no opportunities, nothing happens. I just write down the numbers and fax them to my broker.

Where does the discretion come in?
In deciding where to place the entry, whether the market is supported, how much risk will I assume, and does the trade have a high probability of making money.

What is your risk management like now?
The basic rule that I use is to risk somewhere between 1% and 3% on every trade. I do not remember the last time that I put on a 3% trade, but this is the rule. Normally, I risk between 1% and 2%.

Do you always put in a stop?
Yes, the stop is included as a part of my order.

Where do you place your stop?
When I decide to enter a trade, let's say a long one, at a certain price level, I place a trade usually with a buy-stop order above the market. Sometimes I decide to enter in a line trading concept and put a buy order above the high of three or four days. Then, I place the stop-loss

at a technical level that I expect the market will not return to. This means that if it does, then I am wrong and want out.

You talked about psychology At what point did you realize that the psychology of trading was important?
I realized that psychology was important during September and October of 1996 when I had the time to re-evaluate all of the trades for the year. Even though I was happy with the results, I could have done better. I had missed a few opportunities because I was not following my trading rules. In order for a system to work, you have to follow the rules that have been developed for the system. Even though I was making money, I was upset with myself because I would lose more than I was expecting to lose from my system when it went into a drawdown. Money that is not being made during a drawdown period actually becomes a drawdown. I decided to look into this area.

An interesting observation about trading: when you begin trading, you focus on understanding how the markets work. For example, the exchanges, the orders, the types of contracts, etc. If we say that knowledge is expressed in terms of a percentage, 100% is the knowledge that you need in order to trade the markets in the beginning. It is easy to believe that 100% is how the market mechanism works, which is easy information to gather. However, when you reach 100%, you realize that this 100% is a part of something that is actually 1000%. Upon achieving this level of knowledge, you start again because you now understand that you need a system with certain rules, money management, etc. It is like climbing a mountain while being unable to see the top because there is a forest. You are always climbing to the next level, but you never know where the top of the mountain is because there is another forest obscuring the view.

At some point, you have everything in place - a system that you can trade with the knowledge of the market, how it works, how it operates with the signals and the stops - and you decide that you are not at the top of the mountain. This is when you finally understand that there is more to trading and that most of it is inside of yourself. You cannot see this unless you go there. Unless you get to the point where you have a system that makes money and the money management rules, you cannot see it.

If you had told me that psychology was important in the beginning, I would have thought you were crazy. I believed that psychology had nothing to do with trading. All that was needed for success was study to understand the markets and the rest should be very easy. I am not only speaking for myself but also from what other traders have said about their experience. Traders that actually start making money figure out how they want to trade and start thinking about their inner self.

What did you discover about your inner self that made a difference in being able to follow your rules?
Speaking in general, I would say that trading is a trip of self-discovery. In order to develop in trading, you also have to grow and develop as a person. While improving your trading, you must also improve yourself, your character, and the way you behave. As I developed as a trader, I also grew as a person and learned things that I did not know about myself.

What influences were there in this area for you?
You were a major influence, Adrienne. The seminar and private work that we did together taught me that discipline is not just something that you write on paper and say, "I will be disciplined." It is actually something that happens in your every day life. It is not easy to understand. It takes someone special to make it easy to understand the changes that discipline will bring. What you did in working with me brought understanding not only at a logical level, but at the level of the understanding becoming part of myself.

How much money do you manage now?
I am providing analysis for people trading around $700,000.

Do you want to go on to be a CTA, a money manager?

This is a period of time that is very interesting because I believe I will look back at this period as a turning point. In order to continue in my current direction, effectively I have to become a CTA. For the time being, I am considering all of the options and need to fully examine the tradeoffs.

How do you manage your computing solutions business and trade the markets?

I am a position trader and most of the trading foundation has been established. I do most of the work in a few hours on the weekend. I plan for the markets each week and stick to my daily routine, which includes an hour of studying the markets. Because I trade in a daily time frame, I can check the market activity from the previous week, and make notes on possible setups for the coming week. If a market goes to my order level, then I send the order in to my broker. Of course, if I devoted more time to trading, it would grow faster. Recently, I hired an assistant full-time for monitoring the trades, so I can devote more time to the development of my trading business.

If a young person came to you and wanted to be a trader, what advice would you give him?

It depends upon the person. I think it is important for a trader to start with very little trading capital. If you have very little capital when you lose it, not "if" you lose it, but "when" you lose it, the pain will not be so intense. The lesson is the same regardless of whether you lose $10,000, $100,000, or $1,000,000; you lost it. You get the message. If you want to lose $1,000,000 in order to get the lesson, then you have another type of problem.

A new trader should read everything he can about the markets and learn to make his own choices. Test the system or systems thoroughly. Devote the hours necessary to know the markets. Find a system and trading style that will fit your personality.

If I wanted to be a day trader, I would be the lousiest day trader in the world. Why? I cannot day trade in terms of time. I cannot be in front of the monitor at certain times of the day. If I tried to be a day trader, it would be a disaster. Also, if I was trying to trade in a weekly time frame at this time, I could not do it. Why? I do not like long-term trades and in order to trade in the weekly time frame you have to have a lot of capital. I have found a time frame that works for me. The important thing is to find the system, methodology, and the time frame that fits you.

There are at least a thousand ways to lose money. Write them down as you discover them, and learn not to repeat the same thing again.

If you are smart, you will never make the same mistake twice, but because no one is that smart, you will do the same thing again 4, 10, or 20 times. At some point, understanding will come and you will not make that mistake again. Then, you can move forward to the next mistake. There comes a time when you make so many mistakes that you actually can feel the mistakes and begin to start avoiding them. That is when you learn that mistakes are part of the process and you start making money.

Trading is the most difficult job or hobby that a person can have because it has much to do with personality. It is highly correlated. If you do not have a stable personality, I would advise that trading is not for you.

To be a doctor, you have to study for many years. To be a mechanic, you have to study for a few years. First, you get the degree, and then you work somewhere to get the necessary experience to be a professional. It takes 6 to 10 years to become some kind of professional, and, of course, that does not mean that you will make a significant amount of money as a professional if you just put in the time.

If you consider the time that it takes to become accomplished in any profession, you cannot enter trading and expect to be successful in a few months. Becoming a really good trader cannot be done in a year or even in four years. Everyone likes to think that they will be the exception, but it does not work like that. Some people have beginner's luck and make money in their first trades, which gives a false sense of confidence to commit more money. Some people even quit their jobs thinking that they have found the "golden goose." The system does not work that way. From what I have found for myself, from other traders, and from what I have read, there is a 99.9% probability that you will lose the first money that you trade. If you continue, you will learn that you must study a great deal to learn about the markets, and then yourself. Then, you trade, and lose, and learn. After a period of time, with study and persistence, you will begin to make money.

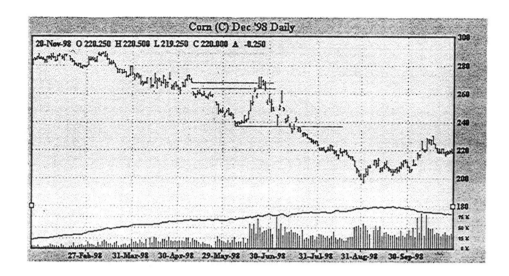

The above chart shows Corn in a downtrend. On the 5/11 we have a gap down day that follows through smoothly and the we have a reaction that closes the gap on the 6/23. Price is unable to take out the last important swing high that occurred on the 5/7 at 274. Then we get two inside days. I sell on the break of the 3rd day at 266 with a stop at 274 and a first target of 240. A 2 to 1 trade with good probabilities of the downtrend resuming.

Because of the increased volatility , I took early profits in this position at 254 and so I had at least a small profit trade at the worst case and left the rest of the position run and exited on 9/3 on a stop profit after the follow through that occurred after the impressive reversal day on the 9/1, for a profit of 3,300 $ per two contracts.

All charts were created with Technical Tools.

140

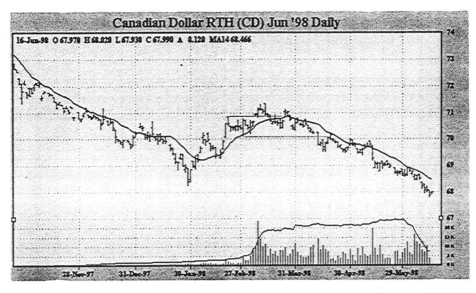

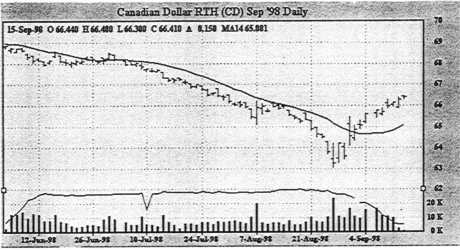

The above chart shows Canadian Dollar in a major downtrend. So, I am looking for an oppurtunity to short CD.

Between 2/20/98 and 3/2/98 there comes a reaction in the downtrend and a zone is formed between 70.85 and 70.12. At the 3/9 CD gaps higher - above the upper zone. In the following days there is some follow through but on the 3/11 we have a reversal day (DOJI also) with short implications. So, I sell short at the 71.07 with a stop at 71.40 for a target of 69.30. The risk is 330$ per contract and the potential profit is 770$ per contract. With a approximately 60% chance of winning the risk/reward is 3.5 / 1 for a high-quality trade. CD continues the downtrend in orderly form and the stop is lowered at 70.30 on the April 14th, the day that it crosses (with a wide range day) the lower zone at 70.12. So from now on the trade is profitable and I follow through it by always lowering the stops. At the 6/12 I roll-over to September and I finally exit the trade on a stop-profit at 9/1/98 (that crazy day) for a total profit of 5950$ per contract. 141

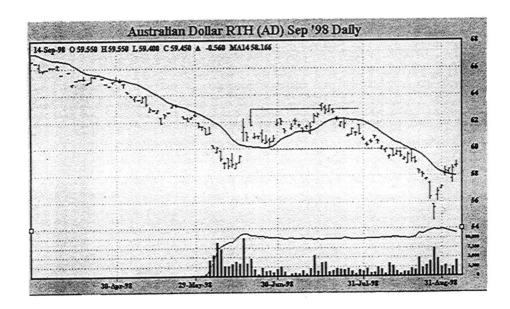

Australian Dollar RTH (AD) Sep '98 Daily

14-Sep-98 O 59.550 H 59.550 L 59.400 C 59.450 Δ -0.560 MA14 58.166

The above chart shows Australian Dollar in a major downtrend. So, I am looking for an oppurtunity to short AD.

Between 6/19/98 and 6/26/98 there comes a reaction in the downtrend and a zone is formed between 63.00 and 60.05. At the 7/16 AD gaps higher - above the upper zone. In the following days there is no follow through. At the 7/22 we have a down gap that closes the gap of the test of the upper zone AND crosses the 12 day moving average. So, I sell short at the open at 62.22 with a stop at 63.40 for a target of 60.50. The risk is 1180$ per contract and the potential profit is 1720$ per contract. With a approximately 65% chance of winning the risk/reward is 2.75 / 1 for a high-quality trade. As soon as AD gaps down at 7/27, I lower the stop to 62.31 for practically no risk. I exit the trade at 60.50 as scripted for a 1720 profit per contract.

MODELING STUDY

CHILDHOOD FAMILY STATUS
- Stelios enjoyed growing up in a middle class family in Athens, Greece

MENTORING - INFLUENCES
- From family - honesty and persistence
- Financial magazines
- Joseph Hart --*The Trend Dynamics Newsletter*
- Adrienne Toghraie--Trader's coach

ENVIRONMENT
- Family supportive
- Supportive wife

EDUCATION
- Bachelor of Science in Law with a minor in Computer Science

INTERESTS - Skills - Abilities - Honors
Childhood
- Inventive with his surroundings
- Football
- Bicycles - breaking them and fixing them
- Basketball
- Gymnastics

Adult
- English
- Reads everything on trading and psychology
- Motorcycling
- Running
- Computers
- Ability for modeling
- Meditation

QUALITIES
- Competitive
- Self-starter
- Organizer
- Persistent
- Quick to adapt to any environment
- Negotiating skills
- Mediating skills
- Ability to help people to get the best out of themselves

BUSINESS EXPERIENCE
- Entrepreneurial from young age
- Computer software and hardware solutions

PHILOSOPHY - SUCCESS BELIEFS
- There are no obstacles that you cannot overcome
- If you set you mind to goals, you will attain them

PROSPERITY CONSCIOUSNESS
- Gives opportunity to talented young people

TRADING EXPERIENCE
- Stocks, options, and futures
- Technical foundation with discretionary interpretation
- Money manager
- Position trader

RECOMMENDATIONS
- *Reminiscences of a Stock Operator* by Edwin Lefevre
- *How to Make Money in Stocks* by William O'Neil
- Shaefer Newsletter for options
- David Kaplan's *Options Advisor*
- Adrienne Toghraie as a trader's coach
- *The Market Wizards* by Jack Schwager
- *Technical Analysis by* Perry Kaufman

TRADER CONTRIBUTIONS
- Makes his clients money
- Speaker at trading conferences

TRADER GEMS - Fundamental - Intuitive - Psychological
- You have to keep yourself updated on new ideas in the markets to have an edge
- When you analyze the recommendations of most financial newsletters, they are very often running in the opposite direction of what they recommend
- You must pace yourself to have the staying power to endure over the long haul
- If you can handle all of your psychological pitfalls, you can adapt to all of the situations the market presents to you
- Perspective on trading expands when you get more experience. First, you think that trading is all about understanding how the markets work. You see this as 100% of the knowledge you need. Later, you realize that it is part of a 1000% system with money management, entries, and exits. Finally, you find out it is all the inner you.
- Trading is a trip of discovery because in order to improve your trading, you have to improve yourself
- In order to have trading discipline, you have to have it in your daily life
- It important to feel the pain of loss in the beginning, so you get the message early with a small amount of money
- A new trader should read everything and make his own choices

  1. Test the system
  2. Know the markets
  3. Find a system that fits your personality and time frame

- There are at least 1000 ways to lose money. Write them down as you discover them and learn not to do them again

145

- When you learn that mistakes are part of the process, you will start to make money and will feel more relaxed
- If you are unstable, do not trade
- It takes 6 to 10 years to be a really good professional trader
- Everyone likes to think he or she will be the exception
- There is a 99.9% probability that you will lose the first trade

FUTURE PLANS
- Become a CTA

TRADER GEMS - Mechanical - Analytical - Technical
- Like many good traders, Stelios trades in the direction of the long term trend
- He combines trading with the trend with Fibonachi retracement levels in order to develop his trading signals.
- Keep risk low--1% to 3% of your account size on any given trade
- Always trades with a stop
- Stops should be based on technical market levels

Murray's Analytical Modeling Study

Trading Analysis
Mechanical--Objective: Use of Fibonacci retracement levels to enter trades in the direction of the trend

Mechanical--Automatic: Charting of indicators used in analysis

Discretionary: Combines trend following methodologies with patterns and Fibonacci retracement to development entries, exits, and stops

Analysis of Stelios' Methodology
Stelios is like many of the other traders in this book. He trades in the direction of the trend using some type of a momentum retracement as his trading indicator. This methodology is common among successful traders. It works well when you can limit your risk and have good methodology to determine the direction of the long-term trend. Like other successful traders in this book, Stelios limits his risk on each trade to a small percentage of his account. His exposure is limited to between 1% and 3% of his trading capital and stops are based on technical price levels. If Stelios believes a trade is too risky, he will not take it.

(See Tom Bierovic's Chapter 14 for discussion on momentum retracement)

Adrienne's Psychological Modeling Study

The Juggler Model

To be a good juggler, you must first start by learning how to handle a single ball. As a young boy, Stelios learned, by taking apart his bicycle and putting it together, how to build from one piece to another to make things work. As Stelios grew up, his copious reading and interests in history, philosophy, and working things continued to develop him into a person who could effectively juggle many activities.

Stelios completed his advanced education by taking a Degree in Law with a minor in Computer Science. Although his legal training is a valuable asset in business, Stelios has never practiced law. Instead, he started his own software development business where he juggles a countless number of balls with ease. In the software development business, you must learn to turn complicated office management scenarios into a simple form and do this in a cost-effective way for the client. Stelios and his company meet these challenges every day and he does this while being a trader, money manager, speaker, and family man.

The phrase "to get something done, ask a busy person to do it" was invented to describe a man like Stelios. When I told him that I wanted to come to Athens, he took on the responsibility of setting up a conference, various seminars, private consultations, as well as interviews in every major newspaper. He manages his time with the utmost efficiency. Starting the day in busy Athens traffic, he gets to work by motorbike.

Stelios has many more balls in the air to juggle than just the ones from his work. He is an athlete who loves football, basketball, gymnastics, and running. He also knows how to party with the best of them. He is a supportive and loving husband as well as a good father to his two small children. He believes in staying in touch with the latest and best information possible to run every part of his life in the most effective, efficient, and happy way. Whenever a friend or family member calls him with problems in their business or personal lives, he is their mentor, psychologist, or coach. Furthermore, he is someone who enjoys every type of activity from the arts to travel.

To Stelios, there are never enough balls in the air to keep him busy. One day he called me to ask whether or not he should go into the tourism business. He was excited by the enormous potential for profit he saw in capitalizing on a window of opportunity in this field. Being a mere mortal, I saw the difficulty in adding one more ball to the mix and talked him out of it. Nevertheless, he would have added this activity to his life.

How does this Juggler Model affect Stelios' trading? He appears to use it to great advantage. This is not to say that everyone would be able to do so. However, his ability to handle so many competing activities at once is a coping mechanism, which allows him to utilize all of the factors and forces in the market to aid in his decision-making. Because he is interested in everything, he has read everything on the markets and is able to synthesize this information into a usable form. With the Juggler Model, he is able to see the world as one of possibilities in which there are no obstacles, only one more ball to juggle. And if you are a great juggler, as Stelios is, you can turn each obstacle into another opportunity. This model can be a very successful one for the right trader.

CHAPTER 6

Bob Watson

The Zen trading warrior - How a "possibility" thinker combined intellectual, spiritual and physical disciplines to create a high percentage return on his investment capital.

Shall we start at the beginning - tell us what it was like growing up.

I was born March 7, 1961, in Orlando, Florida. My parents were employees of a company called Martin-Marrietta in the 1960's. My parents were not well educated having barely finished high school. Despite their apparent lack of formal education, they were innovative and never gave up the dream of working for themselves. They were just trying to make their way in life. We lived outside of Cleveland, Ohio, from the time that I was 3 years old until I was 14. I was a normal kid. I made "A's" and "B's" as a student, and participated in basketball and football. In 1973, we moved to Texas, and I kept up the same grades and played basketball.

What were you like as a kid?

As a kid, I went to work at age 7 throwing newspapers. That was a distinguishing factor that was common throughout my years as a boy. If there was a job that someone would hire me to do, I would do it. From my parent's model, I was motivated to make my own way.

If something caught my attention, I was motivated and would work very hard at it. But if I lost interest in something, not much would get me to pick it up again.

I was an only child. My parents were always struggling to get ahead in life. They wanted to be entrepreneurial, but they were unable to make that happen until I was in high school.

What resources did your parents give you through their early struggles?

They gave me a sense of determination. They also taught me the importance of making good use of the resources that are available to you. My parents came from an incredible disadvantage. My dad was a middle child among fourteen brothers and sisters. His family was taught good morals and character, but their approach to life was so inflexible that it inhibited development. So, the positive thing I got from them was character, and the lesson I learned from their inflexibility was that I could not limit myself by thinking the way they did. I believe that life can be anything that I can imagine.

Where did that lesson come from?

It came from seeing the abject poverty that many of my dad's brothers and sisters lived in. I realized that there was not much difference between the guy that lived on the hill and the people who lived in the valley. My Dad's family saw things almost as a class system, and I believed that I could be unique.

Was your family a traditional family in the sense that they celebrated the holidays together? How was your home life?

They were steadfast, prim, proper, and celebrated all of the holidays in a very traditional way. It was almost a responsibility to be with family on holidays, and fight with them the whole time you were celebrating. This approach to life caused me to rebel and look at things differently.

What made you move to Texas when you were 14?

My Dad got an opportunity to work in an oil-related business where he was in charge. We moved to Houston, which was very much of a booming frontier town versus Cleveland or Pittsburgh. Things were much more cut and dried in the North when compared to what was going on in the South. As a result of the move, I was able to get my driver's license early and enjoy many things earlier in life. Texas was a great place for a 14-year old.

What was high school like for you?
I had the normal student-athlete life with a touch of the rebellious nature. My senior year, I took cooperative education classes so that I could take the minimum number of classes. In this way, I could work, buy a car, and save for college. I wanted to make life more pleasant for myself, which meant working. It was very unusual for a kid to go to school half a day taking physics, analytic geometry, and other college preparatory classes and then going to work in the afternoon.

Tell us about college.
I attended Texas A&M University at College Station and loved it. I went there because I did not want to go too far from home where all of my friends were. At that time, the engineering field offered the highest paying jobs right out of school. I had no idea what an engineer was, nor did I know that Texas A&M had five guys for every girl on campus. Those were terrible odds, and I do not recall that fact being mentioned on the recruiting poster.

Texas A&M University had an incredible sense of history and tradition from over a 100 years of being primarily a military school. I was trying to find myself after a very unsatisfying year in the engineering program. I switched my major to political science and began to explore what I wanted to do with the rest of my life. I found college a bit boring except in the subject areas I enjoyed, like history and law. In the summer between my freshman and sophomore years I enlisted in the Army Reserve to see the world.

Where were you stationed?
I was assigned to Heidelburg, Germany. We traveled to Italy, Switzerland, France, and old East Germany. It was a very interesting time. My responsibility was to research specific countries of national interest and then compile what they called Country Studies.

What was traveling like for you?

I was able to see the world from a German point of view, a Swiss point of view, and an Italian point of view at the age of nineteen. This experience has given me a worldly perspective on issues to this day.

What did you do when you came back to the States?

I went back to Texas A&M and studied political science, which turned out to be boring. Then I went to Houston and worked for my Dad while attending the University of Houston. I studied accounting and earned a degree because it was easy for me.

Did you do any other type of work?

I worked for a couple of firms and went to school at night. One was an oil field concern where I was an oil scout. The college experience was neat for two years, but it was all about playing games. At the time, I was more interested in getting ahead, and the only way I could see that happening was by being out in the workplace.

You finished school, completed your time in the Reserves, and then what happened?

In 1984, I got my first taste of the financial business. I went to work for a company that did financial planning and asset management. After spending about a year and a half working as a financial analyst, I went out on my own and started my own estate and tax planning firm in 1986.

What other interests did you have at that time?

I pursued martial arts as a real passion in my life. I was always athletic and enjoyed building my body and mind in concert with each other. In 1980 I began to study what eventually was called the Chuck Norris system. Studying methods of bringing one's mind and body together has been an important resource for trading.

Are you still training in the martial arts?
Yes, I continue to expand my body of knowledge in several different martial disciplines.

Would you tell us how studying the martial arts relates to trading?
Let me relate it to combat. I remember being hit hard in the opening seconds of a round and then, after regaining my poise, I simply attacked to gain the victory. You never can get through any martial combat without taking some impact, which is a lot like trading. You can never get though a trading week without taking some losses. The determination of a mind and body, united in purpose, is a very formidable weapon. I had done the physical and mental training, but had never combined them with the spiritual aspect of life. Dr. Richard McCall who wrote, *The Way of the Warrior Trader*, is one of the people with whom I have studied. With his Zen-Mind Challenge and Master Quest programs, I have been able to integrate 18 years of martial arts study into understanding how intuition is used in trading. To be quit frank, I never gave intuition its due until its importance was revealed in Dr. McCall's programs.

Do you meditate?
Yes.

Tell us why meditation is important to your trading?
It helps in controlling the emotions and gaining focus. Before this interview, I meditated for 10 minutes to clear my mind and access all parts of my memory and subconscious to enhance my mind/body performance.

Would you tell us about starting your business, the direction it took, and when you started to get into trading?
In 1986, I started a tax and financial planning service because I saw the need for people to have a person with the ability to plan their financial lives.

In 1990, I wanted to manage money and trade United States Treasury Securities, which almost nobody did. My reasoning for the choice of financial instrument was that there is no way for me to blow a client up. When I buy a Treasury security for a client, the securities are purchased at a discount. If the client does not like the way I am handling their funds, he can always hold them until maturity. I cannot hurt them. In 70 years of research, I found some small quirks in the Treasury market. If you build your portfolio correctly, it would be very difficult to have a losing year.

I used my models and concepts to market a Treasury fund. We did a very good job of active duration management using a fundamental approach with 350 million dollars in pure Treasury securities. I found that price was the ultimate indicator of market psychology. I also found that there are patterns and aberrations that continue to occur time after time. I combined these understandings with fundamental research and our firm continues to be one of the leading edge Treasury management firms in the country.

You say, "we," how many people are there?
Scott Hill and I are the two principals in the firm. Four people work here.

Tell us about your trading?
In 1993, the Treasury market was at an all time low. I knew that bad things were coming. But being a long only guy, how should I solve the problem of being long only? How do I take futures and overlay them on the cash Treasury securities market? In May of 1993, I started researching how to offset the downside of the Treasury market. By mid-1994, I had come up with technical trading approaches to offset the problem. I found some aberrations in the Treasury market that allows my clients to reap three to five percent per year over and above normal Treasury returns.

One of the extreme models was in the number of standard deviation units the market is from its moving average. When you start to reach

156

a certain number of standard deviation units, you know that you have a 97% chance of not remaining at that level. This information is useful to a person who is inproportionally long or short in the market. In other words, 97% right does not mean that you are going to make 5 points, but 97% right means that it is time to either lighten up, add on, or hedge up whatever position you might have at that time. It is this type of theory that drives trading today, both as a bond trader for institutions and an S&P trader for a select few clients and myself.

What do you mean by aberrations in the bond market?
Take a daily bond chart and look at a 40-day moving average, drawing a band at plus or minus 3%. It quickly becomes evident that 97% of all closes reside within this plus or minus 3% band of the 40-day moving average. When the market trades at the top of that 3% range, it is either time to lighten up on long positions, drop the duration below my benchmark, or short the market. The converse is true at the bottom of the 3% band also.

What ends up happening in your analysis when it is affected by the speed of market moves? The market moves higher very slowly and the 40-day average gradually expands as it goes?
In most cases, you are looking for moves that are fairly short in duration, 10 to 15 days, and not the slow grind up. If the market moves very quickly when an important piece of news is released, for instance, it is a good time to sell.

Is this happening in the Bonds now? Some of the rallies to new highs are followed by pullbacks of a point or so?
The market is sitting at the 3% band and keeps popping through. It is having a hard time closing above the band, which is interesting. In other words, from a technical standpoint, it is just flat overbought. Time can take the market out of the overbought condition. If prices stay virtually flat for two or three weeks, then suddenly the market has room to expand upward again.

It is fascinating how consistent the 40-day moving averages are at providing good support levels in a bull market and good resistance levels in a bear market. Looking at the 3% band line, it can be used as a buy or sell area. It can be used with other technical indicators to show areas to liquidate positions or at least pare back to reduce risk.

Have you noticed this tendency only in Bonds?
No, it is evident in all markets. Most things tend to regress to their means, which is a pretty common factor in all markets. Markets do not like to stay hyper-extended. For example, if you take the S&P market, you will find that it likes to stay within a 5% to 6% range of the 40-day moving average. You will find that when the market gets to that 5 % to 6% band it is overbought or oversold, and will stall. It does not like it. Very recently in the S&P, we crashed through the band and have had a rough time during August and early September. There were actually multiple days spent below the band, which does not happen very often. It happened about a year ago for a one day, but the only other time it happened and stayed for any period of time was 1987. The rest of the time, the market has respected the bands.

You can use the bands sitting with 15-minute data or 5-minute data, and you are observing something that you have seen over and over. The more years you have looked at the market, the more you can see that things are, in fact, true.

Why do you think the 40-day moving average works?
I think it works because everyone else uses it.

What does being at one with the markets mean to you?
That is a good Zen concept. Picture this concept like a stream of water. If you are one with the market, then you are flowing with it, using its energy to help you be profitable. Your energy and the market are the same. Not being one with the markets means you are swimming against the flow. People that lose money on a consistent basis are fighting the flow of the market.

You are fighting the market because you are almost forecasting the turn.
No. I am taking advantage of a nice brand of neurosis that takes place at those 3% bands. People are buying because they are afraid that they are not going to be in the move.

Have you ever figured out why 3%?
People want to be in the bond market, not because they think it represents a good opportunity, but because they are afraid of equities, and they are afraid to miss the next bond move. That is a fringe element of thought represented in the current price, even though it is not the overwhelming thought represented in the market place. I would say 70% of the people at these levels become paralyzed. They cannot buy and they cannot sell. They are like a deer caught in the headlights of a car.

What else do you use for trading Bonds?
Well, Murray, I use this methodology you sold me called *Taylor* and other patterns that I have found in the marketplace. I am now searching for more recurrent patterns.

Tell us why you are attracted to this particular system?
In essence, I looked at the Old Testament Book of *Ecclesiastes* where Solomon, who was the wisest man in the world, said "that there is nothing new under the sun. There is a time under heaven for all things." I took that to mean patterns and cycles exist occurring over and over again. I figured God must be right about cycles and recurrent patterns, so that is how I began to look for recurrent patterns.

When you looked at *Taylor,* what did you find that you needed to refine?
Taylor was written with no consideration for regression theory. By developing incremental zones above the moving average, you start creating risk zones. For example, if you want to go long 2½% above the moving average, you have created a very high-risk trade. Now,

this does not mean that it will not be a good trade, but it means that it will be a high-risk trade. You need to change your leverage.

You are searching to go long in a market place at the 40-day moving average or lower to give yourself the maximum potential because of risk versus reward. Most people forget that it might be a good idea to have a profit target along with a risk amount when entering a trade. I go into every trade with the idea that there is a profit target attached to my risk.

Do you put that profit target into the market?
No, I do not.

So, if the market blows right through the profit target, you will stay with your position?
Yes, exactly. I will stay at the party for quite some time. I am looking at the easiest money to be gained in the market. In most times and in most market places, there is easy money. For example, you do not buy something one half of a point off of the yearly high with a close stop and expect to make a lot of money when the market breaks out. If you are right, you will be very happy, but if you are wrong, you are going to be stopped out in about 12 seconds.

Actually, you could probably be right and still get stopped out in 12 seconds?
Yes, exactly. You could get both. It becomes a high-risk trade that is not worth playing.

Who else was a great influence to your trading methodology?
George Soros was probably the greatest influence, as he broke the markets down in term of people's behavior instead of purely a numbers game.

Which books stand out to you?
George Soros' *Alchemy of Money*. I do very little as far as reading

the technical information. What I am more concerned with is the psychology of why something does what it does.

Do you have any insight into the psychology of trading the Bonds on report days?

The Bond market has always been a very interesting vehicle to identify what information is in the market and what is not in the market. You get to an Employment report with expectations of 200,000 jobs and the released report shows 390,000 jobs; the first response is the market is down a half a point and the next response is the market is up a point and a half. Traders are saying to themselves "Now, how could that be?" After the report, a few experts are allowed to determine the market psychology. Unfortunately, the experts were brokers telling you what they thought, and not actual money managers. I think the most dangerous thing in this business is the television set.

Have you observed countertrend moves prior to the market moving the direction that you would expect if a report were different than expected numbers?

It depends on the underlying theme in the marketplace at the time. For example, the last year and a half, Bonds have moved counter trend on reports. The two or three years prior to that, Bonds responded to reports the way you would expect them to. The markets change character, which is the oddest part of trying to assign absolute parameters into systemology. That is the end-all system based upon the prevailing psychology of the historical data that you have or the prevailing psyche. The problem with the market is the psyche changes. As the psyche changes, you need to feel what the market is doing, and get into its flow.

And where do you feel it?

Now, we can get really esoteric. I will classify it as a point in my gut. I listen to the floor activity in the S&P when I trade. I can feel what is happening on the floor. I can feel when a wall of trading is coming.

Where specifically do you feel it? Is it in your gut, in your chest, in your head; is it all over your body? Where is it?
It depends upon the intensity level of the trade. Most of the time, it starts out in the gut. But sometimes it is an entire body sensing. It depends on the intensity of the move. Many times the instinct is not localized.

If a trade was rated from 1 to 10, with 10 being best, where is the gut and where is all over the body?
Most of the time, if a trade is truly dangerous, the best intuitive nature I can get is definitely from my stomach. It is the 10 of trades. This is truly the zone, a place you want to trade from all the time.

When you say stomach, are you talking about the lower stomach, below the navel, or higher up in the solar plexus?
I am talking about two or three inches below my navel. From there, I sense more of a market move or market wall. That is where I get most of the gut response. There is a bunch of other stuff that runs around, but most of the time those emotions are just emotions.

When you get a feeling in your gut in that place, then you know that trade is more likely going to be 7 to 9?
Yes.

And when the feeling is not as intense or in other parts of your body, you know it is not going to be as good?
Yes, that is when I get a perplexed look on my face, meaning, "oops." I have definitely pulled in the wrong direction. It is that the market is getting ready to move against my position.

Do you set up time frames for a trade where something has to happen within an allotted time where you are wrong even if the trade is marginally profitable?

Yes. Most of the time, the methodology or system I am trading determines what timeframe I use as exit.

If I am on a one minute chart, and do not see a certain level because of congestion breakouts or high/low breakouts, I expand my time horizon. I use range breakouts because that is where the market has traded in balance, where the buyers and sellers are balanced for a certain period of time before someone decides they want to drive.

Are you taking the breakouts in the direction of the trend or are you countertrending them?
It depends upon the dynamics of the market, but the majority of the time I go with the trend.

How do you know market dynamics by looking at the previous day?
For example, if the high/low range of the market today were small, I would expect the range to expand in tomorrow's trading. If the range were large today, I would expect it to contract tomorrow. It is not always a given, but it is a premise that I begin the next trading day with.

If the market is in a very tight range, will it expand more? Is it linear?
No, it is adaptive, but this area is the specialty of my methodology and is somewhat sensitive and proprietary. The relationship is not perfectly linear, but it is an adaptive relationship. You are looking for people to go from non-committal which is a high/low day with a very tight range. The market is flat and nobody really wants to push it anywhere. The locals are not long or short and people are waiting for the next bit of information to jump on or jump off. When I see this kind of day, I am searching for some kind of market expansion. I am searching for the direction of the market mentality to change radically and to go with it, but always I am careful to remember the end result of the day might be nothing.

You also do statistical studies especially in the S&P. You are watching a trade set up and know you have some probability that the market is going to hit "x" level?

Yes. You start out with precursors going into trades. In other words, I am going to set up a trade and I am looking at certain levels that I can see on an hourly chart and on a daily chart. For example, suppose I am going into a trade risking $750 and a major support level is $500 lower. If I am entering a short trade, I am going to be a little antsy at that support level. I know that it is there and I know that everyone else knows it is there. If the market does not punch through in a certain amount of time, I am out because I know what the trade will turn into.

Do you use the kind of studies that *Taylor* did with the extreme bars, knowing the probability of taking out yesterday's low as a minimum target for a trade?

No, I do not in the S&P. The S&P can be analyzed based upon the prior day's highs/lows and percentages of the range. Some of it is similar to *Taylor* in the sense that he deals with a range and then a percentage of that range.

What can you tell us about trading the S&P Index?

They say that you can climb a mountain and sit and stare at a wall for ten years to find yourself or trade the S&P for six months. Trading the S&P is a total psyche battle everyday. I combine sound methodology with proven systems for discerning repeating patterns in the midst of chaos. What will trading mass do at critical levels. My work incorporates time of day, price patterns, and price levels to generate the best possible trade. As a factor, the time of day is probably as important as the breakout level. If I do not have 80% to 90% of the people in the pit, the chances of having a breakout level from a day's high or low are improbable. With 60% of the pit full, it is almost impossible for a breakout unless there is news. I am blending market psychology and statistics, but I am looking to get the maximum probability that my analysis will be right.

How do you know the number of people in the pit?
I listen to the pit and the guys on the local floor will tell me how many people are there. I use a service called "Squawk Box," which gives me continuous quotes and commentary from the floor.

If you have a light pit, the probability of your methodology working is low?
Yes. What you find is the day trading session in the S&P is from 9:00 A.M. to 11:00 A.M. Central. Not your time, Murray, but Central time 1:00 P.M. until 2:30 P.M. or 2:45 P.M. is the afternoon session when all of the players are there. That is when you see your moves and most of the contract volume that you can use comes into the pit.

In those dead sessions, do you get a chance to place orders at prices that you should not be getting? Or do you never deal with that?
I never deal with that. I just shut down.

Sometimes, I find a safe shorting opportunity around lunch, off of a countertrend rally.
You can see that, but that is more gut trading than it is analytical. I really have a hard time measuring the market's propensity to do anything during those lunch times. Some of those lunch trades start the biggest breakouts that I have ever seen. The majority of the time, they go nowhere and you are creating an artificial anxiety level. I do not want to take on the feeling of being in a trade when I do not know which way it is going to go.

Now, you said something before that you get "antsy." Where in your body do you get "antsy?"
I would say chest and shoulders.

When you feel "antsy," your chest and shoulders feel uncomfortable. You know that this is not the time to be trading?

165

Yes. If I can shake it off, then I know it is not real. If I cannot shake the feeling off, then I know it is something that I had better listen to. That is why it is so important to be in a good mental state. For example, recently I found that my subliminal mind sees more than my conscious mind. I see the world through my intellect and the experiences may not be as the world truly is. Thus, my unconscious mind or subliminal mind is trying to lead me in directions that I do not want to see. I have found an overlay within the past 60 days based upon that theory. I was having a problem with a level of persistent anxiety on certain trades. After observing the problem, I studied my results and found that there was a recurring pattern that was quantifiable.

Do you think that a trade log detailing how you feel and why you got into a trade is important?
It is to me, especially when I start seeing things like levels of anxiety that should not be there. I try to use the "inner man," so to speak, to tell me about things that I may not be aware of.

When we are trading, we are concentrating on what we think is our methodology, but other dynamics in a trade are being picked up subliminally and are not consciously listened to. I am starting to learn to listen to these things. It is another level of intuition.

It is not necessarily another level of intuition. It is a part of intuition. If you want to put intuition at levels, then that is another measure of how you can make it better for you.
Yes, how to turn intuition into action. I always looked at intuition as kind of a fuzzy, little funky feeling that I did not know how to handle.

No, we know that it is in your gut and in your shoulders and it is not good unless you get a feeling that you cannot shake off. If it is real, the feeling will still be there and signals you not to take the trade. When you get the gut feeling again, you go with it.

166

Yes. That is what it boils down to. I have found that I can take my intuition and quantify it. It is better than I could ever do intellectually.

Going back to the personal side, did you get married? Do you have children?
I got married a few times. The first time I was married, I was very young. It was one of those love things, but our general outlook did not agree. She was very wonderful, but it just did not work. There were no kids.

After my first try, I decided that the love approach did not work. On the second time, I tried the analytical approach which was not good at all. The third time around I listened to my gut, and I married a wonderful woman, and we have five kids. We have been together almost eight years. She is my soulmate who was chosen for me and it has been wonderful. It actually gets better every day.

What do you like to do with your family?
With my kids, it is basically anything. We watch TV, play, wrestle; anything that allows me to interact with them so I can see their smiles. With my wife, we do personal growth activities. Anything that we can do to raise our level of consciousness, and improve ourselves. My wife started studying martial arts about 30 days ago with two of our kids. I am integrating some things that made me who I am with them.

Tell us about your company standing now? How much capital are you managing?
We have about 100 million dollars in U.S. Treasury equity. On the trading side, I have around one million dollars in equity for trading the S&P.

What have been your results?
Last year, we were up about 250% on S&P trading. That is not calculated like everyone else's number where you use $10,000 units

to calculate your percentage. Basically, we trade about 4 contracts per $100,000, so it is not super leverage, but it is good leverage. This year, I am probably up between 50% and 70%, but we had lag time because the S&P contract changed as of October 1. We shut down our systems last year for the remainder of the year, and for the first five months of this year because of the contract change. In essence, we shut down and retooled because of the change or at least our perception of change in the overall S&P markets.

What was the change?
The change was in our volatility parameters. We did not actually get it quantified, but we figured that the methodologies that we had been using in the past all blew up. They just did not work.

We stopped live trading for three months at the end of the year after we realized that the system had blown up. We spent five months of this year working on the methodology and getting it right. Now, as we speak, we are hitting our stride where we are making 2% to 4% per day, which is where we need to be.

What criteria do you use for charging your clients?
On the Treasury side, our clients are institutional. We really do not have criteria for charging our clients for trading. We are currently trading with my money, and a couple of close friend's money.

Do you want to be a CTA?
It depends on whom you talk to. There are people that want me to be all things to all people, but it is difficult dealing with the regulations involved with being a CTA. I am looking for special people to work with and for in commodities trading.

Now that you have a lot of money, what are you going to do with it?
We give approximately 20% to 25% of my income per year to charity. Once my family is relatively secure, I would like to give 70% over the next several years.

168

What do you like to give to?

I give to churches, children's homes, and various charities with special emphasis on kids. With the rest of the money, I would like to get completely out of debt and use the money to continue to evolve spiritually. My interest in life is not in more stuff. Stuff does not do anything for me. I have had lots of stuff, and you have to take care of your stuff.

Trading has become a means to an end. It provides me with the means to do what I want to do, and a challenging art to master.

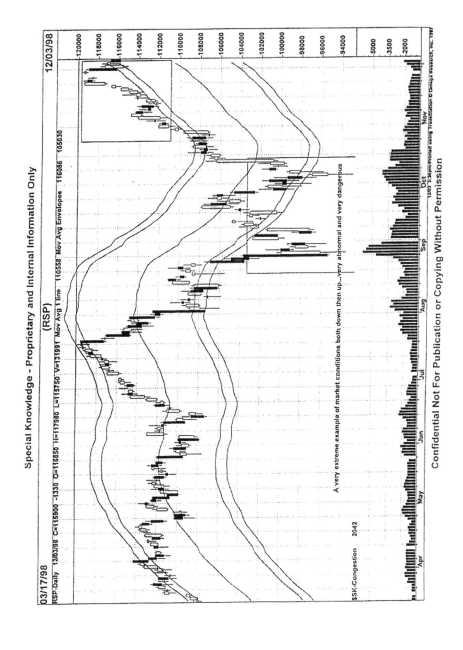

Special Knowledge - Proprietary and Internal Information Only

(RSPZ8)

10/14/98 11:45am   10/15/98 1:45pm

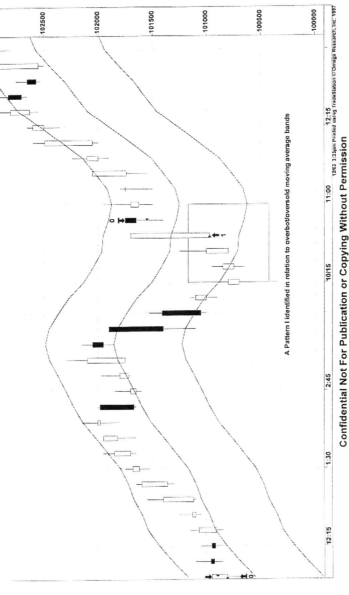

A Pattern I identified in relation to overbot/oversold moving average bands

Confidential Not For Publication or Copying Without Permission

171

Special Knowledge - Proprietary and Internal Information Only

(US)

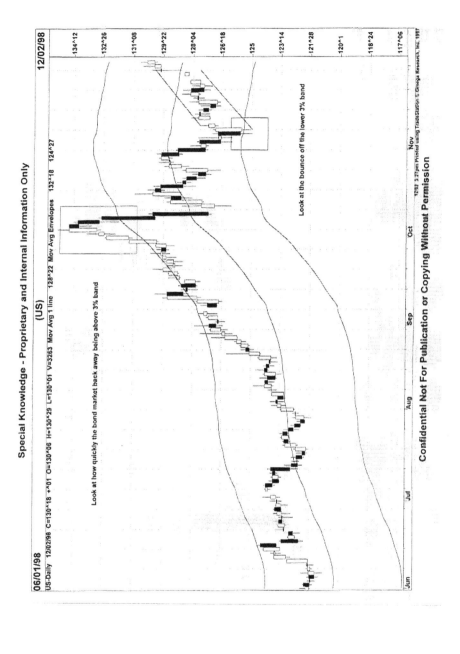

Confidential Not For Publication or Copying Without Permission

172

MODELING STUDY

CHILDHOOD FAMILY STATUS
- Bob's family struggled during his childhood and worked into middle class as a teenager in Houston, Texas

MENTORING - INFLUENCES
- Parents had entrepreneurial spirit even when things were hard
- Parental influence--determination and making good use of available resources
- Dr. Richard McCall--*The Way of the Warrior Trader*
- Supportive wife

ENVIRONMENT
- Only child
- Moral character
- Extended family's inflexibility influenced him to become more flexible
- Steadfast, prim, and proper
- Traditional

EDUCATION
- Good student
- Began with engineering and computer sciences
- Studied political science
- Earned degree in accounting
- Worldly prospective because of travel while in military

INTERESTS-Skills-Abilities - Honors
Childhood
- Baseball
- Football

Adult
- Martial arts
- Mediator
- Has read extensively on trading
- Personal growth activities

QUALITIES
- Highly motivated as a youth to make his own way primarily with things that interested him
- Spiritual
- Patient
- Persevering

BUSINESS EXPERIENCE
- Had newspaper route at seven
- Worked throughout high school years
- Military intelligence - research
- Financial planner and analyst
- Own firm - estate and tax planning

PHILOSOPHY - SUCCESS BELIEFS
- Life can be anything you want it to be
- Anyone can be unique
- You make life more pleasant for yourself by working
- There is a profit target attached to my risk in every trade that I take
- More concerned with the psychology of why does something do what it does rather then technical information

TRADING EXPERIENCE
- Money manager
- U.S. Treasury Securities
- S & P Index
- Technical/Discretionary

RECOMMENDATIONS
- *Taylor Trading Methodology* by Murray Ruggiero
- *Trading for a Living* by Alexander Elder
- *Alchemy of Finance* by George Soros
- *The Crowd* by Gustave Lebon
- *Way of the Warrior Trader* by Dr. Richard McCall

TRADER CONTRIBUTIONS
- Makes clients money

PROSPERITY CONSCIOUSNESS
- Donates to churches, children's homes, and various charities with an emphasis on children

TRADER GEMS -Fundamental - Intuitive - Psychological
- Meditation help to create focus and control emotions
- Price is the ultimate indicator of market psychology because it is a true reflection of what traders feel
- When you find an aberration in the market you must take action
- Most things tend to regress to their means
- People who consistently lose money in the market are fighting the market
- Markets change character so there is no 'end all system'
- The most opportunity in S & P trading is when the most traders are in the pit - from 9 A.M. to 11 A.M. Central time, and from 1:00 P.M. to 2:30 P.M. and I trade during those times
- Large breakouts during lunch generally go nowhere and create artificial anxiety
- My subliminal mind sees more then my conscious mind in trading
- Keeping a log gives information on patterns of anxiety and where you go wrong in trading so you can correct it

FUTURE PLANS
- Continue to evolve spiritually
- Give a larger percentage of income to charity

TRADER GEMS - Mechanical - Analytical - Technical
- The bond market is mean reverting
- If we take a 40-day moving average, prices will normally be contained within plus or minus 3% of that average
- This mean reverting concept is valuable when locating a place to lighten up a market position
- The basic reason that this mean reverting concept works is when the market is rising or falling too quickly it becomes overbought at +3% or oversold -3%
- The Bond market will rarely stay outside of the bands for more than a few days
- In the S&P500, this mean reverting effect occurs at 5% to 6% off of the 40-day moving average
- Bob trades T-Bond futures by combining the Taylor book method with other patterns, and concepts such as regression theory and reverting the to mean
- Bob balances the risk potential of a trade with its potential profit. For example, a long signal in T-Bonds near the upper 3% band would not represent a low-risk trade. If the signal occurred below the 40-day moving average, it could represent a great risk/reward trade
- When developing a system, it needs to adapt to changing themes in the market. As the themes change, you need to be able to feel what the market is doing
- Bob also tries to predict tomorrow's range. His predictions are based on the concept that the range also reverts to the mean. Low range days lead to high range days and high range days lead to low range ones. This relationship is not a simple linear one

Murray's Analytical Modeling Study

Trading Analysis
Mechanical--Objective: Interpreting the mean reverting price bands and price chart patterns

Mechanical--Automatic: Mechanical trading systems

Discretionary: Listening to the market activity and commentary from the S&P500 pit on a "Squawk Box"

Analysis of Bob's Methodology
Most of Bob's work is proprietary, but luckily, some of it was based on my work on the Taylor Trading Method. I will overview the methodology here in this chapter.

George Douglass Taylor published a manual known as "The Book Method" in 1950. This work has inspired many price-based swing-trading strategies used by professional short-term traders. These strategies include the work of Linda Bradford Raschke, Larry Williams, and Toby Crabel. What is exciting about Taylor's ideas is that they have withstood the test of time unlike many trading strategies.

Interest in this method was fueled when it was discussed in George Angell's book *Winning in the Futures Market*. In 1994, Traders Press republished Taylor's original work. This new edition included a reprint of the chapter on Taylor from George Angell's book as well as comments by Linda Raschke published in Club 3000. Taylor's trading methodology is really a combination of concepts that work together to produce reliable short-term trades. The concepts discussed in Taylor's original book include some of the following:

1. Only take short-term trades of 0 to 3 days based on price action

2. Only trade when the odds are on your side taking small, consistent profits out of the market
3. Trade short-term reversals based on price action around recent highs and lows
4. Study price movements relative to the past three days open, high, low and close
5. Study the length of upswings relative to downswings.
6. Ignore the news
7. Study the longer term trends of the market, both the direction and the intensity
8. Study the seasonal effects on the price action of the market
9. Study the concept of the 3, 4, and 5 Elliott Wave sequence and how it affects short term price movements

Most people who study the Taylor methodology do not integrate all of these concepts because of the difficulty in understanding his writings. Luckily, for the few who have taken the time to learn his methods, he was a much better trader than writer.

The first part of Taylor's trading method is based on price action around recent highs and lows. This part is based on the concept that most markets have a three-day rhythm. Sometimes the market will have an extra beat or two, but this three-day rhythm occurs often enough to be of value as a trading tool. Taylor's pattern consists of three types of days that follow a sequence. The first was called a "Buy Day," where the low is made early and the market trades higher and closes near the high of the day. Next, we have a "Sell Day" in which the high is made first and the market closes lower for the day. Often, the high made on the buy day will act as resistance. Finally, we have the "sell short day," where the high occurs first and the market opens near the high and closes near the lows for the day. Figure 1 shows an example of an ideal three-day cycle in sequence.

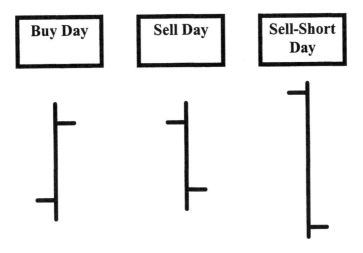

Taylor's concepts work because most traders place stop orders at recent highs or lows. When the market takes these levels out, and reverses, all of the traders who place orders at those levels would lose money.

Taylor's Three-Day Cycle

Taylor believed that markets followed a three-day rhythm. This rhythm existed often enough that it can give an edge in trading. In one of our systems inspired by Taylor, we detect this rhythm by locating a ten-day low where the market closes in the lower 20% of its range. The next day is a buy day. After that, the cycle is set and every third day is a buy day. The market should cycle though the pattern Buy Day, Sell Day, and Sell Short Day. This cycle is not perfect and does shift. We can confirm where we are in the cycle by requiring the market to close in the lower 20% of the range on a Sell Short Day. We would buy the market on next day just below today's low on a limit order. If the market does not close in the lower part of the range, we would push the cycle forward one day and buy on the next day if tomorrow closes in the lower 20% of the range. Our sell days are confirmed when the market closes in the upper 20% of the range. This method is very adaptive and resets our cycle every time the market sets a new ten-day low.

Other issues

Taylor's trading method combined many different factors. For example, he looked at the overall trend. When the market was in an uptrend, Taylor's method added one day to the rally cycle. During down trends, he added one day to the decline cycle. Taylor also knew that countertrend moves would not occur until previous lows were exceeded in downtrends and the previous high was exceeded in uptrends. He also looked at something like Elliott Waves. He labeled the Real top, which was the top of Wave 3, and the actual top which was the top of Wave 5. Another issue that is very important is that down openings are bullish and up openings are bearish.

Taylor Trading Methods and Seasonality

Taylor's original trading methods were applied to the grain markets, and he used seasonality to filter his trades. He looked at both the overall seasonal trends as well as month of year effects. It may be hard to believe, but month of year has a large effect even in today's markets. Month of year effect is a powerful filter for trading systems in most markets.

In the S&P, volatility is higher around triple witching than normal expirations. For this reason, this method makes more money when volatility is high and works better during March, June, September, and December. Another seasonal factor in most financial markets like the S&P and T-Bonds is day of week. About half of the total gains in the S&P500 have occurred on Monday. Friday is the only day of the week with a downward bias.

Developing a simple Taylor-type system
We can use the work of Taylor to develop a trading system for various markets. I have developed systems using the work of Taylor for both the S&P500 and T-Bonds. My work in T-Bonds is what Bob Watson has based his T-Bond futures trading system on with proprietary modifications. Taylor used a three-day rhythm in the market, but some markets like T-Bonds have a five-day rhythm. This is an important point and extra time periods lead to the existence of a fourth type of day called a breakout day. During a breakout day, if the market takes the high or low out by just one tick, we want to go in the direction of the breakout. The five-day rhythm in the T-bond market is set by an "N" day low where the market closes in the lower 20% of the trading range. This occurrence sets the first buy day. Recently, I have started using cycle analysis to set the value "N" to identify where the Taylor rhythm starts. When the rhythm does not match market conditions, we do not trade. Let me show you a Taylor Shell system coded in TradeStation Easy Language.

```
Inputs:Key(10)
Pts(3),             Pt1(0),             Pt2(1),             Pt3(2),
BLev(.40),SLev(.80),Ct(3),BuyFilt(TRUE),SellFilt(TRUE),Hold(-
1);
{Key how many days to use to start Taylor count}
{Pt1, Pt2, Pt3 is what day in the Ct count sequence, Ct is the number
of days in a sequence, default is three to test the given three rules}
Vars: Lowbar(0),Seq(0);
If (High-Low)>0 then value1=(Close-Low)/(High-Low);
If Low=Lowest(Low,Key) and value1<.2 then Lowbar=CurrentBar;
{Find current day in sequence}
Seq=Mod((CurrentBar-LowBar),Ct);
{These are the classic counter trend rules for buying and selling}
If value1<BLev and Seq[Pt1]=0  then buy("B1")  at low -NPts
points limit;
If value1<BLev  and Seq[Pt2]=0  then buy("B2")  at low -NPts
points limit;
```

If value1>SLev and Seq[pt3]=0 then sell("S1") at High+NPts points Limit;
{If Hold is -1 then exit at next day's close, for the S&P500 you exit at today's close}
{Other markets do not have the range so you need an overnight hold}
If Hold=-1 then begin
If BarsSinceEntry>1 then exitlong at close;
If BarsSinceEntry>1 then exitshort at close; end;
Exit
{Hold the market for N day before exiting a position}
If Hold>1 then begin
If BarsSinceEntry>Hold then exitlong at close;
If BarsSinceEntry>Hold then exitshort at close;
end;

This system has rules coded for the basic three-day Taylor counter trend patterns, but they can occur anywhere in a "Ct" count day sequence. This system shell using a Ct of 5 was the starting point for the T-Bond system which I sold to Bob. It is missing two patterns which I added plus several filters, but if you have TradeStation, optimizing this system on the T-Bond market could be a very profitable project.

George Douglass Taylor was one of the most brilliant technicians of the 20th century. His methods have passed the test of time and continue to work to this day in markets which did not exist when he developed them. Often, the works of old masters are overlooked. Maybe the Holy Grail system has been found, but we cannot see it because it is lost in the forest we call "technical analysis."

Adrienne's Psychological Modeling Study

The Possibility-Thinking Model
Bob was raised in a family that was more aware of the impossibilities than the possibilities in life. As an intelligent and observant young boy, he was determined not only to escape the limitations of poverty but the limited and rigid thinking which accompanied it. Slowly, the world of possibility opened up before him as he did whatever he could to make money, starting with a paper route when he was seven years old.

From his parents, Bob took some very important qualities which contributed to his Possibility-Thinking Model - determination, character, the ability to use the resources at hand, and an appreciation of the entrepreneurial spirit. But, he was highly motivated to take these qualities and go his own way.

Another factor that contributed to his Possibility-Thinking Model was the fact that his parents never gave up on their dream of working for themselves until they had achieved it. Dreams rub off on many children because they see their parents striving for something and unconsciously, it becomes important for them, too. Also, as the only child, Bob was more likely to identify with his parent's dreams than if he had been the fourth or fifth child.

When Bob's family moved to Texas, it was to an open culture where Possibility-Thinking was in the air for him to breathe. The rebellious part of him was motivated to get moving on his dreams. Rebellion is an essential ingredient of the Possibility-Thinking Model. You must have some rebellion in you to work against the norm.

By the end of his high school years, Bob worked half the day when he saw the possibility of making money for school. The career he selected offered the best possibility for making the most money immediately - engineering. His stint in the army opened up even

183

more possibilities by introducing him to the world. All of these early experiences reinforced a model that Bob could derive possibilities for success wherever he looked.

Even from his passion for the martial arts, Bob was able to derive possibilities to improve his trading. Once, when he had received a blow in a match temporarily knocking him down, he realized "you never can get through any martial combat without taking some impact, which is a lot like trading. You can't get through trading without taking some losses. . . .The determination of the mind and body united in purpose is a very formidable weapon." Meditation helps him to understand how intuition is used in trading and how to control emotions and gain focus. Possibility-Thinkers want to enlist others in thinking because the power of a like-minded group not only ignites the potential for each individual; it is essential for the original Possibility-Thinker to reach his potential. On the other hand, if everyone's thinking is negative, the negativity reinforces the group's thinking, like his extended family, and limits everyone's potential. For that reason, Bob seems to have made it a goal to bring other Possibility-Thinkers into his life.

How does this model influence Bob's trading? He went into Treasury Securities because there was no possibility of blowing up clients in that type of investment. While it looked too safe to be interesting, Bob looked for possibilities to make solid returns. What he found were aberrations, which opened up possibilities to make money. When a Possibility-Thinker looks for what is wrong to make it right, he will find ways to do it. Bob heads one of the leading edge Treasury firms in the country. Bob believes that the people who lose money on a consistent basis are fighting the flow of the market, while Possibility-Thinkers go with the flow looking for the best, the easiest, and the safest possibilities to materialize.

People with this particular model know that all things exist and they just need to discover what already exists. Bob was looking for patterns and found them. When a Possibility-Thinker is in alignment with himself and takes the signals from his neurological system, the answers will be there. However, if they are to keep in tune with the universe, they must keep their minds and bodies healthy in order to receive the answers.

Bob understands that his conscious mind is limited to his intellect, and that the subliminal mind, when aligned, opens up possibilities to find quantifiable patterns not previously seen. Through his martial arts training and meditation, Bob has attempted to reach the point where he is not limited to understanding. As a result, he makes a high percentage return on his trading capital. This success has led him to even greater Possibility-Thinking, seeing the potential to use his earnings to do much more than just getting more "stuff" which means very little to him. The end result of Possibility-Thinking is prosperity consciousness. Bob's goal is to give 70 percent of his profits to charity. Possibility-Thinking is one of the key ingredients to realizing top performance in trading.

CHAPTER 7

Ed Pomeranz

Caviar to schnitzel - How an immigrant created great wealth before the age of 20 in the import/export business and went on to be one of Europe's top money managers before the age of 30.

Shall we start at the beginning? Tell us where you were born, about your family, and some things about what you were like as a child.

I was born into a wealthy family in Odessa, on the Black Sea, in what was the Soviet Union in 1969. My father had studied Business Administration and had a supermarket. My mother was a housewife.

My parents spoiled me. I was used to having caviar and other delicacies, which were beyond the means of other people in the country. This became a problem when I started in kindergarten. I was offered black bread, butter, and cheese for lunch and I threw it away from the table, because I wanted salmon and black caviar.

My family immigrated to Austria in 1976, when I was seven years old. The atmosphere was not pleasant in Russia for a Jewish family in the middle of the Cold War.

Tell us about your childhood in Russia just before you left. What were you interested in as a little boy?

As a little boy, I liked to play chess and ice hockey. I was a mama's boy, and did not like it when she was not within reach. One day, my mother left me with my grandfather when I was about four years old. At 2:00 A.M., I started to cry because I wanted to go home to my mother. My grandfather did not know what to do with me, so he taught me how to play chess. By 7:00 A.M., I beat him. My family realized that I had a special talent and took me to a chess club in Odessa. When I eventually beat everyone, they asked me to leave

187

the club, explaining to my mother that there had been enough Jewish world champions in chess. The first money I ever made was from playing chess.

How old were you?

I was eight years old. It was 1977, and we had recently moved to Austria. I was playing football in the garden with some other kids and saw an older man playing chess. I went to him and explained that I wanted to play with him for money. We played for two dollars a game. For each move, he would take fifteen minutes and I would take five. That is how I started playing chess for money. Now, as an adult, I no longer play chess at that level.

Tell us about your family's move to Austria. How difficult was the transition?

It was a difficult transition because I could not speak German. We moved to Vienna, Austria, in November 1976, and school had already started in September. In the Austrian system school started with primary, then gymnasium, followed by the university. If you finished a class with a bad mark, you had to repeat that class. I was fortunate that I always had teachers who believed in me and I passed the classes. They always said, "This guy is clever enough that we should take him to the next class." After some years in Austria, I could speak German, but my grammar and writing was still bad.

What did your father do when he came to Austria?

When we came to Austria in November, my father was wearing his summer clothes. Odessa was still very warm at that time of year. We were a wealthy family when we left Russia, but we could not take anything out of the country with us. Basically, we moved to Austria with the clothes on our back. The border guards would not even let me take the ice hockey equipment that I loved so much. Initially, my father supported us by going from store to store selling caviar and champagne that he had bought from other immigrants.

What other interests did you have while you were going to school in Austria? Any other sports or games?
I started to play table tennis and developed that game to tournament level. Then, I got involved in boxing for 2 years.

How were you doing at school?
I finished gymnasium as an "A" student and was the head of the student body for four years. By this time, I was already interested in the investment business and helped to organize fund-raisers for the school. They let me be responsible for the money. I wanted to invest the money in stocks, but they told me I was crazy and did not let me do it.

I was 17 years old and in my last class in high school. I was working at a gasoline station and made my first $1,700. This represented the beginning of my financial career; I started to invest in stocks.

How did you do?
It was 1987, and I was doing quite well until the Crash in the stock market. Three friends each contributed $1,700 to trade. Our investment grew to $15,000. Of course, we lost everything in the Crash because we did not know anything about the importance of money management at that time.

What did you do from there?
I studied Business Administration at the university. While I was attending the university, I worked as a stock analyst in an Austrian bank and also traded stocks. It was a heavy load to study and work at the same time.

We analyzed companies and sent our findings to a large Japanese investment house. At this time, we were analyzing a beer company that had many undervalued real estate holdings. For this reason, we advised them that we felt that the stock of the company should go up in value.

189

My bookkeeping teacher taught us what it meant to have properties in a company that were undervalued, giving us an example of a stock that had gone up in price. I understood why the stock had gone up because we had done the analysis for the investment firm and had sent it to them. When the Japanese firm started to buy the stock, I understood the whole thing, but it was a little too late!

I was 20 years old and because of the experience with the investment firm, I became more interested in technical analysis. That is when I began working for a bank as a dealer on the Austrian Stock Exchange. I was the head of the desk at 21 years old, which was very young for the position. This is where I started to make my money in stocks, but not really with a system. I looked at charts and made my decisions based on gut instinct.

A little later, my grandfather had a heart attack. I left my financial career to help my family in the import/export business. I worked with my parents for 1½ years to help them build their business in Russia.

What type of business did your family have?
My parents and my grandfather had a supermarket and a gasoline station on the Austrian/Yugoslavian border. When the war started in Yugoslavia, the border was closed, and they lost almost everything. All of this happened immediately after the announcement of "Peristroika" in Russia, and I began to help with the import/export business.

What were you importing and exporting?
It was 1992 and 1993. We were exporting consumer goods to Russia, and we were importing some commodities.

Which commodities were you importing?
We were importing urea from Russia.

How did you do financially?
I did very well in import/export. After I built the business, I left the company to pursue my primary interest, which was trading.

After the Crash, I started making some money back in the markets. There was a big bull market in stocks when I was trading on the Austrian Stock Exchange before I started with the import/export business. How I made a lot of money is an interesting story.

Before Austria joined the European community, you could maintain anonymous stock trading accounts. With my coded account, I started to trade stocks. The bank mistakenly booked between $80,000 and $90,000 to my account. When I noticed this amount of money in the account, I went to the Chief of the bank and told him about the mistake. Since it was an anonymous account, I could have withdrawn the money because the bank did not even know my name. The Director was so surprised that I would return the money, he told me that he would leverage my account. This was like having unlimited credit. My account became very healthy after one year. With what I know about money management now, I would never have taken those same risks again. I was very lucky.

Were you one of the people who thought the Russian reforms were going to work and life was going to be wonderful?
My parents and I had a very different opinion about the future and its opportunities. I was always thinking ten moves ahead like I did when I played chess. I tried to explain to them that it was not enough to be in the Western world and do import/export trade with Russia. Russia was not Africa, and was going to learn Western business practices very fast. My parents needed to go into Russia to establish their business and have their own supermarkets there.

They were of the opinion that it would take many, many years before they would be able to find people in Russia that they could trust to manage because it would take them so long to understand the

Western financial system. Since we were of differing opinions on that matter and I did not see a future, I left the company.

At the time, I did believe that the reforms were going to work though. That is why I encouraged my parents to go to Russia for business to establish their roots. For the last six or seven years, I have been right, but in the last few weeks, I have been wrong.

When did you get interested in futures?
While I was working in the import/export business, I became less interested in stocks and more interested in futures. I was interested in all kind of futures -- financials, metals, commodities, but I had no clue about how they were traded. I had a friend who told me that he was very good in futures. So, I gave him a part of the money that I made to trade with the idea that I could learn from him. To make a long story short, he lost everything. However, I met one of my business partners, Christoph, at the brokerage firm where he was trading.

I thought if this guy can lose my money, then I should try trading the futures markets myself. At least if I lose, then it is my fault. At this time, I started working to understand the business of investing and learned that I needed a game plan if I was going to succeed.

How did you do?
In the beginning, it was very difficult because I wanted to repeat the success I had enjoyed in the stock market. My experience in the stock market had been buying at the bottom and selling at the top. With futures it did not really work that way.

I was financially healthy during this time, but I did not have a real job. I applied for a job with CA Global Futures AG, which has recently been renamed to Bank Austria Creditanstalt Futures Group. This is the brokerage firm where my money had been lost. From that point, I started again.

Christoph and I started to develop ideas for trading strategies. I was interested in developing a game plan for trading with money management rules. I wanted to be a mechanical trader, but I was interested in having fun in my life, which meant that I was not mentally ready for being disciplined. I knew that if I was going to trade successfully, I needed to have discipline. So, I decided to have a computer maintain the discipline for me.

Imagine how it was in Austria at the time. There were few programmers with whom you could share ideas about trading. It was hard to trust people to not steal your ideas. Fortunately, an old friend gave me the name of a programmer that he felt I could trust. This man programmed my ideas and it became the system that we are trading now.

Was your first system basically a trend following system?
Yes, the first system that I designed was a trend following system.

Do you still trade by following the trend?
Yes. The system applies breakout principles. As you know, when you miss a winning trade, it creates more pressure than being in a losing trade, since you do not want to lose any opportunity. I tried to trade every market, but I began to realize that I did not need to always be in the market and I did not need to pick market bottoms and tops.

You are trying to capture high probability pieces?
Correct. I want to be in the markets where I have the best mathematical probability of success. We have started to use filters to trade the markets and it has changed the outcome of our trading. We are still trading the same model, applying the same breakouts to the markets, but we are using filtering techniques on the breakouts.

What filters do you use?
It was not a filter to go against the trades, but it was a filter to go or not go with a particular market. We were checking how a market

performed in the past for a certain period of time. We had two models. One model was trading across all 65 markets. After the model went to a certain level, the market was trending and the probabilities were very high that it was going to continue trending. We started to trade this market based on our analysis.

Were you using a random walk?
No. It was a combination of rates and average win to loss ratio analysis. When the ratio went over a certain figure, we started to trade the market.

How old were you when you developed your system?
I was 24 years old when I developed my system.

Tell us about the development of your business. Were you trading on your own?
I was trading on my own, but not with the mechanical system that I was developing with my programmer. After he put everything together, i.e., entries, exits, money management tactics, then the computer traded the system automatically.

When did you decide to go on your own?
I started to trade on my own on November 28, 1994. This was when I started to develop my own business.

What is the name of your company?
My company is called FTC, Futures Trading Concepts. I was trading a managed account of $750,000 double leveraged to $1.5 million. The money in the account came from friends. I did not go out to customers to ask for money at this time, because I had a system, but I did not have a track record. My partners and I were all in our twenties and we needed to prove that we could handle the responsibilities that come with managing funds. In the beginning, I was concerned about our trading discipline and the consistency of our results. I felt an enormous responsibility for managing the funds of others.

You were trading a 100% mechanical system?
Yes, I understood that I had no chance for success in discretionary trading because of my bon vivant lifestyle. At least I was able to understand the problem and was good at following the rules of my mechanical system, so we did very well.

Do you still trade 100% mechanical?
Yes, I still trade 100% mechanical, but after a certain period I want to include some discretionary decisions as well. Over the years, I have seen many chart formations and other indicators that I thought presented a good opportunity to trade. These kinds of indicators would be difficult or impossible to program, but I would like to take advantage of them in the future.

Did any of the new elements that you have added to your system estimate a probability that you really should not take a trade or indicate that drawdowns occur in a given environment?
We have a filter, but we want to divide the filter into long positions and short positions. For example, we will use a move in the D-mark and in the dollar. The move is going to happen in the U.S. dollar and the position is in the dollar short against all major currencies. It is a move that is going against the odds. We are talking in futures terms. It is the first trade to the long side for the D-mark and the dollar is in a run. For the last 2 ½ years, all of the trades in the D-mark have been to the short side. There have been no trades to the long side that were good. We took this trade because we are still in the developing process on this part of the system. I was not really feeling comfortable when I took the trade, but now it is going in our favor. I still think the odds are not with us being short.

So, you have a mechanical system that says take the trade, but your internal system says, "I'm not so sure!"
Yes, I have my personal interpretation of the market, but I always stick to the system.

How many people did you have when you first started to develop your business?
There were four people involved when I first started.

When did you become a Commodity Trade Advisor?
In November of 1994, I gave my first order for the managed account and on May 1, 1996, we started the Bahamian Fund. We are still not registered with the Commodity Futures Trading Commission or the National Futures Association, but we have complied with all of the rules since 1994. From the beginning, I was thinking ahead. To raise money in the United States, you need at least thirty-six months real time track record.

How much money are you trading with now?
We have approximately $15 million under management.

Tell us about your track record in percentages?
In 1995, our return was 20.8% net to the client after all costs, of course. In 1996, our return was 17.9% and in 1997, it was 47.5%. In 1998, we are up approximately 13.1% as of September.

When you filter are you filtering out periods in which the market moves sideways?
No, I am not filtering the time when the market is sideways. I am filtering out when the market is trending long-term.

So, you are only taking trades in the direction of the long-term trend?
Yes, correct.

You are saying that if you are not making money on long trades, you take all of the short trades. If you are making money on the long side, only take the long side?
Yes, now we have come to the conclusion that we cannot mix long positions and short positions. You can have good movement on the long side of a market, but cannot trade it because you lose

196

everything on the short side while you lack diversification. It makes more sense to divide the analysis into long and short, and to trade in the direction of the trend because you get more diversification.

If you trade both sides of the market, you are going to have one side that is going to break even for you.
Correct. That is what we have determined from our studies and experience.

It sounds like you are following some of the work that I did in my *Cybernetic Trading* book?
Yes, we are using some of the ideas presented in your book.

Who was your biggest influence as far as trading itself?
Richard Dennis.

Why would a mechanical trader find the psychology of trading important? Why would you want a Trading Coach when you are a mechanical trader?
There is a lot of stress involved in trading. Having techniques to reduce the stress helps you to make better choices and see opportunities. Trading is not only about developing systems and trading those systems. It is more than that. The competitors of championship level chess prepare for a match with the same physical workout as a person preparing for a boxing match. You need to be physically and mentally prepared to be consistent in following your trading rules.

Psychological support helps you to make the right decisions not only when you are trading, but also when you are in the developmental stages of a system. When you develop a system, you go through a lot of information. Being psychologically fit is a key to each next level of success. You may have something that works presently, but if you do not keep on learning and investing time in research, you can find yourself behind. That is why I am happy to have you as my trading coach, to help me face all of these challenges.

I think you are trying to say that there is a certain mind set in being at one with the markets. A discretionary trader has to be at one with the markets all of the time in order to be a great trader. A systems developer has to be at one with the market that he is analyzing when developing a successful system. As long as a trader's system is evolving, the developer needs to feel comfortable trading the system, to understand why it works, and to see things that other people do not see to base the system on a valid premise relating to how the markets work. You have to be at one with the markets as you build a system.

You are absolutely right, Adrienne. Maybe the best comment to your statement is a good example: We were really spoiled as young guys having good results in our first years of business. In 1998, we had good months in January and February, then March through July were five losing months in a row. You asked me why a mechanical trader would need a coach? I think many people in the same situation would have overruled their system at this time. I do not need to tell you that 1998 has been a really crazy year with unbelievable volatility. I have never seen this kind of market movement. You need to be psychologically fit to deal with difficult times. I know that for continued success, I need to keep working on myself. I owe that much to the people who believe in me and entrust their money to my company.

Tell us about the lessons that you have learned along the way that have been vital to your success.
The most important lesson that I have learned has been in the last three or four months. Shall we start from the beginning? Coming from a wealthy family, I was spoiled and always had a lot of luck in my life. Everything always seemed to go in my direction. Do not ask me why or how, I do not know. Even with a couple of setbacks along the way, whatever I touched eventually went in my direction. I always felt that I had "The Midas Touch."

In the last three to six months, from February on, I started to lose. I was always used to making money. We proved our system to be a successful, top system. I was very proud of my accomplishments. The lesson came when everything seemed to be going against me. I realized that I was not guaranteed success in life, just because it was always there before.

Whenever I made a great deal of money, I had a tendency to abuse myself with excesses. During a drawdown period or any difficult period in life, I realized that you have to make healthy choices so you can make the best decisions and have the stamina to handle the challenges. Everyone has to give something up to achieve great things in life. That is what I learned from you, Adrienne. It is necessary to negotiate with your different parts and give each and every part what it needs to support good trading. If you put everything into trading or just into having fun, the other parts will stop supporting you and your efforts.

So, did you get married and have children?
I have been with my wife for 14 ½ years, but we got married five years ago. We have two boys who are 5 and 2 years old. Now I know that there is more to life than just going out and having fun.

Where do you want to go from here? What are your goals for your business and your goals for your life?
My business goal is to have 100 million dollars under management in different trading approaches. I would like to keep on trading at an earning to drawdown ratio between 2 ½ and 3 to 1.

My passion and drive is to be considered one of the top traders in the world. That is what I would like to achieve.

What is your ranking as a money manager?
I can tell you where we were in 1997. In *Futures Magazine,* we were ranked number one. In a rolling window of 12 months, we were trading the Bahamian Fund and ranked between number one and number six for the year 1997.

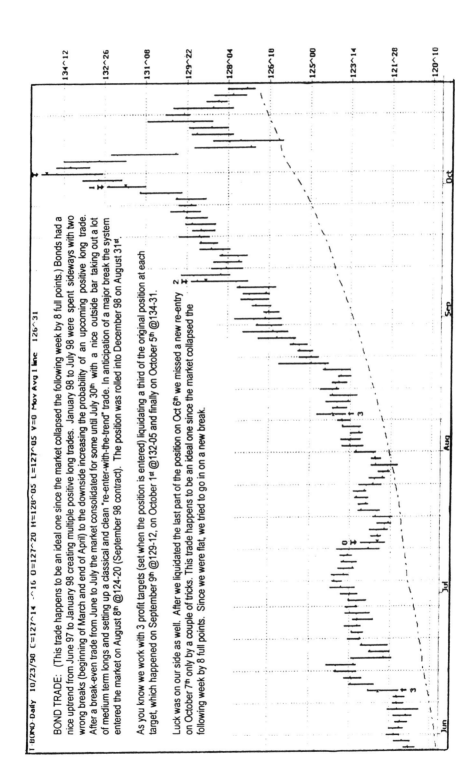

1-BOND Daily 10/23/98 C=127^14 ^16 O=127^20 H=128^05 L=127^05 V=0 Mov Avg 1 line 126^31

BOND TRADE: (This trade happens to be an ideal one since the market collapsed the following week by 8 full points.) Bonds had a nice uptrend from June 97 to January 98 creating multiple positive long trades. January 98 to July 98 were spent sideways with two wrong breaks (beginning of March and end of April) to the downside increasing the probability of an upcoming positive long trade. After a break-even trade from June to July the market consolidated for some until July 30th with a nice outside bar taking out a lot of medium term longs and setting up a classical and clean "re-enter-with-the-trend" trade. In anticipation of a major break the system entered the market on August 8th @124-20 (September 98 contract). The position was rolled into December 98 on August 31st.

As you know we work with 3 profit targets (set when the position is entered) liquidating a third of the original position at each target, which happened on September 9th @129-12, on October 1st @132-05 and finally on October 5th @134-31.

Luck was on our side as well. After we liquidated the last part of the position on Oct 6th we missed a new re-entry on October 7th only by a couple of tricks. This trade happens to be an ideal one since the market collapsed the following week by 8 full points. Since we were flat, we tried to go in on a new break.

200

MODELING STUDY

CHILDHOOD FAMILY STATUS
- Ed's's experience has covered many socio-economic levels. He began his life in a wealthy family in Russia. When opportunity called for them to escape to the West, his family became poor in Vienna, and he has grown to wealthy in Vienna.

MENTORING - INFLUENCES
- Richard Dennis was his biggest influence in trading
- Adrienne Toghraie--Trader's coach
- Amy Ballon--Spiritual coach

ENVIRONMENT
- Teachers believed in him
- His family treated him as if he were a star
- Everyone always said he was clever
- Supportive wife and two children

EDUCATION
- Business Administration

INTERESTS -Skills - Abilities -Honors
Childhood
- Champion chess player
- Ice hockey
- Made money when he was a child
- Speaks Russian, German and English
- Tournament Table Tennis
- Boxing
- Head of student body
- Organized fund raisers for school

Adult
- Table tennis
- Jogging
- Meditation

QUALITIES
- Fun and funny
- Enterprising
- Competitive
- Negotiating skills

BUSINESS EXPERIENCE
- Worked at gas station
- Import/Export

PHILOSOPHY - SUCCESS BELIEFS
- Believes he is very lucky
- You have to have a plan in order to be successful
- How you live your personal life will affect your trading success or failure
- You have to give up something to get something

PROSPERITY CONSCIOUSNESS
- Jewish charities

TRADING EXPERIENCE
- Stock Analyst
- Head at desk - Dealer on Austrian Stock Exchange at 21 years old

RECOMMENDATIONS
- Private consultation with Adrienne

TRADER CONTRIBUTIONS
- Gives other young people an opportunity

- Makes money for his clients

FUTURE PLANS
- Expand business and personal growth
- Get a degree in history

TRADER GEMS - Fundamental - Intuitive - Psychological
- You need to be physically and mentally healthy to be a consistently good trader
- Before you begin any technical studies, you have to handle psychological issues or it will take you a longer time to be a trader and you will have to handle them anyway
- A trader's coach helps you to maintain balance
- Being psychologically fit prepares you to be ready for each next level of success

TRADER GEMS - Mechanical - Analytical - Technical
- Ed trades a basket of markets using a system which enters off of filtered breakouts
- Ed system tries to capture pieces of these long-term trends
- Ed does two things in his trend following system which many other trend following traders do not:
    1. He evaluates the results of long trades and short trades separately
    2. He uses these results to decide if he will take the next trade in a given direction
- Ed's system is basically mechanical except for adding classic chart pattern recognition, which cannot easily be programmed into the analysis
- Ed trades the currencies using the dollar index as an intermarket and only takes trades in a direction counter to the dollar index since the dollar index is negatively correlated to the currencies
- Ed trades in the direction of the long term trend

- He uses the equity curve of an unfiltered system to filter the signals of his new system. He keeps a separate equity curve for both long and short trades.

Murray's Analytical Modeling Study

Trade Methodology Analysis
Mechanical--Objective: Identify classic chart patterns and evaluate current system performance unfiltered to filter actual trades

Mechanical--Automatic: Mechanical trend following trading system
Discretionary: Interpretation of some signals

Analysis of Ed's Methodology
Ed Pomeranz's trading methodology is a classic Turtle-like trend following methodology with some twists. Ed basically trades a channel breakout using the Dollar Index as an intermarket for analyzing the currencies. Ed did not give us the details of his system, but we will test this basic concept. Our simple system for testing this concept is as follows:

Input: EntLen(10),ExtLen(10),Len(10);
Vars: DXAve(0),DXMom(0);
{DX is the dollar index}
DXAve=Average(DX,Len) of Data2;
DXMom=Close of Data2-value1;
If Relate=0 then begin
If DXMom<0 then Buy Highest(High,EntLen) + 1 point Stop;
If DXMom>0 then Sell Lowest(Low,EntLen) - 1 point Stop;
end;
Exitlong at Lowest(Low,ExtLen)- 1 point stop;
Exitshort at Highest(High,ExtLen)+1 point stop

This system is a channel breakout system, which requires the Dollar Index to confirm the breakouts for trading the currencies. This confirmation only allows long trades when the dollar is below a given moving average and short trades when it is above. It also allows the optimization for different channel periods for both entries and exits.

Let's test this concept on the Yen. First, we will optimize a classic channel breakout system on the Yen for the period 1/2/86 to 9/14/98 using a 14-day breakout to enter a trade and an 18-day to exit. This system produced the following results for our analysis period with no deduction for slippage and commission:

Net Profit	$116,570.00
Trades	114
Win%	45 %
Ave Trade	1022.54
Drawdown	$ 16,668.75
Profit Factor	2.05

This system does well for trading the Yen over our development period, but the $16K drawdown was a little high. Let's see what happens if we require that the prices be below a 20-day moving average to short the Yen and above the 20-day moving average to buy the Yen. Using this filter, our results are:

Net Profit	$123,397.00
Trades	85
Win%	46 %
Ave Trade	1451.74
Drawdown	$ 9,868.75
Profit Factor	2.61

Comparing the results with and without the Dollar Index filter for trading the Yen, we see that not only does the filtered system make more money, the average trade is about 40% higher. The drawdown was also reduced from over $16,000 to under $10,000.

Trading Using the Equity Curve
Ed uses an equity curve for long and short trades separately and uses this information to filter trades. This concept works because trades show serial dependence in a channel breakout system. Ed originally incorporated this method after reading about it in Chapter 10 of my

book, *Cybernetic Trading Strategies*, published by John Wiley and Sons. One basic concept for using this information is to only take long trades when the current equity on the long side is above its "N" bar moving average. Conversely, short trades are taken when the short trade equity curve is above an "N" bar average. There are many other concepts for using equity feedback and this is a fertile area of research in development of trading systems.

Ed's long-term trend trading methodology will produce steady returns over the long-term, if you can live with the drawdown characteristic. Using equity curve filtering methods, we can cut these drawdowns without greatly reducing profits. If you are trading a five to ten year long-term horizon in a tax-deferred IRA or SEPP futures account, the 30+% returns per year that these methods can give will be well worth the occasional 20% to 30% drawdown that must be endured.

Adrienne's Psychological Modeling Study

The Recognition Model
The cream always rises to the top and that is our recognition model for Ed Pomeranz. As the son of a wealthy Russian family, Ed was put on a pedestal and told that he was special. In fact, his family treated him as if he were a star. This level of praise and attention at such an early age established Ed's lifelong pattern of needing recognition. To get the kind of recognition that he required meant that he would have to be the best of the best. As a child, when Ed did not receive the attention that supported his model of the world, he would do whatever was necessary to get similar attention in some other way.

As a four year old, Ed did not want to be far away from his mother. One lonely night away from his mother, he stayed with his grandfather. By morning, he has learned to beat his grandfather at chess. Ed's love of chess and the recognition it brought him led to competitive play later on. It also taught him how to plot strategies which required him to think ten steps ahead. This experience was the start of a series of outstanding performances by which young Ed felt he had to live in order to get the recognition he needed. Later, after moving to Austria while not knowing the language, he still managed to excel.

As he developed his recognition model, Ed learned that being the best he could be to others prompted them to bring out the best in him. Their support and encouragement gave him an edge in overcoming any shortcomings he had. His teachers loved him and saw his potential. To this day, Ed recognizes the importance of people bringing out the best in him. In school, Ed was the head of the student body. From this experience, he learned that one of the best ways to get recognition was to be a leader. People who want recognition thrive on taking on responsibility and overcoming the most challenging circumstances. Ed proved this point when he took over the responsibilities of his family's business when he was in his early twenties. Naturally, his leadership made the difficult business of import/export thrive and gave him the next ingredient for recognition, a deep pocketbook. So, where would a young man who has proven himself as a leader, successful businessman, and champion chess and table tennis player go next? Where else but the markets.

The recognition model is a very strong model for success and achievement. The drive for recognition provides a constant source of energy and motivation toward the completion of goals and successful outcomes. For a trader, this is a very attractive model. Although this model drives a trader to success, the emphasis is not directly on money. Naturally, this goal can only be reached by making money. However, by taking the direct focus off of money, it reduces the level of greed and fear in his trading which tend to sabotage results.

The problem with the recognition model is, of course, that it is a double-edged sword. On the one hand, it can be the impetus for great success. On the other hand, it can be a trap. For Ed, it was both. It brought him the rewards of achievement and success. It also meant that once the rewards came, Ed would have to have the biggest and best in his surroundings - which introduced Ed to the best wines, the best food, the designer suits, and, in fact, to the "designer everything." This great abundance of material success inevitably led Ed to a fast-paced life. So, while Ed's excellent performance was carrying him to the top of the money management world, he was also living the life of a bon vivant. Unfortunately, this life style required as much time and energy from Ed as his career did. Even though he had achieved so much success and recognition before he turned thirty, his excessive lifestyle caught up with him. Fortunately for Ed, the recognition of being the best at what he did was more important to him than leading an excessive life style.

Once again, Ed handled this conflict in the smartest way possible by taking on a healthy lifestyle and, basically, becoming the Boy Scout necessary to maintain top performance as a money manager. He has always recognized the importance of developing his psychological stability for successful trading. Ed realized during this time that the only way he could balance his desire to lead a rich and happy life and to be successful in his work was by being totally systematic in his trading. Now that Ed is on his healthy/spiritual path, he is looking forward to becoming a master trader and developing his intuition as an additional edge.

As part of his recognition model, he continues to attract people into his life who support his need for recognition. He attracts the staff who are able to bring him recognition. But, in addition, Ed himself is willing to do whatever it takes to gain recognition. He will work as many hours as it takes and do the hard stuff in order to get an "attaboy" from the important people in his life and from the trading industry.

CHAPTER 8

Neal Dietz

The "Systems Man" - How an innovative restaurateur used this ability to make mucho enchiladas in the markets as a broker and money manager.

Can you tell us about your childhood and about growing up in your family?
I was born in Newburg, New York, in 1955. We moved down to Westchester, which is just outside of New York City. Until I was 18, I lived in the area between Port Chester and Mamaroneck, New York, which is on the Long Island Sound.

My father died of leukemia when I was 8 years old and I am not really sure what he was like. The things I remember most about him are that he smoked Winston brand cigarettes and drank schnapps.

That must have been a very difficult time for your mother, what happened then?
After his death, my mother, my two brothers, and I moved. We lived together for another four years. Then, one night after dinner with a friend, a drunk driver who was driving 60 miles per hour in the wrong lane struck their car head-on. My aunt and uncle, who lived just a couple of miles away, took the three of us in.

Did your aunt and uncle have children?
With the addition of the three of us, there were six kids in the household, but it was not like growing up in *The Brady Bunch*. It was the 1960's, and my aunt and uncle had three extra kids laid on them, shall we say. There were three boys added to their boy and two girls, which made for one crazed household. We all got spun off to the wind.

213

Tell us about your uncle and aunt?

My uncle was the vice-chairman of a large regional department store chain in the New York City and Long Island area. He was a workaholic and helped expand a two-store operation that his wife's father had started into an extremely successful department store chain.

My aunt was a school teacher. She taught third and fourth grade during that same time.

Did you like sports as a kid?

I played every sport in the world. I was good at most of them and really excelled at a couple of them. Being good at sports helped me get through the trauma of having two parents die at an early age and changing schools three times before I even got into high school.

Were you good at games?

I liked backgammon, but I much preferred card games, like hearts.

What can you tell us about your college years?

My brother likes to say that people should not ask where I went to college; they should ask what college I did not go to. I was on a ten-year plan. I would go to school for one year, skip three, go back for one year, and skip three more. My first year out of high school, I went to American University with the intention of getting a degree in political science with a psychology minor. That strategy lasted exactly one year. At the time, I really did not want to go to college, but it was my way of getting out of the house. After I quit school, I sold encyclopedias to the military for about six months, then worked as a furniture store manager in New York.

My brother called me and asked to borrow some money when I was in the middle of my college career. After I finally stopped laughing, he told me that he wanted to open a restaurant. He had just graduated from Ithaca College. After some discussion, I decided to loan him the money with the contingency that I came as part of the package because I was not attending college at the time.

What year did you start the restaurant?
We started the restaurant in 1976, when I was not old enough to own a restaurant with a liquor license. One interesting fact that I discovered fifteen years later was that my father and uncle also opened a restaurant in New York City when they got out of college.

Did you continue your college career while you were working in the restaurant?
Yes, I did. I went to Ithaca College for a semester and changed my major to business administration. Following that, I left Ithaca College and went to Arizona State. Then, I decided it was time to get serious. In 1978, I moved to Boston and did 2½ years work in one year and a summer at Boston University where I earned degrees in accounting and finance.

What experience was brought into running a restaurant?
We had never been in a restaurant except to eat, but between the three of us, we made one great restaurateur. At first, we worked on instinct by what we liked to eat. I believe that our restaurant was one of the first soup, salad, and sandwich bar type eateries that became so popular in the 1980's. It looked something like a TGI Friday's. The restaurant has been successful over the years and is still open today.

What were these talents that made one good restaurateur?
Jerry, my brother, who called me for the loan, is an extremely innovative cook. My oldest brother, David, is probably the world's greatest day-to-day restaurant manager because he has exceptional organizational skills in addition to an ability to handle people.

What skill did you contribute to this trilogy?
I was the "systems man" and to this day I am a "systems man". The development of a successful system for the restaurant came from me

leaving the business for two years and working at several different places while collecting ideas. I completed this process while finishing college. When I came back to the business in 1979, we began to implement my system and the restaurant really hit its stride.

Would you explain what you mean about a restaurant system?
We standardized and mechanized the order process from the waiter, to the bartender, to the kitchen, and back again. We also changed the space planning in the storage area by creating the first layout for computerized inventory. We ran a food operation with a cost basis of 29% in the days when a McDonald's operation was running at about 35%, and we were still able to heap food on the plates of our customers. It was a clean, lean, and well-run operation. During this time, our sales went from about $350,000 to $650,000 per year.

Did this improvement in the business make life more exciting?
No, I got bored after about three weeks and was ready to open another restaurant. This was the beginning of the end for me in the restaurant business. My idea of a successful business was to own 49% of one hundred restaurants, but my brothers wanted to own 100% of one restaurant. After that, I began to change the focus for my contribution by spending the next two years managing the money of the business.

What do you mean by "managing the money"?
When restaurants work well, they generate loads of cash. This happened in 1981 and 1982, when money markets were at 16% and the stock market was going down and never coming back again. In those days, it was easy to make money by throwing it in a money market at 16%.

When did you actually start trading?
In 1982, I told my brothers that it was time to take some money and put it in the stock market. This happened right after the federal reserve rate had been cut for the third time.

I always had an interest in following the stock market, but I had never invested. One day, I wrote down five stocks that I thought were good investment candidates. As I recall, we had about $100,000 sitting in the bank. I told my brothers that we should take $50,000 or $60,000 of the excess funds and invest it in these 5 stocks. They looked at me like I had four heads. After the market took off, I convinced them to buy two "hot" computer stocks recommended by our broker. Of course, these stocks blew up, but the experience made me realize that I had the bug.

It was shortly after that I decided to leave the restaurant business to seek my fortune in New York City. I knew that I was never going to get my 100 restaurants and I refused to be 30 years old waiting tables. I told my brothers to keep the restaurant and the money. I was going to do what I wanted to do, which was managing money in the markets.

Do you think your uncle's entrepreneurial spirit affected how you viewed your work?
Absolutely not, my uncle was the typical company man and even though it was his company, there was no real entrepreneurial spirit that I think I garnered from him.

What do you trade - stocks, mutual funds, commodities?
I have traded everything actually.

Tell us about your trading history?
I walked into the Prudential-Bache office in New York City to interview for a job. I did not know that their company was taking my uncle's business public at the time. When the Vice President of Operations realized the relationship, he suggested that I should work in my hometown. I told him I wanted to work in Boston and he responded that there were no jobs available in Boston. Always liking a challenge, I drove my car to Boston. Upon my arrival, the Boston fixed income manager reiterated what the VP had told me to which I replied, "I can't believe you don't have one desk."

217

Prudential had just opened a new office outside of Boston and he gave me the name and number for the manager in that new office. In 1983, I was installed at Prudential-Bache. In those days, you had to take "broker in a box," which was basically a self-study course for your Series Seven license. I finished the course in about a month.

Why did you decide to become a broker?
There were two primary reasons. The first reason was that all my money was in the restaurant and I needed to earn a living. The second reason was that I find it just as easy to trade other people's money as my own. If you can make it work, why not do it. You get the best of all worlds. I risk my money in the same way as I risk my clients', and I have the benefits of being a money manager.

When I worked at Prudential, they had just come out with the Index options a year or two before.

Back in those days it was easier to make money in trading options.
You can still make money in trading options. I think it is not any harder. We still make a lot of money trading options, but there are some differences. In those days, we were trading Index options. In the morning, I would come and sit down at my desk and read Martin Zweig. I was also very intrigued with Robert Prechter's Elliott Wave studies. I would listen to the two of them and if we were bullish, we would buy calls and sell puts to pay for them. If we were bearish, we would reverse the position and buy puts and sell calls.

Was there ever a day when you were dead wrong and got your lunch handed to you?
Yes, actually, and what was even worse than that was the day when I was dead right, but was out in the country.

Tell us the build up to those stories.
I traded from February 1985 until March 1986, without a big loss. I am one of those bizarre people who likes to study statistics, while I

also have the ability to feel the movement of the market. There are things that you can see happening in options when they are about to turn. We traded options on that basis, backed up by Elliott wave counts and Martin's work. I was one of the larger options traders on the East Coast for Prudential trading only OEXs on forty to fifty discretionary index option accounts. Intuitively, I was able to cut the losses short and let the winners run. In March 1986, I got to experience for the first time a gap opening down when I was long the market. At the time, I was managing the money of a woman who later became my wife. She handed me $18,500 in February 1985, and in February 1986, her account was around $74,000. On that day, the account went from $74,000 to $66,000 and I discovered fear.

How large were your trading positions at that point?
We would probably average 300 to 400 contracts on each side of the position.

How much were you managing for yourself?
My account was fairly small. It was the beginning of 401K plans, so I was putting my money into that vehicle. I had $40,000 and was trading five lots for myself. At that point, I was probably the most leveraged person that I had.

Did you continue to lose after that day?
That was the beginning of a long slide that took me in many different directions. We won, we lost, we stayed even, and this continued until late 1987. Interestingly enough, we had the huge run up in early 1987, and I was up virtually nothing for the year going into October.

In 1987, when we were not making any money, people were beginning to get a little ticked off at me. I had gone through the classic situation, I had made a lot of money and thought I was God even though I had no real system in place. What had saved me was a very good intuitive sense of the market and a basic accountant's money management skill. In October, we went up for the year in a week and a half in a of couple trades. We bought the OEX 310 puts and caught the first 300 points down in the market. That one trade made the year.

Now, tell us the second story of how you missed a trade when you were out of the office.
There was a rule that if I was out of the office, no account could have an open position. The Monday before the Crash, we rolled our put position down a couple of strike prices and made an extra $5 to $10 off of that and on Wednesday closed the whole position out. We were going to Jamaica for the weekend. At 11 P. M., just before taking the shuttle on to New York, I said, "No one is going to be in the office when I leave, I am going to make a call from New York and buy myself 5 puts before we go to Jamaica. I will buy them now and deal with them when I get back." My wife looked at me and said, "You're going on vacation. You can buy something when you get back." The puts that I was going to buy were trading at $2.50 when I left and were at $197 when I returned on Tuesday!

What happened when you came back to the office?
I almost quit and went out on my own because the office manager would not let me sell options. The only people who made money in options for the next six months were the sellers. The volatility factor of the market had gone through the roof and the liquidity had completely left the market. The market was rigged against you from then on unless you could sell the options. That is when they changed the margin requirements and that is also when I decided to go into trading S&P futures.

What was the transition like?
When I was trading Index options, I was making money for the clients and for myself. Option commissions were great and commodity commissions were low. I found in transition that I was working hard and not getting paid for it. That is when I decided that

I wanted to have my own operation because I believed that I could do it for myself.

What was the most important thing you learned from working with clients?
One of the things I discovered about clients was that while they were risk takers and aggressive people, they really only wanted to keep from losing their shirts. They were not the big risk takers that they thought they were.

What was the business like after that?
The business really calmed down. Trading the futures and S&P Indexes taught me that I had no system. I had gotten away with my intuitive ability before, but now I was in the "big kids' league." You really do not want to play in their league without knowing what you are doing and that required a good system.

Did you continue to stay with Prudential?
I walked away from the futures business and became a stock and stock option trader/investor exclusively for myself. I also built a managed money business with my partner. The fee based managed money business is the business I am in now with my partner and have been since 1989.

How did you manage that transition of walking away from the business?
I walked away from trading index options. I did not walk away from the business of trading. We developed an entirely different business with my existing client base. I am one of those people that walked away from the Index options craze of the 1980's without blowing anyone up or getting sued. I was able to retain most of my clients by sitting down with each of them and telling them the market is still where we can make money and how we were going to do it.

How was the business different?

The transactional business was coming to an end. It was the dawn of fee based or managed money in the equity business. We converted hot money accounts (aggressive trading - options, futures, etc) to portfolio management where we managed all of their money. We were beginning to have good diversification and charged a fee for management. We would find what people wanted and provide it for them. For instance, corporate executives would ask me, what is this 401K thing? I did not know anything about it, but found out for them. What developed from that is a mutual fund timing system for the more aggressive clients who wanted to trade mutual funds using the same kind of analysis that we do now.

Outside of that, I managed private money trading both stocks and stock options and sometimes T-Bond futures.

What year are we talking about?

That started late in 1989. We spent about a year making the CBOE rich by trying to trade spreads, which is fool's play. It got to the point that it was too expensive. The premiums were outrageous, and it was not worth the trouble. We hatched this whole thing during that time period.

When did you meet your partner?

In 1989, I met Ed. We combined our businesses in 1990, but stayed at Prudential-Bache until the end of 1994. In 1995, we moved to Advest, which is more of a boutique kind of house where you can do your own thing.

How did you choose Advest?

We went out and interviewed seven or eight different firms ranging from Merrill Lynch to Alex Brown. We checked the entire spectrum from old-line wire houses to discount commission houses. We were looking to go to a firm where we could do what we wanted and not worry about the company and its position. In other words, we wanted to establish a company within a company, which is what every broker and money manager does. It did not make sense to go out on my own. If I had my own shop, I would get paid more than I do now, but I would also have to worry about the headaches involved with owning a firm. I have a back office that runs everything for me.

Do they take a percentage of your fees?
Yes, absolutely. But they have no say in the running of my business.

You were basically a stock trader?
Excuse me, but I am a stock and an option trader. That is why I said nobody trades index options anymore except the institutions. Now, if I want to trade the market, I go and pick the five stocks with the highest relative correlation to the NASDAQ, DOW, or S&P. Then, I buy options on those stocks. I get the same bang for my dollar, if not more, than I used to get out of the Index. I do not have to trade as much and the premiums are not as high. That is why I said that you can make money trading options, because the stock options have less premium in them. There are certain stocks that have literally become commoditized; Intel, Microsoft, and General Electric, for example. I run a program that ranks the relative strength of the top 120 S&P stocks on a regular basis. When we get a buy signal, we can grab the top five and buy options on them.

When did you start developing a system?
To date, I have read about a zillion books on investing and I can tell you about everything from point and figure charting, to candlestick analysis, to Elliott wave counts, to Gann angles. I read a book by a man named Nicholas Darvis, who was a ballroom dancer in the 1950's, and studied point and figure charting. About the same time, I also read a very interesting book by William O'Neil who must have read that same book. This was the beginning of actually developing a system and the first effort was a kind of bastardization of William O'Neil's method, which is now known as "Growth Momentum Investing."

You build a base, break out of the base, and get long when the breakout is confirmed.
Absolutely, but we also follow a volume indicator in addition to the breakout.

How did you develop your system to make it your own?
I realized after 6 months of analyzing the market his way that stocks were not all that different from the S&P Index options. Each stock has a personality of its own, and you can watch a stock and the way it acts. You can start from that point with his base and the break out pattern and get a sense of what a stock is going to do. From there, we added a pyramiding methodology, which does not make the system any better, but refines it.

Basically, I took O'Neil's methodology and folded in candlestick analysis as a way to refine it.

Now, do you use any kind of mechanical system by itself?
I use AIQ buy and sell signals because they are very basic and very good. With my methodology, I tell people that I offer them the discipline they do not have themselves. If purely trading futures or options, I believe you could take the AIQ system methodology by itself and put together a pretty decent buy and sell methodology. Most of my clients are looking for something else though. They are building long term portfolios and want above average rates of return with below average risk.

So, you never tried to get O'Neil's methods programmed?
No. I run the AIQ system, and I spend the first 20 minutes of my day figuring out which way I think the market is going.

How do you do that?
I will start from the AIQ buy or sell signals, and then use simple confirmations like phase and moving average convergence/divergence, which in other words is basic trend following. I am your

basic trend follower. I just want to know how far along we are on the fear/greed spectrum. Are we into manic greed or manic fear? There are a couple of methodologies that I have developed using their numbers which also help to confirm really good buy and sell signals.

What are they based on?
The AIQ system is the basis, but it is a black box system. The black box buy/sell signals come up a buy or sell just like any black box system. But, there is also the equity portion of the system where it breaks down groups and sectors. It measures the MACD directional movement indicator of each of the groups and sectors. We have taken the percentages that are generated on both a daily and weekly basis from this data to get confirmations of overbought and oversold conditions, which are amazingly accurate. In terms of confirmation, on top of confirmation, this analysis gives me an idea where we are on the fear/greed spectrum.

If somebody wanted to trade stocks and did not want to spend too much time studying, they could buy AIQ and be a chimpanzee?
Yes, I think they could, to be honest with you. But, I have refined the system.

You believe someone would not get killed or hurt just trading AIQ?
Yes, this system, just as all systems and statistics, is only as good as the people using it. Most people forget that no system works all the time. Without proper money management and stops, you would get killed using a near perfect system.

Have you ever overridden AIQ?
I do not take the equity trades from AIQ. That is a totally different system. I just use their box to do the charting. I do not use their equity methodology. I use the black box signals that it generates as a starting point for making my buy and sell decisions.

You are using the general market timing model from AIQ?
Correct, as a starting point as to how invested I want to be.

How do you define the breakout?
I am looking for a large flat line followed by a wake up call. When I define this to a client, I tell them I want a stock that has been consolidating into a tighter and tighter range with volume dropping to the point where the stock is somnambulant. Then, I want to see a breakout that nobody can explain and the bigger and more bizarre the breakout, and the larger the volume, and the less anybody can explain it the happier I am.

If you get a big volume breakout because of news, would that worry you?
Big volume breakouts because of news are fine, but I do not like them as well as big volume breakouts that nobody can explain. This is only the beginning and is what I call the wake up call. We will take a look at the fundamentals, but the only fundamentals that I am concerned with are earnings. Other than earnings, there are no fundamentals that matter. As long as the company is earning money it is fine with me, but I do not want to be buying a stock of a company formed by nine guys in a van in Maine who have an idea that they think is going to work down the road. Please remember that my degree is in Accounting and I know how to lie with statistics.

What about the valuation of a company in terms of what it is worth if liquidated?
It is bull! You know it is bull, and I know it is bull. Value is what the market says the stock is worth every day.

What would you do if 1973 happened again?
I would never get a confirmed breakout. Look at the charts. You could not put together a consolidation and a breakout in 1973 if your life depended upon it. You would have gotten a sell signal. All the

buy signals that came up would never have confirmed. I would have spent all of my time shorting the market instead of buying it.

Do you short the market?
Yes, I do. I do not short a bull market, but I short.

What if you saw 1987 happen all over again, would you short that market?
If 1987 happened again, we would move to cash. We do short stocks and buy puts on the options side of the market because I am a firm believer in gravity.

Iomega has had some fun.
I had a client who was long Iomega. If you remember, it had closed at a pre-split price of 48, opened the next day at 55 (higher high) and closed at 49(reversal). I called my client and told him it was time to sell Iomega and go short. Then, I realized that I had this whole cadre of clients who were so young that they did not know what shorting a stock was because they did not know what a bear market was.

How much money are you managing now and how much of your own money is under management?
Right now, direct money under management is about $24 million, and indirectly we have over $100 million under management. I have all of my own money under management; the amount does not matter.

What has been your rate of return over the last five years?
The rate of return for my conservative accounts for the past 5 years has mirrored the S&P. My conservative accounts do not want to out perform the Index. They just do not want to get their butts kicked.

What is your volatility?
Back in the summer of 1996, when the market decided to take a tumble, the average NASDAQ stock was down 30%, the average S&P stock was down 18%, and we were down 7%. We try to

227

average about half of the volatility of the market on the down side while maintaining most of return on the upside. Our aggressive accounts usually average well above the S&P Index.

Why would someone like you want a trader's coach?
I had been through hell this last year. My seven-year old son was diagnosed a year ago with ADHD (attention deficit hyperactive disorder) and is bi-polar. This is bad in adults, but horrendous in children. He is actually doing really well now. After we got him settled down in the middle of last year, my wife was diagnosed with breast cancer. In addition to these problems, my aunt and uncle, who raised me after my parents were gone, both died of cancer within 5 months of each other.

Two days after learning that my wife had breast cancer I was sitting in my office looking out the picture window into the garden. There was an electrical storm at the time and a lightening bolt struck and every phone and computer in the office went dead. I walked over to my partner and said, "God is really gunning for me. Unfortunately, He has lousy aim, so I would watch out if I were you." That basically sums up how last year went.

The problems from last year were not the only reasons that I started soul searching. I still suffer from the memories of that day in 1986. I let my stops go and sometimes I am not strict enough with my discipline.

Is it because you were beat up by the market once in your life?
No, I have been beat up other times. What led me to Adrienne was the fact that I had let a stop or two go while in positions and would watch myself do it. I would watch 50% to 150% gains drop to losses and just sit there and watch them. I had talked with psychologists about the problem and had done considerable intro-spection. I had also read Adrienne's articles for a long time. Occasionally, I would forget what was going on around me and start acting like an amateur.

One day, I put together a chart of every single stock transaction where I had failed to enter the stop, added up all of the money lost, and looked at the pattern that evolved. I realized that I had been banging my head against the wall for years. I am sitting here outperforming 90% to 95% of my peers: can you imagine where I could be if I was not sabotaging my efforts.

In November of 1996, I called Adrienne and we did some preliminary phone work while I was still in denial that there was a problem. After going through the problems of 1997, the situation came out and really became inflamed. Finally, I decided to get to the bottom of the problem because I realized that I have the potential to be great. I knew that I was wasting my abilities if I did not take the time to figure it out.

I went to see Adrienne and she beat the hell out of me. We did some work and things are improving. Adrienne asked me when I left, "What did you learn?" I said, "I learned that you can hand me the flashlight, but only I can walk down the path. I need to do my own work." I meditate now twice a day and it centers me. I am working on becoming more organized and removing the clutter from my life because that is part of what was getting in my way.

I have decided that I am going to focus on the most important things of life. My real trading goal in life when I started was to be able to do this for myself and support my family in the style that we have been accustomed to. If everyone walked out of the door tomorrow, I believe that I am capable of being successful. I am getting to the point where I may even go back into futures trading.

Have you ever thought of putting money in a SEPP account?
I cannot put money into a SEPP because I have a 401K plan, and I am connected to a company that provides a pension. One of the primary reasons that I left Prudential-Bache was that my largest asset was being managed in a 401K by them with an average annual

rate of return of 6% from 1985 to1994. I wanted access to manage my own assets. Now, I manage virtually all of my own tax-deferred assets

Where do you want to go from here?
Remember what Jessie Livermore said, "The money is not in the trading, the money is in the sitting." One trader you interviewed on tape impressed me. He talked about trading commodities on a long-term basis. It was a concept that I had never heard anyone discuss before because it seems that every futures trader is trying to catch the next 8th or 32nd. That interview got me interested in getting this part of my life back together and going back into futures trading.

What type of futures markets would you look at trading?
Bonds and the S&P Index are the most likely because I already work in that arena. I learned long ago that diversification in futures trading can be hazardous to your wealth. In other words, trade what you know!

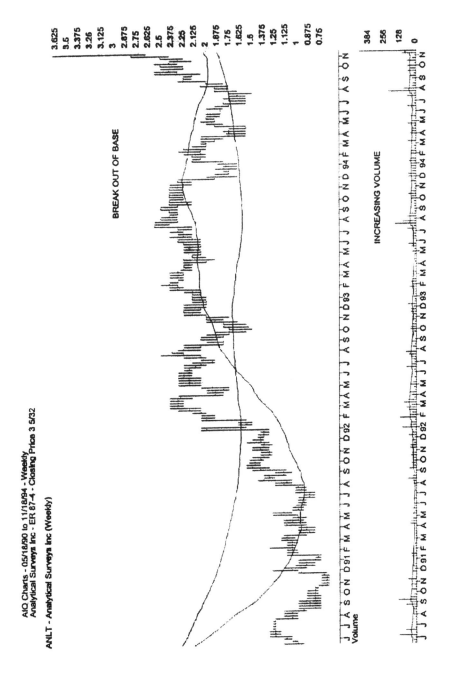

AIQ Charts - 05/18/90 to 11/18/94 - Weekly
Analytical Surveys Inc - ER 87-4 - Closing Price 3 5/32

ANLT - Analytical Surveys Inc (Weekly)

BREAK OUT OF BASE

INCREASING VOLUME

Volume

MODELING STUDY

CHILDHOOD FAMILY STATUS
- Neal experienced middle class to upper class Westchester, New York

MENTORING - INFLUENCES
- Workaholic, highly successful uncle who raised him
- Robert Prechter - Elliott Wave
- A trader who talked about trading commodities on a long term basis
- Adrienne Toghraie--trader's coach

ENVIRONMENT
- Father passed away when he was eight
- Mother was killed in car accident when he was twelve
- Two brothers
- Raised by aunt and uncle who found it difficult to handle the needs of six children

EDUCATION
- Changed majors and schools for 10 years
- Studied political science and business administration
- Accounting and finance degree

INTERESTS - Skills - Abilities - Honors
Childhood
- Played all sports - excelled at some
- Games - Backgammon - Hearts

Adult
- Finished brokerage Series Seven qualifications in one month
- Loves to study statistics
- Mediator

QUALITIES - CHARACTER STRENTHS
- Innovator
- Fun and funny
- Never gives up
- He knows what he wants
- Chutzpah
- Survivor
- People skills
- Tacks towards goals

BUSINESS EXPERIENCE
- Sold encyclopedias to the military
- Furniture store manager
- Restaurateur at 19 years--innovator in operations
- Fee based money management business

PHILOSOPHY AND SUCCESS BELIEFS
- Believes he will survive and succeed regardless of what he does
- Believes in creating a win/win situation with everyone
- Learns and modifies from experience to make better choices
- Looks at things from the perspective that everything is a starting point

PROSPERITY CONSCIOUSNESS
- Gives to homeless and orphan causes

TRADING EXPERIENCE
- Discretionary trader
- Broker
- Money management
- Has traded everything
- Was once a large OEX options traders

RECOMMENDATIONS
- *The Disciplined Trader* by Mark Douglas
- *Winning on Wall Street Amongst other Things* by Martin Zweig
- *How to Make Money in Stock* by William O'Neil

TRADER CONTRIBUTIONS
- Earns clients money

FUTURE PLANS
- Looking forward to trading the World Equity Benchmark Securities because that is where the future action is going to be
- Wants to live long enough to have a 10 handicap in golf--*will probably die a broken man* (see I told you - a funny man)

TRADER GEMS - Fundamental - Intuitive - Psychological
- Most people who invest with money managers are risk averse
- Each stock has a personality
- Earnings is the only fundamental worth looking at
- Diversification in the futures market can be hazardous to your wealth
- You can hand a trader the flashlight, but only he can walk down the path
- It is important to let go of the clutter in your life
- Keep it simple

TRADER GEMS - Mechanical - Analytical - Technical
- You can buy the big cap stock options, for example Intel, Microsoft, and General Electric, and get more bang for your buck by putting this type of basket together rather than buying the index of stock option futures
- AIQ, a computer program which generates buy and sell signals on the stock indexes, is a good point to start as a market timing model for trading

- Combines AIQ signals for general market timing with basic trend following from a consolidation to trade stocks
- Looks for large flat market formations on declining volume followed by a breakout on good volume. He also adds candlestick patterns to this analysis
- He likes breakouts on good volume especially if it is for unexplained reasons
- Neal's goal is to match or exceed the performance of the S&P500 with less risk

Murray's Analytical Modeling Study

Trade Methodology Analysis

Mechanical--Objective: Identification of consolidation patterns ready for a breakout in a given stock

Mechanical--Automatic: Uses AIQ signals for market timing

Discretionary: Combines AIQ indicators with patterns on individual stocks to produce trading signals

Analysis of Neal's Methodology

Neal's concept is that you only buy stock when the market is positive and then, you also select stocks with good chart patterns. In theory, this should outperform the market on a risk-adjusted basis. His basic stock system looks for a breakout from a base confirmed by volume, which is a classic trading method for stocks and many trending commodities.

The problem with making this type of methodology mechanical is that it is not easy to mechanically identify the basing pattern. This is one reason that Neal has not made his system mechanical. In my October 1998 article in *Futures Magazine,* I wrote about Richard Dunnigan, whose work has allowed us to develop a mechanical definition of a basing pattern. Research in this area is just beginning, but could someday allow us to develop 100% mechanical systems based on the concept of breakout from a consolidation period.

Adrienne's Psychological Modeling Study

The Maximizer Model

How does a young boy get noticed with six children around? Any way he can. Neal had a difficult beginning, losing his father and mother at a young age, and having to adjust to the already love-stretched family of his uncle and aunt. While Neal did not find his uncle's life appealing, his uncle's success in developing a profitable department store chain provided Neal with a good model for problem solving and innovation.

As Neal grew up, he developed an interest in virtually all sports. He did not hone in on just one sport, but participated in all of them. He approached college with the same broad brush strokes, flipping from one major to another. From each playing field, he picked up information, strategies, and other useful ideas.

What did Neal do with all of this diverse experience and training? He used it to develop a model for coping with whatever life handed him. When his parents died, he learned that you could survive regardless of whatever happened. Later on, he learned that not only could you survive but you could also turn each situation, no matter how bad it seemed, into an opportunity to get something out of it. In other words, Neal developed the Maximizer Model. Neal learned how to make lemonade from lemons. He studied the hand that was dealt him for the best way to maximize its returns. Maximizing your hand could mean turning it into a winning hand or it could mean finding a way to minimize the inevitable loss. Or it could mean that at the very least, you could find a way to laugh at the universe.

Being a maximizer requires you to be a very inventive, creative, problem-solving individual. Those qualities, in turn, require you to know a great deal about the world around you. You cannot be a great maximizer if you are not a realist because you cannot wish a bad situation into a good one. You have to have courage and self-confidence. In Neal's case, he has all of these qualities.

Neal loves to play the card game of Hearts. Anyone who plays this game knows that the great players are dealt a hand and must have a strategy for minimizing your losses in a bad hand and the courage to "Shoot the Moon" in order to win really big and eliminate your competition. The game of Hearts is very much like being in the markets. You are dealt a hand and you have to have your psychology in order. There are factors you cannot know in advance or control. On the other hand, you play the odds with your system. It's a great game for someone working from the Maximizer Model.

Throughout Neal's life, he has been presented with major challenges to his coping ability, ranging from the deaths of his parents, to his wife's cancer, to his young son's neurological problems and the recent deaths of the aunt and uncle who raised him. While most people justifiably resort to the "woe is me" response to this stream of tragedy, Neal takes the hand he is dealt, maximizes the situation, and finds satisfaction and pride in his ability to maximize it. In fact, he even takes pride in his wife's ability to cope with her cancer and come through the ordeal. By deriving pleasure from the results of his maximizing each situation, Neal has expanded the model so that he is even more likely to apply it in his life.

Professionally, Neal has used the Maximizer Model from the time that he started up his restaurant business with his brothers. He looked around at the situation, figured out the strengths and weakness of each person involved, and saw a way to maximize the situation by having everyone work from his own strengths. With his new trading partner, he has done the same thing by working from their respective strengths.

When you work from the Maximizer Model, the goal is to maximize the situation. Reaching the goal does not come with limitations or rules for how to reach your goal. Therefore, the model allowed Neal to become a broker, trader, and money manager. It allows him to use all of his resources, and it allows him to take risks. Since the goal is to maximize the outcome, the model naturally puts a brake on those risks so that they do not reverse your progress or take you out of the parameters of the situation. For that reason, this model has allowed Neal to become a very successful money manager who maximizes return without incurring too much risk. His approach is much like that of a quarterback's approach to a play; here's the situation, this is what we want to achieve and this is the strategy that will maximize our chance of getting there.

Neal has also applied this model to his strategy for developing his own business within the structure and protection of a larger business, thereby maximizing his situation. He did not try to develop a new business because he saw the potential for return within the present situation.

Finally, he has applied his Maximizer Model to his trading. In his own words, you can see him putting the model to work: "Now if I want to trade the markets, I pick the five stocks with the highest relative correlation to the NASDAQ, DOW or S&P. Then I buy options on those stocks. I get the same bang for my dollar, if not more, than I used to get out of the Index." Once again, with 20/20 vision, Neal has assessed the situation and found the best way to get the most out of it - and enjoy himself in the process.

CHAPTER 9

John Fritz

Born to be special - How a poor son of immigrants
applied his training as a physicist
to discover wealth in the markets.

**Tell us some things about yourself and your family. Where were
you born? What were your parents like? What were you like as
a child?**

I was born in Detroit, Michigan. My grandparents came to the
United States from Hungary. My family was quite poor. In our
neighborhood, I would guess that probably half of the people over
the age of 35 spoke little or no English. My father quit school in the
10th grade and my mother quit school in the 8th grade. My mother is
the eldest of 8 brothers and sisters, and has always been a very
strong force in my life. Recently, she said to me, "After
experiencing the first three months of your life, I knew that you were
extremely special." She always knew how to encourage that special
something that was within me.

What did she mean by that?

She saw that I was the brightest baby she had ever seen.

Tell me about your early influences?

We lived in an apartment above my grandparents who spoke no
English. My mom encouraged me to excel in school, especially in
math and science. She instilled in me the belief that I could do
anything that I wanted to do. She also let me know that it might take
a lot of work.

Mom worked on the Ford assembly line for 25 years putting
together cars manually. About a year ago, I happened to see a
special on Public Television about the Ford assembly line workers.

The program had these large, burly guys talking about quitting their work because it was too physically demanding. My mother worked on the assembly line for 25 years, and they did not give women any breaks. Her motivation was to get us into the suburbs where the environment was better than the city.

What did your father do?
He was a manual laborer. His job was cutting out and assembling work gloves. Later his company promoted him to a sales position.

What did you like to do?
I liked sports, but I was not very good at them. I did extremely well in grade school in my studies.

When did you finally move?
When I was about 12 years old, we moved to Lincoln Park, which is a southwestern suburb of Detroit. We moved from a neighborhood where I zeroed in on my schoolwork because there were not many kids my age to a neighborhood where there were many kids in my age group. Then, schoolwork became less important to me, and I more or less coasted through high school.

What happened after high school?
After I graduated from high school, I went to the University of Michigan. Ann Arbor was a real eye-opener for a kid who was raised in a large extended family where most of the people were politically quite conservative. The University of Michigan really expanded my horizons. While there, I became interested in politics.

What did you do after you graduated from college?
I could not get a job, so I went to school for another year to get a teaching certificate even though there was no reason to believe that I would be a good teacher. I remember answering a question from a student fully and completely during my first year of teaching. That experience stirred something within me, and I went back to school

telling people I wanted to get a Masters Degree in Education, but my real aim was to get a Ph.D. in experimental physics.

Was there a professor who particularly inspired you?
I was fortunate to have had a wonderful professor who happened to stutter. Everyone in his classes zeroed in on his stuttering, but me. I was enthralled with what he was saying and got an A+ in the class.

What kind of work did you do while you were in school?
The first year of graduate school, I taught a lab course in the Physics Department. During the 1960's, physics was a major area of research and university physics programs were well funded in an effort to generate interest in research. I was paid to teach physics labs my first year of grad school. Later, the National Institute of Health paid my tuition and $5,000 per year to work on a major experiment that my thesis advisor had proposed.

Tell us about this experiment?
It was an extremely difficult experiment. We were looking at the structure of a molecule that was important in the chlorophyll cycle. It is called ferredoxin. We were doing radiowave and microwave irradiation of samples and checking for how green plants absorbed energy. The study was the precursor to Magnetic Resonance Imaging (MRI), which does half of what we were doing. We were also performing the same tests on the electrons, protons, and neutrons of the sample. I did not find out until we were about two years into the experiment that the world's expert on the subject had said that this experiment could never be done at a university, because it was too difficult to perform. We completed the experiment and solved the problem.

We worked primarily with spinach and parsley. Biochemists would go to the Detroit Farmer's Market, buy 150 pounds of spinach or parsley, work on it for a week, and come up with perhaps a half an ounce of the substance that we worked on. I was getting burned out from all of the time that I spent in the lab. I could not see myself working in the physics setting for the rest of my life. I completed my Ph.D. in 1969, and remained for two more years to finish the experiment.

Did you consider yourself to be an exceptional physicist?
No, not at all. To be an exceptional experimental physicist, you should start building radio sets when you are 4 years old and fixing cars when you are 8. I struggled with the technical side of experimental physics. The physicists did not have many interests other than their work. I had many outside interests like politics, and I was also skiing and running.

So, where did you go from there?
In 1971, I began looking for a way to use the research skills that I had developed to earn an affluent lifestyle. I started by looking at the stock market, but was really confused by 4,000 to 5,000 different stock issues that were out there clamoring for attention. In that time frame, there were no big, fast personal computers that could analyze this many stocks at one time. If you will recall, the first IBM PC was marketed in 1982, and it was nothing like the machines that are available today.

I knew that the futures market was lurking out there somewhere, but from things that I had heard, it seemed either immoral, illegal, or both. I shied away from the stock market because it seemed too big to understand. When I realized that you could concentrate on just a limited number of commodities, I began to understand more about the futures markets and with that understanding, my feelings changed. Eventually, I decided that the futures market was for me.

What was it like at the beginning of your trading experience?
I performed research and put together a system to trade, but found it difficult to find a broker who would take my $5,000 account. Tom Bechtel, a wonderful guy at Merrill Lynch, decided to take my account. He loved "wackos" with trading systems. We have had a

good relationship for 24 years. Two years ago, I managed to lure him away from Merrill Lynch to work with me.

As a physicist, I wanted to understand one system really well. Most of my calculations, at that time, were done on a school computer because it was very difficult to crunch numbers in a timely manner without access to a good computer. I developed a trading system on frozen pork bellies, but I was not ready to support myself in trading. My savings were about to run out, so I returned to teaching chemistry in public high school.

Did you trade while teaching?
I was trading part time.

Were you successful at trading initially?
In 1979, I hit a big coffee trade. I think I made about $75,000, which was really good money for me at that time.

How much money did you have in trading?
In 1980 and 1981, I was in really good shape because I had saved money to build a decent size trading account. That was about the time that I started trading full time.

What kind of system were you trading then?
It was actually an early version of an opening range breakout system. I would take the opening price plus so much for a buy signal or the open minus so much for a sell signal. I have not done this for 14 or 15 years, so I do not remember some of the details. I used this system before I ever saw anyone use it.

I was trading coffee in the late 1970's using the same idea, but the parameters were different. I looked at a fair amount of data and decided what constituted a breakout from the opening range and what was not a breakout.

I got registered with the Commodity Futures Trading Commission in 1983, and the National Futures Association in 1984. Tom, my broker, helped me raise some money to begin trading.

How much money were you trading back then?
I was trading a couple of $25,000 accounts. About this time, I took my computer and moved off to San Diego, California.

Where was your focus at that time?
I was focusing primarily on pork bellies. I noticed that pork bellies drifted higher under low volatility for a long time and slammed down under high volatility. I included this observation in the trading system. Somewhere in the period between 1983 and 1986, pork bellies drifted lower and totally broke this filter rule.

Instead of drifting higher under low volatility and crashing down under high volatility, they just drifted lower and I missed some very good trades on the downside. Because of the market conditions, I think most traders lost money during that time and I did, too. I kept looking to buy during low volatility and the market continued to drift lower. It was a bad situation. Somewhere around 1985, I decided that I hated losing money and was never going to trade again.

Tell us about your loss experience?
It really hurt me, and my trades (or lack of trades) caused some of my clients to lose nearly half of their money. It was very hard to lose money for other people. After that time, I went back into lab work.

How did you get back into trading again?
One day, I wandered into a nearby lab and found a book called *Software Companies in Michigan*. There was a company called Micro Futures listed in the directory. I called with the intention of getting a part-time programming job. The man I spoke with, Jeff Miller, worked with MJK Associates. He wrote software that helped

MJK customers get daily futures updates and he resold historical data on floppy disk. He was one of the first people to do this in the industry.

MJK, are they a vendor that sells data and telephone updates?
Yes, they are. I wrote a letter expressing an interest in working with Jeff. About a month later, he called and said he was tired of trading from home and that he was moving to Chicago to trade T-bonds on the floor. I wanted to buy the company, but the asking price was too high. Jeff and I negotiated a lower purchase price and with my mother's financial help, I bought Micro Futures.

It took me about 8 months to get the business back under control because he had let things go. I started working on trading systems that I could use to trade my own money.

What was wrong with your original systems? Why did they not work out for you?
The thing in the original systems that killed me was the filter. Filters are a certain general parameter, which serves to keep you out of trades. There was a very long filter trend in pork bellies, which changed abruptly, keeping me out of good trades, and putting me into bad trades. I have never used a filter on a system since then. A filter can make you lose the big trade, which is very bad for a long-term trader.

In a system, you want to set up the procedures in such a way that you do not eliminate any possibilities. The idea is to let the data tell you where to go. Setting up flexible research procedures and letting the data lead the way is a very common approach in physics research.

I researched long-term and short-term systems, and the data showed me that a long-term approach was clearly the best way for me to trade. While there is randomness in the market, there is some predictability in longer term trading.

Where did your progress take you from there?
I decided to diversify.

I developed a system for eighteen markets and started to build a client base again. My first two clients came from Micro Future's mailing list.

It was very important for me to establish a proven track record that I could show to potential clients. It was in October 1989, when I began working with the eighteen market long-term portfolio. That is what I have been doing since.

How has the system done?
The first 15 months of trading the system were fabulous. Then, I went into a 15% drawdown until the spring of 1992, when my drawdown went to 57%. At that time, it was back into research to figure out ways to trade better. I must mention that this was a bad time for many long-term traders because of the markets that we had during this time.

Where do you get your ideas for trading?
My style seemed to be to work very hard, process a lot of data, look at a lot of graphs that summarize the performance of the ideas that process the data, then let it perk in my brain for awhile. I have very often said that all of my best ideas come when I am not working. They have come when I am taking a shower, driving, but most often when I am walking in the woods. I used to be a musician, and I love jazz. I played alto saxophone and clarinet. The improvisational training from jazz has helped me to be flexible in recognizing new ideas in the markets.

What part of your system is discretionary?
None of my system is discretionary. It feels like I have spent 30,000 hours on the program (this is 9 years at 10 hours a day) and feel that there is no reason to override the program because all of my ideas are already in the research. The only time I have ever used anything

that looked like discretion was when I was short in crude oil and heating oil just before the Persian Gulf War. I bought some options to protect myself. In fact, the system handled that whole thing quite well.

Who influenced your trading style?
There really is not anyone in the futures industry who determined my style. I did not start out wanting to be a long-term or short-term trader. As much as possible, objective handling of the testing of futures data has determined my style. For me, research style determines trading style. With that said, an interesting and very important characteristic that physicists seem to have is an exceptionally strong connection to the real, physical world, since that is where they work. I think this leads to an unusual discipline where, after a brief initial disappointment, they are usually pleased to find out that a wonderful, beautiful idea they have is wrong. Some people have this sense to a degree, but since physicists know that the physical world will continue on its own path, independently of how they think it should work and there is a real sense of relief to find out that they are wrong as soon as possible. Only then, can they start in another direction, which may possibly be right. This all seems so obvious, but with all the witchcraft and astrology and psychic hotlines around, maybe most of the rest of the world does not really think the way physicists try to.

Is that a triple moving average system?
Yes, but I use five averages, even though you really do not need five. However, all of the averages have to reverse before I take a trade.

During the research period from 1991 to 1994 when I worked to improve my original system, I continued to use simple concepts, a large amount of data, a small number of parameters, and the same parameters and approach for all markets. Many ideas worked when applied only to the data used to develop a system, but failed when applied to out of sample data. Usually, a complicated system with more parameters would work well on the training set and fail miserably on the test set. As the testing moved to simpler and simpler concepts, the system evolved into a multiple moving average crossover system.

Some people may initially be surprised that this is a new system based on moving averages. I would like to describe why I believe that moving averages are not simple. The problem with this type of analysis, of course, is how to select which moving average or combination of averages to use.

In order to get good results when testing a new system, very complicated ideas are often used to somehow pound the reality of trading into submission. Physicist Richard Feynman probably says it best, "If it's simple and elegant, it has a good chance of working. If it is complicated and messy, it probably won't work."

Why did you go to moving averages, when really you started as an opening range breakout sort of guy?
I found it very difficult to close out a trade when using the opening breakout concept and it did not seem to work for many markets.

What are the biggest mistakes that you think most traders make when developing trading systems?
There are a number of problems that I find in technical research coupled with system testing and development. Typically, very complicated ideas with too many parameters are used in order to obtain good test results over too short a testing period. Most people look at only a few years of data and if the results are good, they think they have discovered the Holy Grail. I have processed about 400 years of commodity data in a research run. Some traders use just a few years of data, adopt 6 to 8 parameters, adjust them all to fit the data, do not use out-of-sample data as a test, and think they have a system. When four parameters are chosen that give good hypothetical results, but small changes in these parameters give

much poorer results, I would question the robustness of the system. Testing like this can be compared to working on the edge of a cliff. Another problem that I have seen is optimizing individual markets using different parameters or approaches.

You want to make sure that changing your parameters has little affect on your results?

Yes, people use different parameters or different methods to find parameters for each market. If you do that and have 20 years of data in each market, you are essentially running 20 years at a time. I set up procedures to find the parameters that I am looking for. The program simply reads in the stream of data and it does not care which market it is reading. It treats them all the same. It may come out with different moving average parameters, but the same software is used to determine coffee and gold trades.

It is not an optimization? You are not picking highest profit to generate your parameters?

Clearly, a good idea used in a naive way can lead to greatly over estimated gains and under estimated equity declines. I believe that a major strength that this system has is that it uses a large amount of data, very few parameters, and handles the system developmental data and out-of-sample test data in a realistic way.

What do you think about women in the markets?

I remember reading some years ago that women traders were in the great minority as futures traders. They said that percentage-wise they were much better than men at getting good results and the reason that this was true was that men get excited over the possibility of large profits and women recoil from the risks. I think I have a real feminine side because I look at risk all of the time.

Are there any more observations about technical research that you would like to make?

I disapprove of reporting system results only for the time period used to develop the system. You get your wonderful optimum parameters and make the assumption that these parameters would have made so much for the time period, and of course, that is a joke. Although I do not use neural networks very much, everything that I have done for the last 4 or 5 years has been with the neural network idea of setting aside a training set to find the parameter. Then, I do not care what it does during that time period because it must work on data that has never been tested before in the test set. Do you know how many people are doing that?

That is a standard practice for people who really know what they are doing. There are people who cheat because it is easy to build these systems with wonderful results. People who are purchasing systems want to see minimal drawdowns, and they do not care how much curve fitting must be done to get there.
I agree that careful testing is standard practice for people who know what they are doing, but what percentage of commodity trading advisors really know what they are doing? My guess is ten to fifteen percent. What prevents me from doing bad research? I trade more than fifty percent of my own net worth in just the one program I offer to the public. Therefore, I have no reason to cheat.

How profitable has your trading been the last three or four years?
My revised, diversified system did very well in 1995. It was up 81%. 1996 and 1997 were in the 15% to 25% range. I think 1992 was my only losing year.

How much money, besides your own, are you managing now?
I am managing about one million dollars. It is very hard for me to raise money.

You have decent numbers. Twenty percent puts you in the middle to upper crust of Commodity Trading Advisors.
Yes, I know. Tom and I have put together a pool for which I am the only trader. I tell prospective clients that our money is traded right

with theirs. To me that should be a powerful selling point, but it just does not seem to register with many people.

Tom believes that we are not able to raise much money because the stock market has been so good. I believe that I have outperformed the stock market over the last five years. Also, I am not willing to take time from my research to travel around the country to raise money. I have had a few offers from at least three people who could raise a significant amount of money for me to trade, but I was not willing to agree to the payout they wanted for themselves.

How have you done when you adjust your risk, like calculating Sharpe ratios?
I do not calculate Sharpe ratios. I calculate a ratio of average yearly return divided by the worst drawdown.

Would you explain what you mean by an adaptive moving average?
We had talked about adaptive moving averages. Everything that I have seen indicates that it takes at least 10 to 15 years of data to find a good moving average. The moving average can change over time, but very, very slowly. I use more than 10 years of data to find the moving averages that I am using.

So, have we talked about system volatility?
Let me give you the numbers. The combined systems for 8 1/3 years, which is all of the trading that I have ever done with the long-term diversified system, was up 25.8% per year compounded return including the 57% drawdown in 1992. The refined system, which has traded for 3 years, is up 35% per year with a 42.6% drawdown. Coffee was unmanageable last year.

As you are adapting your system, are you adapting it in terms of net profit or drawdown? What's your measure?
My measure of merit is always yearly gain divided by worst drawdown. I still work full time to try to improve my trading.

Looking again at your system for a brief second, is it 5 moving averages? Is it the single crossover?
Yes.

Walk me through the process of how you would adapt your parameters?
I am not using the word "adapt" anymore.

Evolve?
The parameter is extremely stable because the number of years that I use may change it by small amounts and slowly. That is where I am in continued development right now.

Let us suppose that we are using a single moving average crossover system. You would develop the moving average over 15 years of data, and then trade it over the next how many to see if it worked?
I take about 15 years of data and break it into six-month intervals. I take 120 moving averages and find the gain over the drawdown for each of the 120 moving averages for a six-month interval. Then, I slide forward one day and repeat the process.

So you are optimizing the moving average, finding the best one for the past 6 months?
Yes. And I slide it forward one day at a time for 15 years.

How do you decide which moving average to use? Do you use the one that appears most often in the results?
I go back and process these 3,655 six-month intervals for each market that I trade and shift them forward one day at a time. I find the moving averages, which range from 2 days to 300 days. I have established a procedure, which is proprietary, to find the best moving average for the period. I test the result on the next day, and slide everything forward by one day and add the new day's data to the set.

So you are building a bigger and bigger mesh, and at the top of the pyramid you are using the whole 15 years?
Right, but it is only to find the parameter for the next day after each interval. So I use a training set and a test set, but they slide forward one day at a time. This is not cheating. Now, I have 15 years of data for 21 markets and I set out to find a procedure, which optimizes those 300 to 400 years of data in the same way for every market.

Of course, the proprietary part of your system is how you combine all of these results into one set of numbers?
Yes. It is simple though. I call it Fritz's criterion.

How often do you repeat this process?
Because it changes so slowly and in small amounts, we add 2 weeks of new data to 20 years worth of existing data. There may be a 5% change twice a year, up or down.

So, we are talking 21 to 22 days?
Yes, a change of about a day in 21 days.

I will talk to you more about adaptives. The problem with adaptive moving averages is the problem with moving averages. I have tried to find out the moving average to use as a function of velocity and volatility. I do not follow windows or cycles.

You do not believe in cycles?
What was the cycle preceding the Gulf War? What was the cycle that preceded the last coffee freeze? Some fundamental events happen and the market responds to those events. I think of myself as a long-term, purely technical trader who trades on changes in fundamental events.

You could probably find a long-term weather related cycle that works for the coffee freezes.
You would probably need 2,000 years of data.

Do you trade on daily bars as opposed to weekly or monthly?
Yes, but I use close only rather than high, low, close.

Do you look at multiple time frames at all?
No, returning to what I said about the problem with trying to adapt a moving average is that when you have learned the information about the volatility or velocity that is important, it is too late, it has gone somewhere else. I have tried things like sliding the data forward and backward by one to four weeks. You can find a place where there is a beautiful correspondence, but it is the same problem you have with the moving average, you are always too late.

My trades are always about 3 weeks or so late. We just reversed the Canadian dollar after being short for 13 months. What works in my method is that I am consistently about three weeks late, but I hold the trade for an average of four months. I think that is why long-term traders are successful because their percentage of error when they enter a trade is relatively small. When you are talking about a day trader, if he is wrong by half an hour in a trade that is held for a few hours, they do not do well. I am usually off in timing by about 20%. I cannot make it better than that even though I am still working on it.

Do you use continuous contract data?
I put together what I call a continuous contract, but it may not be what you think of as a continuous contract. It works just like a rollover trade. On a certain day, I find the offset between the two adjacent contracts, add or subtract the offset to the new contract, and string them together.

You do not propagate back through to create a true back-adjusted contract?
No, but it is not a blending problem. We rolled April heating oil and crude oil yesterday. We were short going into the day, so we bought the April contract to cover the short, and sold the June

contract on the open to stay short. That is exactly how my continuous contract is compiled.

What happens in a standard back-adjustment is that you dress up the gap, but propagate it back to the beginning of the database so that you can string the contracts together and the current bar is at the right price.
There is no reason to have it at the right price because you are only concerned with price difference.

You are trading from the continuous contract data when you can place your order. In using a moving average crossover system, price does not matter. However, if you are doing something where price does matter, such as buying on a stop, then it is important to have the right price. That is the reason why you propagate the difference when you roll contracts back to the beginning of the database.
I use large stops. In my case, the data stream works exactly like a rollover. If the system says the stop should be $2,000 off of the close on this day, then the program goes back and finds the actual contract and subtracts $2,000 from the close, and that is the stop.

Do you do any sort of "Monte Carlo simulation" or anything on your money management?
No, I do not. I really have not used any type of "Monte Carlo testing" at all.

You have not estimated the worst case drawdown for the system based on "Monte Carlo simulation" or any statistical method like that?
No.

Is there a reason for that or have you just not gotten to it?
No. I think the reason for that is that I have not only matched my trading style to my personality, but I have matched my research style to my personality. I am always calculating gain over drawdown, and

optimizing in a way that is honest because I am trading with my money.

What are you looking forward to?

I think I will always be trading futures. I am just fascinated by the process of trying to get closer to the truth. I really do not have many material needs, but I do have a very beautiful house in mind that I would like to build in the woods in the country, probably near Ann Arbor. And I would like to meet a very special woman and get married again.

Compounded Monthly Returns for the Trading Programs of John W. Fritz, Ph. D.

LOG (Compounded value of an initial $1,000 investment) : COMBINED SYSTEMS

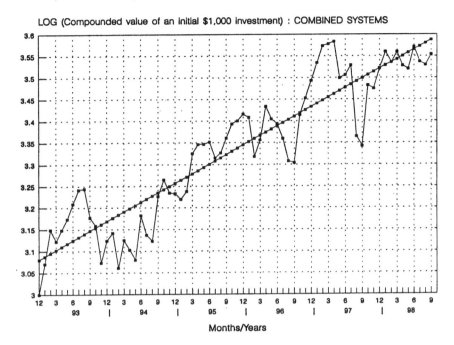

Months/Years

This graph is an attempt to display the cumulative "Net Monthly Rate of Return" from the end of December 1992 to the end of April 1998 as reported on pages 12 and 13 of the Disclosure Document of John W. Fritz, Ph. D. dated June 19, 1998. In addition, the performance has been updated to the end of September 1998. The graph assumes an initial deposit of $1,000 on December 31, 1992 and compounds the monthly rate of return up to September 30, 1998. Returns for the Original Diversified System were used for January 1993 to December 1994. The return for January 1995 (the first month of trading for the Revised System) used the combined performance of the Original and the Revised Systems to find the return for that month. Returns for the Revised Diversified System were used for February 1995 to September 1998. Since the data gives a compounded return, the logarithm of the cumulative return is plotted. The smooth curve is a least squares fit to the log of the data.

		Yearly Rate of Return	Worst Decline
Original System	12/92 to 10/95	30.7%	-34.4%
Revised System	12/94 to 9/98	27.5%	-42.6%

Please note that this graph uses the Net Monthly Rate of Return for the Actual Monthly Composite Trading Record and therefore, does not perfectly represent any single, actual trading account, since different accounts started at different times, paid different commissions and earned different rates of interest. However, the performance IS FOR ACTUAL TRADES. This graph IS NOT A COMPUTER SIMULATION of theoretical trades. The National Futures Association requires the following addition:

PAST PERFORMANCE IS NOT NECESSARILY INDICATIVE OF FUTURE RESULTS

Some people may initially be surprised that my trading system is based on moving averages (MVAs). I would like to show why I believe moving averages are really not that simple. The problem, of course, is how to select which moving average to use. I have heard some traders claim that the moving average used is not terribly important as long as a person uses a moving average consistently. I strongly disagree with this comment. To show why many research projects might fail, I would like to describe the problems involved in developing system parameters. The two graphs below are the summary of the results of a computer program. They are actually a summary of the hypothetical results for using 63 different, separate moving average sets.

The time frame used to make the top graph is from 12-31-79 to 12-31-89 and it may be considered to be the training set. The time frame used to make the bottom graph is from 12-31-89 to 10-31-94 and it may be considered to be the test set. For both graphs, the horizontal axis represents the MVAs used and the vertical axis represents the average profit per year. The market shown is the Japanese Yen and $80 commissions were used when any trade was closed out in the program and when contracts were rolled forward.

The first problem with the top graph can be seen even before it is compared to the bottom one. It shows a peak profit of $7,631/year for MVA=10.48 and a slightly lower peak profit of $6,751/year for MVA=33.09. Unfortunately, for intermediate MVAs (20 to 25) the profit drops to around $4,500/year. Two peaks separated by a valley seem very difficult to handle. Should one use MVA=10.48 or 33.09 for the Japanese Yen? I would have been very surprised if the test graph also would have shown this strange behavior.

The bottom graph tests whether the first graph, if used in a naive way, can predict future profits. Unfortunately, this second graph does not show two profit peaks with a valley in between. In fact, if either of the optimum values for the MVA found in the training set is used, the results for the test set are very poor. MVA=10.48 gives a profit of $4,123/year and MVA=33.09 gives a profit of $3,859/year. What is even worse is that the MVA range from 20 to 25 gives very good results (about $7,000/year). The peak gain per year is $7,753 and is found at MVA=24.82. If a researcher only reported the results of the training run, they might report that future profits from trading the Japanese Yen were expected to be $7,631/year (when a 10.48 MVA is used). The bottom graph shows why this statement is extremely misleading. Of the 21 futures markets I considered, the graphs for the Japanese Yen are about average in terms of how poorly the earlier training graphs can predict results for the later test graphs.

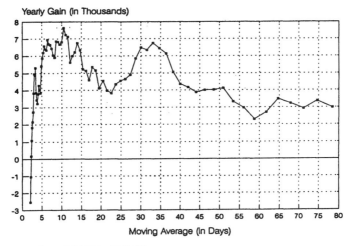

Japanese Yen from 12-31-79 to 12-31-89

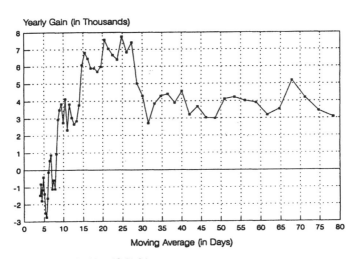

Japanese Yen from 12-31-89 to 10-31-94

The numbers given on the horizontal axis are for the shortest moving average in the multiple set of moving averages.

As a final comment to illustrate why the predictions of some trading systems might fail, I ran two computer trading simulations to show how bad research can lead to very poor projections.

A) I call this run the "naive" run, because it includes almost all of the test set (12-31-89 to 11-30-94) in the training set (12-31-79 to 10-31-94). It incorrectly uses data in the future to find parameters by hindsight. However, it is in fact obvious that this data from the future is not available for real time trading. I call this kind of research "cheating". It found graphs like those shown above for the Japanese Yen for all 21 markets by using data from 12-31-79 to 10-31-94. Then the program selected the moving average for each market that gave the highest yearly gain. This is called the "naive" run, because almost the entire test set (12-31-89 to 11-30-94) was a part of the training set (12-31-79 to 10-31-94). The results are shown below in A).

B) I call this run the "consequences of cheating " run. The only difference between this example and example A) is that now the research is done correctly because the training set and test set do not overlap. Only data from 12-31-79 to 12-31-89 (training data) is used to determine MVAs. The MVA used for the test period from 12-31-89 to 11-30-94 (test data) is simply the one that maximizes the gain during the training period as in A) above. For example, the top graph above shows that MVA=10.48 was used for the Japanese Yen. Here, the test set is not included in the training set, but the MVAs used were chosen in the same very naive way as in A). The results are shown below in B). This shows that the good results in example A) were only obtained by doing bad research. Therefore, another method of selecting parameters must be found within the framework where the training and test sets do not overlap.

The yearly gain and largest equity decline projections for the period 12-31-89 to 11-30-94 are shown below:

System described above	Yearly gain	Worst decline
A) The naive run	$104,665	$45,204
B) The consequences of a cheating run	$34,612	$81,295

Clearly, a good idea used in a very poor, naive way can lead to very greatly overestimated projected gains and greatly underestimated projected equity declines.

264

MODELING STUDY

CHILDHOOD FAMILY STATUS
- John experienced a poor childhood in Detroit, Michigan, but moved to middle class through his parents' diligence.

MENTORING - INFLUENCE
- Parents had little education
- Mother knew how to bring out special abilities
- Mother said that he could do anything he wanted to do, but it would take a lot of work
- A physicist who worked with him on his approach to trading

ENVIRONMENT
- Very supportive mother

EDUCATION
- Extremely good student as child especially in math and science
- Master's Degree in Education
- Ph.D. in Physics

INTERESTS -Skills - Abilities -Honors
Childhood
- Liked sports but was not a good athlete
- Musician - played alto saxophone and clarinet

Adult
- Politics
- Skiing
- Running

QUALITIES
- Improvisational skills in jazz music

- Feminine side makes him always consider risk
- Integrated Right and Left brain thinking
- Introvert
- Shy

BUSINESS EXPERIENCE
- Taught lab in the physics department
- Special physics research project
- Taught high school physics and math
- Bought a software company

PHILOSOPHY
- Believed I was super bright
- Quote from physicist Richard Feynman - "If it is simple and elegant it has a good chance of working. If it is complicated and messy it probably won't work."

TRADING EXPERIENCE
- Futures trading
- Registered with NFA - CFTC
- Money manager

TRADER CONTRIBUTIONS
- Makes money for his clients

FUTURE PLANS
- 10 wooded acres to build a gorgeous dream home
- Trade forever
- Get married

TRADER GEMS - Fundamental - Intuitive - Psychological
- It is important to test data over a very long period of time
- Use one set of data to develop and a different set to test it
- Quote--"Since we are dealing with the real, physical world, we have an unusual discipline where we are relieved and celebrate

when we find out that a wonderful, beautiful idea we have is wrong. Some people have this to a degree, but since physicists know that the physical world will continue on its own path, independently of how we think it should work, there is a real sense of relief to find out that we are wrong as soon as possible. Only then can we start in another direction which may possibly be right."

TRADER GEMS - Mechanical - Analytical - Technical

- John started his trading career using a simple opening range breakout system, which he added filters to. One example was that pork bellies drifted higher under low volatility and fell under high volatility. The problem was that this volatility affect changed during the mid-1980's and filtered out good trades while signaling losing trades. From that point on, he no longer used filters. The problem was that filters can make you lose the big trades, which is bad for a long-term trading strategy.

- John stopped using opening range breakout because it did not work was well as trading a basket using the multiple moving average concept. He started to use a multiple moving average crossover system. John uses five moving averages. He requires them to all line up to take the trade. We can see an example of this type of system in the triple moving average crossover system which comes with Supercharts or TradeStation in our analysis section.

- This type of system combines the concepts of a channel breakout with a measure of trend following because it requires the shorter term moving average to line up to take a trade

  1. To enter long Shortest>Middle>Longest
  2. To enter short Shortest<Middle<Longest

- John feels that the biggest mistake most system developers make is that they have systems with too many parameters and too few trades in testing. It is also important that small changes in parameters not produce large changes in results.

- John develops systems using three sets of data; a development set, a testing set, and out-of-sample set. He uses walk forward testing to develop parameters to use for the next six months and evaluates how well the set of parameters did by testing the results during out-of-sample testing. He uses 10 to 15 years of data to find the set of parameters to use. He rolls this forward one day at a time for the 10 to 15 years of data.
- His optimization is based on the ratio of average yearly returns to worst drawdown.
- He allows small changes in parameters on any given reoptimization. I think, although he does not make it clear, that he develops the best parameters over the basket and not on any one market. This is why his parameters evolve rather than adapt because changes are slow. Using his methodology parameters only change about 5%, two times a year.
- John's work is based on the close only.
- John's trades are very long term, sometimes they can last over a year

Murray's Analytical Modeling Study

Trade Methodology Analysis
Mechanical--Objective: Not known, could exist in selection process for moving averages

Mechanical--Automatic: System is 100% mechanical

Discretionary: None, why guess when you have numbers to back you

Analysis of John's Methodology
John Fritz uses a classic trading methodology which is to trade a basket of markets with a trend following method. John's method is a multiple moving average crossover system where trades are taken when the moving average crossovers line up in time. Buy when shorter length averages are above the longer length averages in order, and of course the shortest average must be above all of them to generate a signal. The reverse is true for the short side.

In the classic system, they use three moving averages. John uses five. This type of system reduces to a type of channel breakout with a trend filter built in. The trend filter component is based on the moving averages having to line up. This requires the market to be moving a given direction for a relatively long time, which is a type of trend strength indicator. Let's look at how the classic three moving average crossover system works in TradeStation on two different markets using the same parameters.

Our simple classic system is as follows in TradeStation Easy Language
Input: Length1(10),Length2(15),Length3(25);
IF (Average(Close,Length1)[1] < Average(Close,Length2)[1] OR Average(Close,Length2)[1] < Average(Close,Length3)[1]) AND (Average(Close,Length1) > Average(Close,Length2) AND

Average(Close,Length2) > Average(Close,Length3)) Then Buy on
Close;
IF (Average(Close,Length1)[1] > Average(Close,Length2)[1] OR
Average(Close,Length2)[1] > Average(Close,Length3)[1]) AND
(Average(Close,Length1) < Average(Close,Length2) AND
Average(Close,Length2) < Average(Close,Length3)) Then Sell on
Close;

We used the following set of parameters for the Yen and Crude Oil,
with the following results over the period from 1/1/80 to 9/14/98.
Length1=10, Length2=15, Length3=25.

Once again, to judge the bias created by this system, we have not
deducted slippage or commission. You can add your own since we
have net profit and total number of trades included in our analysis.

	Yen	Crude
Net Profit	$181,775.00	$49,086.00
Trades	147	124
Win%	49 %	43 %
Ave Trade	1236.50	395.00
Drawdown	$ 13,612.50	$10,020.00

These parameters do well on the Yen and acceptable on Crude Oil.
In John's trading, he finds the parameters to use by optimizing his
parameters over the basket of markets in a walk forward manner.
This process of how he adapts his parameters is what makes John's
work successful. In our example, we used a relatively short moving
average period. John allows the moving average period to reach as
long as 200 days. It can be statistically proven that this method will
produce profits, but the drawdown characteristic of this method can
range in the 20+% area. This is too risky for many traders, but over
the long term with a 5 or more year time horizon, this system
methodology can help us live better when we retire than we did
when we were working.

Adrienne's Psychological Modeling Study

The Focus Model

John Fritz had the best kind of start for a trader. His mother believed in his abilities and believed that he was special. She showed him by her example that you could set a goal, focus on it, work hard, and achieve it. A second experience in his background helped him to increase his ability to focus. When he was young, he lived in a poor neighborhood where there were no children his age to distract him from his studies. This experience allowed John to learn how to focus on an intellectual pursuit early in his life. These experiences created the Focus Model, which John later used to great ends.

Although John did not put this Focus Model into affect during his high school and college years, the turning point in his life came while answering a question for a student shortly after graduation from college. John suddenly realized how important and satisfying it was for him to understand something deeply. Returning to get his Ph.D. in Physics, he was given an experiment which required him to focus completely on a nearly unsolvable problem. However, John was already psychologically prepared to focus on this assignment. In addition, John's Focus Model was honed by the experience of being in a physics graduate school program. Scientists spend long hours totally focused on their work, which is often tedious and unrewarding. They are searching for the most difficult to find solutions among large bodies of data. They cannot do this work without the ability to shut out the distractions of the world around them. Despite the fact that John had outside interests beyond the lab, he still completed his experiment and his degree, a testimony to his ability to keep focus.

Then, John finds his way into trading. However, he is put off by the vast and confusing appearance of the various markets. What factor seals his commitment? In his own words: "When I realized that you could concentrate on just a limited number of commodities, I began to understand more about the futures market and with that under-standing, my feelings changed."

With John's Focus Model to guide him, he wanted "to understand one system really well." From that time on and off, John worked very hard on developing and trading systems that were mechanical and grounded in "the real physical world." These systems require the same kind of testing that any thesis in physics would require to prove or disprove its validity. John's experience in graduate school led him to develop the simplest solution in order to achieve results which could be replicated, but only his model for focusing on the outcome could carry him through the demanding procedures with 400 years of commodity data and arrive at a system which produces such outstanding results.

CHAPTER 10

Alta Wood

Living the real bull market
How a poor widowed rancher's wife invested her way
to an affluent retirement.

Tell us about your family, where you were born, what it was like at that time in your life?
I was born in Perryton, Texas in 1921. Perryton is in the northeast corner of the Texas Panhandle and was a brand new town at the time with a population of about two thousand people. I have four sisters and two brothers. My father was a carpenter and my mother was a housewife. It was not a very exciting life, rather average I would guess.

Did you get along with your brothers and sisters? Was it fun having that many kids around?
We all seemed to enjoy each other. Mother looked after us children, father worked to support us, and we went to school.

How did you do in school?
I was not a brain, but I always made good grades. I went to school in Perryton until I reached the fourth grade. My sister was attending college in Goodwell, Oklahoma, and so my mother, my sisters, and I moved there while she was in school. In the summer, we would return to my Dad's farm outside of Perryton. My last two years of high school, I lived in Oklahoma City because my father lived there.

What were your interests as a kid?
I liked to read anything and everything, and I liked music. Sometimes, I would hide the light under the covers of the bed, so I could read because my father did not think we should read after we went to bed. I read a lot.

273

In school, did you have any interest in sports or any other activities?

Not particularly. When I was in Oklahoma City, I just ran around with my girlfriends. Of course, there was not a lot to do, but we did not know that. We made our own fun.

Did your father work for himself as a carpenter?

Yes, he worked for himself building houses. He has the unique distinction of having built the first house in Perryton, Texas.

After high school, what did you do?

I worked at a little store here. Then, World War II came along and I married Neil McGarraugh. I had two sons by him.

Did you become a housewife?

Yes, Neil was a farmer and rancher. He worked on a ranch 26 miles south of Perryton that was owned by his father. His father died shortly after we married.

In 1958, Neil was killed in a tractor accident. I was left with two small boys, ages 9 and 11, and a ranch to care for. We raised cattle and farmed wheat on the ranch. In the wintertime, we lived in Perryton, so the boys could go to school. There were no buses at that time, and we would have had to drive 52 miles round trip if we stayed at the ranch. On the weekends, we went back to the ranch, and we spent our summers there.

How many head of cattle did you take care of?

At the time that my husband died, he had between 300 and 400 head of cattle.

And you took over that responsibility?

Yes. When he passed away, I hired hands to work the ranch. They usually were not the most desirable workers because it was hard to get someone to come out to the country and stay. I ran the ranch until my boys were able to take it over and operate it themselves.

The first year after my husband died, I went to Amarillo to buy cattle. A man, who was a family friend, said he would help me buy them. So I bought cattle that year. I think people thought I had a lot of money, but I did not. Even though I had a ranch, the taxes seemed to take everything that I made. My mother-in-law received the income from the ranch, but I got to pay the estate taxes. That was kind of hard.

Is that when you started getting interested in trading?
Six months before my husband passed away, we had bought a little apartment in Canadian, Texas. He was leasing some pastureland down there for the cattle to graze. After he passed away, I continued to use a bank there to make deposits.

One day when I was in the bank, an officer of the bank asked me to join a stock club that had been formed in this small community. It was 1960, and fifty people had formed a stock club. He probably had someone that had to pay off a loan because he wanted me to buy this $1,500 share of the club. I had never done anything like that, but thought that it might be a good learning experience. The club met once a month, but the men in the bank were the ones who made the decisions of what to buy and sell. Each club member had to pay $25 per month. I had not been in the club very long when some of the members decided to disband because they did not like the way things were being handled. According to the by-laws, they could not just sell everybody out, so thirteen members stayed and continued the business.

One day when I was in the bank, one of the officers wanted to sell me a stock called Transcontinental Gas Pipeline. I wondered if he was trying to cheat me, but I bought it. It was around $2,400, and I had not had it very long before it split. At the time, I thought all stocks did that. You bought them and they split. That was my first stock purchase outside of the stock club. I decided that I would put $5,000 in the market to see what I could do with it. If I lost the money, it would not be the end of the world, but it would be nice to turn it into something.

Did that $5,000 investment include the $2400 and $1500 that you already had in the market?
It did not include the $1,500.

I went to the Merrill Lynch office in Amarillo. I had never been in a stockbroker's office before. They sent me to a young broker named Alan Robertson. I do not think he had been there more than a few days. Later he told me that I was his second customer. On January 10, 1961, I bought 35 shares of Pioneer Natural Gas for $25. On March 10, 1961, I bought 50 shares of Stone and Webster at $61. Then, I bought 50 shares of Southwestern Public Service at 30 1/8.

What criteria did you use for making the decision to buy these stocks?
All of my stock choices were local companies. I liked to read *Forbes Magazine* and Stone and Webster was a highly recommended stock in that magazine. There was a stock column in the back of the magazine that I liked to read.

So, at this point, your stock selections were made with other people's recommendations, or were local companies that you could investigate?
I did not have long-range communication, I did not know what to read, and I certainly did not know anyone that bought stocks. I just felt that a company like Pioneer Natural Gas was a solid company in the area that had good management.

How did you make buy decisions?
In taking care of my business, I met people who did business with other businesses. I had some dealings with some of the oil companies in leasing properties for oil exploration rights. Diamond Shamrock was one of those companies and I bought 50 shares of their stock.

I always read the paper, and I checked the listings of stock purchases that senators made. I know that I bought some Loral Systems stock at one time because I noticed that senators had holdings in that stock. I figured that they might know something that I did not know. The main way I made my decisions to buy stock was by what I read.

You were buying stocks based upon a feeling you would get from what was said in newspapers and magazines?
Yes.

Tell us what happened from there?
It seemed that I never had the time or money to invest a great deal at any one time, so I accumulated stocks. Every time I would get a little money put back, I would buy a little stock. I never sold very much. I just accumulated it, which I still do today.

Were you in the bear market in 1973 and 1974?
Yes.

Did that upset you? Did you sell any of your stocks then?
No. I felt that the companies I held stock in were good companies. They were the same good companies that they were when I bought them. If the market went down, it did not upset me that much.

If I know that I own stock in companies that are good, then I am going to stick with them.

What would make you sell a company?
If I feel from my reading that I should sell a stock, or if there is something else that I would like to buy that I feel would be a better investment.

Now, we are in the 1970's. Did anything change then?
I just kept buying and hanging on. You only need one or two good stocks to really do well.

And how were you doing?
I was doing pretty well. I just kept buying and holding stocks and sold very little. I still had a lot of stocks. Once in a while, I would sell.

How much have you increased percentage wise?
In 1997, according to Merrill Lynch, my return was 51.7%. This year has not been quite as good, but it has still been all right.

Did you ever have a losing year?
I am sure that I have had. If you have a profit with a very low cost basis then no matter what the stock market says, you are still ahead. That is my thinking. I have some stocks that I really cannot afford to sell because I have nothing in them. It would cost me so much to sell them because of taxes. For example, consider Pfizer. When I bought it I probably had $2,400 in it, and now it is worth close to $300,000. It would cost me a great deal to sell that stock in terms of tax on long-term gain. At one point, I used a margin account to buy some stocks and it cost me about 5% to borrow the money, but I was getting over 5% out of my stocks.

What lessons did you learn along the way that made it better for you to pick stocks?
I learned that you should be patient and not be greedy. For example, I learned to not run in thinking you are going to make a bunch of money very quickly. People sell too fast. I think selling sometimes can cost you a lot of money. I remember when I started buying stocks, I just knew that the market would hit 1,000. I just knew it would.

How did you know it?
I just felt it.

Where did you feel it?
I just thought that it had to. I thought the companies were good. Once I started buying stocks, it seemed that everything I touched or

did made me wonder what company produced that item. From that thought, I would think about the company that produced the item and how sound was the company as an investment? I always looked up all that I could find about a company that I was buying.

What other lessons did you learn?
I think all young people would be surprised at how their money would grow if they would just take a little money each year and invest it.

Do you think your approach would be good to use to save for your kid's college education?
Oh, yes. I think it is good for anything. Everyone needs a savings plan. If someone would just take $1,000 per year and invest it. They would be amazed in a few years at how much money they would have. Once people start saving, it makes them want to save a little more if they can.

So, the advice you would give to someone is put some money away in stock and let it stay there and accumulate. Many people put money in stocks, but they will not get the gains. What do you do that makes the difference?
I think people need to read more about the companies they are investing in to understand the company more fully. People have such fantastic libraries and publications that are available to them. If they would just read more, I think most anybody could do exceedingly well.

What would you recommend a new trader to read?
I like to read *Fortune*, *Barron's*, and *Investor's Business Daily*. I read anything that I can that has to do with the companies that I hold stock in or might be interested in buying. One time, I took a trip to Australia and they had one business channel on the plane to listen to. I heard about this one little company called Alza that sounded awfully good to me. They had a little patch that could do wonders for people because it could be used as a method to administer

medications. I bought that stock and paid for my trip to Australia just by listening to that one program.

It sounds like you can get emotionally involved in something because you feel that it just makes sense. The company's concept or idea of what they have makes sense and that makes you want to invest with them.
Yes.

What else do you look for when you are making a decision to purchase a stock?
I do not get too excited about companies that have mountains of debt.

What is the difference in the way you would choose a stock now as opposed to the way you would choose a stock when you first got into the business?
When I first got into the business, I really did not know what I was doing. I just felt that it was a good thing to do, but I did not know where to go look for good ideas, suggestions, or to gain knowledge on the markets. Now, if there is a company that I have any interest in, I find out what other people have to say about that company. I also take the time to research and find out as much about the company as I can.

How would you do that? By going to the public library?
We did not have much of that type of material here, but I did subscribe to publications. When I first started out, I relied mostly on magazines like *Forbes*. That is a great magazine.

Do you think Forbes still gives out good information?
I think *Forbes* is an excellent magazine. I think *Fortune* is a super magazine also.

What about newletters? Did you follow any newsletters?
There was a man in New Jersey whose name was James Lampineau. He published a newsletter that I believe was called *The Income Builder*. I had a friend in Amarillo whose brother-in-law had just died. She asked me to read these letters that her sister-in-law had sent her. They were copies of newsletters that this Mr. Lampineau had written that her brother-in-law had received. After reading them, I called him and found him to be very low key. I told him that I had read his newsletter, was very impressed with it, and wanted to subscribe to it. I thought that he gave really good advice about stocks to buy.

Dick Davis another newsletter writer, I have taken his newsletter at various times, and I also like *The Value Line Survey*. I will take a newsletter for a time, then change, because I like to get a variety of ideas.

Over the years, what would you say has been your average return?
Since 1960, I would say my average return has been 20% or more. In the last ten years, I have been buying a lot of medically based stocks that have done absolutely fantastic.

Did you learn about those companies before buying them?
I bought Lily, Pfizer, Merck, Warner-Lambert, and Medtronic. I like to buy stock in companies making products everybody uses. Everyone tells me how sick they are. I keep hoping they are buying the medicines of the companies that I have.

What has been your driving force? Why do you invest? What are your goals?
When I started investing, I thought that if I could ever make $50,000 I would be in the same league as the Rockefellers. They would not have anything on me.

Well, obviously you have made a lot more than $50,000.
That was my first goal. I thought that if I could achieve that amount, I would be a total success. My next goal after that, was $100,000.

Now that you are in the class of the Rockefellers, what is your goal from here?
Giving it away to my children and grandchildren.

Do you have any goals besides making money?
I like to make money better than anything else.

What do you enjoy about the markets?
I enjoy everything about the market. There is nothing about the market that I do not enjoy. I like to watch the market. I like to hear about what different companies are doing in the market. I think it is totally fascinating. Everything you touch is the market. Anything you do is the market. I think it is exciting to be a small part of it.

How many hours a day do you spend working with the markets?
In the mornings, I get up and watch CNBC. That is a must. I spend three or four hours a day easily on the markets.

At one time, did you put a lot of time into it?
Until my children were grown, I could not invest very much time or money because I did not have much of either, but I still was very interested in the market. Whenever I had extra time, studying the market is where I would spend it. I would spend time every day studying the market, and I still do that.

Have you ever looked at a chart?
I used to follow Standard and Poor. That was one chart that I received and followed. No, I really just 'fly by the seat of my pants.'

Do you consider yourself just trading stocks based on fundamentals?
Yes.

Would you look at the price earnings, net profit, etc?
Yes.

So you are basically just trading off of the fundamentals of the stock and holding them?
Yes.

For example, when IBM dropped to $46 a share, did you buy it then?
No, I did not buy IBM, but I have stock in Intel.

Why would you choose not to buy IBM?
I think I bought IBM for my sons when they were in high school. They had a little money in high school, but then they sold their stock when they started buying cattle. I do not know for sure. I just have not bought it, but I think it is a terrific company.

What does your family think about your investments?
When I first started buying stock, they thought that I should get out of it. There was no one that I knew who bought stocks, so I did not mention stocks to people in conversation. All I ever heard about was the Crash of 1929.

But that did not discourage you at all?
No, I wish I had been there, I would have bought.

What do you enjoy doing now besides working with the stock market?
After my sons took over the farming and ranching operations, I have traveled a lot. I started traveling, enjoyed it, and have been all over the world several times. On a trip to Europe, I met two ladies who happened to be executive secretaries at E-Systems. I had *The Wall Street Journal* with me that day and looked it up for them. I bought that stock because this woman was going on and on about the systems this company produced. That stock purchase paid for the trip.

How many stocks do you own at this point in time?
I probably own at least fifty or more.

And most of these stocks are purchases that you made over a period of time and are just sitting on?
Some of them are. Pfizer, I have had for many, many moons. Tyco Lab, I have had for eons.

What was your biggest money maker?
Tyco Labs. Last year, a company from Bermuda bought Tyco Labs. When a foreign company buys your stock, the government makes you pay capital gains tax on the stock whether you sell it or not. That was really a low blow. I had to pay 20% on my earnings.

What do your sons do now?
My sons both farm and ranch near Perryton.

Now, you live in two places, Amarillo and Perryton?
Yes, I also have five grandchildren and I love them all dearly. I think they like me, too.

Are you teaching them about stocks?
Yes. I have one grandson and stock is all he has ever heard. He is now an analyst with Scott-Stringfellow in Richmond, Virginia. He is very sharp. He is 24 years old and attended Texas Christian University. After college, a friend of mine in Dallas named Don Hodges of First Dallas Securities hired him as an analyst, but he received an offer from Scott-Stringfellow that he felt he could not turn down. He is also a pilot and flies everywhere.

All he ever heard was stocks from his Grandmother because his parents had separated and he stayed with me a lot. Now he loves it. He has the background in the markets that I lacked.

I am sure that I will not be like anyone else that you have interviewed. My advice to readers is, "You can do it, I know you can. Anybody can if you just use your head a little."

MODELING STUDY

CHILDHOOD FAMILY STATUS
- Alta Wood experienced a middle class upbringing in a newly settled region of the Great Plains in Texas

MENTORING - INFLUENCES
- Family enjoyed each other's company
- Father entrepreneurial

ENVIRONMENT
- Four sisters and two brothers

EDUCATION
- Self-education--read books under the covers

INTERESTS - Skills - Abilities - Honors
Childhood
- Read anything and everything
- Liked music
- Imaginative in creating playful activities

Adult
- Likes to make money better then anything else
- Loves to travel

QUALITIES
- Resourceful
- Risk taker
- Gutsy
- Street smart
- Independent thinker

BUSINESS EXPERIENCE
- Worked in retail store
- Housewife to rancher
- Managed a farming and ranching operation

PROSPERITY CONSCIOUSNESS
- Loves to give to family

TRADING EXPERIENCE
- Stock club
- Fundamentalist equity trader

RECOMMENDATIONS
- *Forbes' Magazine*
- *Barron Weekly*
- *Fortune Magazine*
- *Investors' Business Daily*
- All other newspapers

TRADER CONTRIBUTIONS
- Taught grandson to be a trader

FUTURE PLANS
- Plans to keep enjoying the process of making money, traveling, and enjoying grandchildren

TRADER GEMS - Fundamental - Intuitive - Psychological
- Find out what political representatives are buying
- Buy good stocks and hold them for the long haul
- Do not sell a stock if it cost you more to sell
- Be patient and not greedy
- Research companies thoroughly in newspapers and libraries
- Invest every year while watching your money grow
- Invest with companies that are not heavily in debt
- Buy stock in companies that make things that people use

- Realize that if you own a domestic stock that is bought by a foreign company, you pay capital gains tax on the transaction even if you do not sell the stock
- Anyone can make money in the markets if they use their head
- Long-term stock trading can be very profitable by looking at fundamentals
- Study fundamental information such as price-earnings ratios, net profits, etc. You should buy companies with good fundamental strength and hold the stock as long as the fundamentals stay strong
- Learn as much as possible about a company and its product line before investing for the long-term

Murray's Analytical Modeling Study

Trade Methodology Analysis
Mechanical--Objective: Analyze the strength of the fundamentals, management, and product line of the company stock to be purchased.
Mechanical--Automatic: None

Discretionary: When to buy a company with good fundamentals based on price action

Analysis of Alta's Methodology
Alta Wood has a trading style that is perfectly suited for people that do not want to be traders, but have long-term goals of money for retirement or college funds for their children. The problem with this system is that you must stick with good companies though bear markets. One way to make Alta's plan work is by using dollar cost averaging. An example of this is investing $200 a month in a dividend reinvestment plan. These plans, which many large companies will have, allow people to buy stock without a broker, and then use the dividends from their stock to purchase more shares as dividends are paid.

Dividend Reinvestment Plans (DRIPs) and Stockholder Investment Plans (SIPs)
Charles Carlson, CFA, and Editor of *The DRIP Investor Newsletter* estimates one thousand companies offer Dividend Reinvestment Plans and Shareholder Investment Plans. These plans allow shareholders to purchase stock directly from the company and bypass the broker and commissions either through dividend reinvestment or additional voluntary cash investment.

It is not surprising that many investors have not heard of these plans and the advantages that they provide. They are fairly new investment vehicles, and it is also unusual that a stockbroker would recommend a stock purchase where no commission is involved.

There are two different types of plans. One requires the use of an outside bank trustee with the shares being purchased on the open market with the issuing company subsidizing the transaction cost. The second type of plan that allows the shareholder to purchase directly from the company may provide for a discount in the stock price, which gives a substantial advantage to the subscribing shareholder. It also provides the corporation with a benefit because it reduces the cost that would be incurred in a typical capital raising transaction.

Here are useful investment rules to remember when considering a Dividend Reinvestment Plan:

- Remember that when you sell, two bad things that can impact your portfolio over time are going to occur. You will incur transaction costs and tax liability if there is a gain in the stock.
- Be patient and maintain a long-term perspective--Dividend reinvestment investing is a marathon and not a sprint
- Take advantage of stock price dips to add to positions in a quality dividend reinvestment plan

There is a large amount of information about Dividend Reinvestment Plans and Shareholder Investment Plans on the Internet.

Adrienne's Psychological Modeling Study

The Model Common Sense

Alta Wood began trading in stocks at a time when women were generally in the home, which is where she started. However, the death of her rancher husband threw her into a situation where she had to sink or swim. What kept her afloat was a combination of personal qualities, the most important being her Common Sense and resourcefulness. Alta's background was the kind that provided her with strong models for doing the sensible thing. Farming and ranching depends upon a combination of hard work, realistic thinking, combined with a strong faith in the future and the ability to solve problems with the resources at hand. One of the important influences in creating this very grounded mentality was the fact that her childhood "wasn't a very exciting life." She did not have the instability in her life which forces many traders to trade for excitement and drama.

This unexciting childhood and her parents' willingness to do the very hard things as a way of life provided Alta with the models upon which to draw. When faced with the challenge of investing for the future, Alta was not victim to greed or the need for excitement that sabotages the efforts of so many traders. Alta loved making money, but was content to let it happen over an extended period of time. Once again, the experience of a farm and ranch, where crops and livestock grow at nature's pace, provides Alta a Common Sense Model for investing.

When we talk about Common Sense, we are referring to the ability to see things the way they are and to access our sense of what is happening without the distortions that come from our own desires, prejudices and emotions. Stripped of these filters, a person with Common Sense can make decisions based upon the facts and be guided by his or her own goals and intuition. Intuition is a very important component of Common Sense because it is the feeling you get based upon the collection of unconscious cues from the environment. When a person is not well grounded psychologically, they are often not in touch with their intuition or it is distorted by emotions.

For this reason, Alta was able to select companies for their potential as long-term holds. She took what she knew about the way the world works, did her research, bought her stocks, and held them while they grew. It sounds simple, but it is very difficult for most people who need constant action and rewards to keep them interested in the process.

Some other factors in Alta's life which created her Common Sense Model were the fact that she had to deal with two of life's hard realities - death and taxes. Her husband's death at an early age, and the fact that she was liable for the estate taxes due on her land kept her thinking very grounded to experience. The other factors have to do with the fact that farming is a very tangible experience. You have land, crops, and livestock. You can see them, touch them, and watch them grow or die. This keeps your thinking very grounded in reality. When Alta discusses the companies in which she invested, she looks at the factors which are tangible. Do they make products she knows and understands? Are they as fiscally responsible as she has had to be to keep her ranch afloat? Is their management as sensible as she is? When Alta says, "I really just fly by the seat of my pants," she is not referring to the haphazard and self-indulgent gambling so many traders engage in. Alta has learned to rely upon the Common Sense Model that she has developed over a lifetime.

CHAPTER 11

Al Gerebizza

His own genie in a bottle - How he used motivation
to penetrate the institutional market and
build a lucrative money management business.

Where were you born?
I was born in Chicago at Columbus Hospital. We lived right in the heart of downtown Chicago, off of Grand and Wells. Our neighborhood was made up mostly of immigrants. In fact, my parents were both originally from Italy.

What are your most poignant memories of your parents from when you were a child?
My father made great home-pressed wine. I have been a wine drinker since I was three years old, which explains my current collection of wines. My father passed away when I was 5 years old. He died of carbon monoxide poisoning. From what I understand about that situation, my parents had an argument and my father went out drinking that night. He fell asleep in the garage with the car engine running when he returned home.

His passing was very tragic for you and your mother. Did your mother remarry?
My mother remarried when I was 12 years old. She married a man who had never been married even though he was in his mid-forties. He was a good provider and was generally a good man, but we never did any of the father-son kind of things. Beside his work and reading the newspaper, he had no interests that we could share.

What was your mother like?
My mother was a tough lady who was very hardworking. She had to be tough and hardworking, because her life was very difficult. My

step father was her third husband. Her first husband passed way from cholera when she was still in Italy, and she had a son and daughter to raise. Now, at seventy-five with three husbands who have preceded her, she does not care to marry again.

Can you tell us something about your brother and sister?
My sister got divorced after five years of marriage, and as a result, went into seclusion. My mother ended up raising her daughter. Because of the closeness of our ages, she was like a sister to me. My brother and sister are both 15 years older than I am.

What was it like when you were a kid growing up in Chicago?
We lived in a nice home, but in an area where the kids were in gangs. After my father passed away, my mother sold our house and we moved to a better neighborhood. It was very fortunate for me that we moved, because if we had stayed there, I could have gotten involved with the gangs and the problems related to them.

I struggled through grade school because I had a difficult time with many of my subjects, especially algebra. My mother and stepfather knew nothing about algebra, so there was no one to tutor me. All through grade school, my grades were not good.

What were the activities that you liked after school?
I liked sports. I liked baseball and football, but my favorite sport was ice hockey. Even when it was 15 degrees below zero, I would want to play. I enjoyed riding my bicycle and doing anything that was action related.

Did you have any major disappointments as a child?
One of my most disappointing experiences occurred when I played Little League baseball. It was very big at the time, and I signed myself up to play. Parents were not as involved with activities as they are today. I remember telling my mother about my uniform, which I was so proud of. She did not show any enthusiasm for my playing

baseball. I cannot think of a time when anyone came to see me play in Little League or any other activity. My coach did not put me in the field to play very often, but there was a time that I had an opportunity to show that I was a good player. I was in right field and the ball was hit right to me. When I tried to field it, it went straight through my legs. That experience made me feel as low as I could possibly go. I was so embarrassed about it that I did not play any more Little League baseball.

Did you ever have an opportunity to recover from that blow?
At the beginning of my sophomore year in high school, I finally picked myself up and said, "I am going to turn myself around and try out for the football team." My dreams made me a football hero. But, after two weeks of playing football, I shattered my ankle in seven places. This was another major let down for me towards being a sports hero.

Did you have any great experiences?
One of my best experiences of all time happened when I was 13. I had joined the Boys' Club of America, and went to summer camp for a whole month with a couple of my friends. It was great to be outdoors.

I learned a big lesson at camp by picking a fight. I wanted to show how tough I was, so I acted like a bully. The kid that I picked to fight beat me up instead.

It was probably a treat getting out of the city.
I hated being in the city. Any opportunity that I had to get into nature, I grabbed. When my father was alive, we would go to Wisconsin. If they told me on Tuesday that we would be going to Wisconsin that coming weekend, I would sit at the window every day dreaming about that cottage on the lake among the trees.

What was it like going to high school?
Even though I went to a Catholic boys' school, I hung out with a rough

crowd that liked getting into fights and brawls. The boys' school was next door to the Catholic girls' school, but it was almost impossible to mix with them socially. So, we traveled into the other suburbs to date girls there and see if we could cause a bit of a ruckus.

Did you have any part time jobs while you were in school?
I was always trying to maximize my time and earn as much money as I could. I would do almost anything to earn money. I sold vacuum cleaners for a month or two. I had a job as a stock boy in one of the local grocery stores, which was a fun job. Then, I worked in the delicatessen at a grocery chain. I liked that job and stayed with it throughout high school. I made better than average money and worked as many hours as I could get. Everyone liked me because I was a very good employee.

After high school, what did you decide you wanted to study in college?
In college, I studied architecture with a minor in business. I really loved the business courses because I had good teachers who gave me good practical applications. One of the instructors had several side businesses such as a Christmas tree business during the holidays. He was a big influence on me because he demonstrated what he was teaching by earning money in many ways. He was a good example of making more money by working harder and smarter. I did not like being paid by the hour. I like to have the incentive of making more money by consolidating my efforts.

Did you feel this was possible in architecture?
No, there was not much money in it for starters, and I did not have the patience to wait for 15 or 20 years hoping to be one of the few that made an exceptional living at it.

What did you do after college?
A friend's father owned a car dealership in Chicago. He talked me into working there for a short time after I finished college. I was sold

on working for him because there was a new car that came with the job. What 22-year old guy would not want a new car? It was a good experience for me because it taught me how to relate to people. I would recommend selling cars to anyone, at least for a short period of time for that very reason. There are not many jobs that are older than horse-trading, and that is what car sales is all about. I did not like selling cars too much, but I did well at it.

Where did you go from there?
After six months of selling cars on the floor, they decided to put me in the finance department. That was a smart move for them because I liked putting deals together. I increased their revenue from car sales drastically in just 3 months. The year that I spent in their finance department was a valuable learning experience for me and continues to be useful in my career as a money manager.

What brought your time at the car dealership to an end?
I met someone while working at the dealership who worked at the Chicago Board of Trade. When he described his job, it was very intriguing to me. About a month later, my parents invited friends over for a Christmas dinner and their daughter brought her fiancé, who was a soybean broker. I must admit that I was impressed by his expensive jewelry and his Mercedes-Benz parked outside. That meeting solid-ified my interest in finding what it took to work at the Board of Trade.

A few weeks later, I started working as a runner for a company called Reynolds Securities. Several years later, Reynolds Securities merged into Dean Witter Reynolds. Eventually, I became a trader and that has been my passion ever since.

How did you develop yourself into a trader?
I saved enough money from being a runner to buy a seat at the Mid-America Commodity Exchange for $15,000. I held that seat for four years while trading there. I did not have enough money to trade for myself, so I got a job as a licensed broker to handle client accounts.

My seat increased in value to $35,000 because of the hot markets in the mid-1970's. I naively thought that my seat would someday be worth one million dollars. Did I learn a big lesson? One of the brokers who had traded there for a number of years told me, "You had better sell this seat right now because it's the highest it's gonna get." He was right. Seat prices went from $35,000 down to $20,000. Even though I made a small profit, it was a major trading experience for me.

What kind of trading methodology were you using and how did you do during that time?
My methodology could best be described as the Gerebizza "Seat of the Pants" Methodology. During the 1970's, high inflation rates drove a strong trend in the markets. It was during the time when the Russian purchase of soybeans pushed the market up to all-time high levels. These were euphoric times in the commodities markets, and everyone wanted to be a commodities broker. I was making good money trading from the information that I was getting from other people.

Where were you getting information?
A friend was working for a major trading company who bought and held. They were buying billions of dollars in soybeans at the time. One of the head officers of the company told me, "Just buy soybeans and hold onto them because they are going to skyrocket." That was my approach as a long-term trader, just buy the stuff and watch it go up. Well, I gained another good trading experience from this time. You guessed it. The market turned on a dime and headed down. Fortunately, I stopped myself out and lost $10,000 of what I had made. At that time, $10,000 was a lot of money to me, and the experience left me devastated.

Where did you go from there?
I worked with Jack Sanders at the Chicago Mercantile Exchange. He was a very influential person in my life, because he was very supportive of my efforts. He helped me lease a seat at the International Monetary Market in Chicago. This was good for me because I

believed that the financial markets had more potential than the agricultural markets at that time. Fortunately, I was right.

Why were currencies attractive to you?
Currencies just seemed to fit me. I liked the fact that I could make up my own contract sizes and did not get charged a commission. I traded the Swiss Franc and the Deutsche Mark.

Did you have any mentors to model in currencies?
One of my mentors was a gentleman who traded heavily in foreign currencies for the Bank of Argentina. He taught me the fundamentals of currency fluctuations.

What trading style did you use when you got into currencies?
I tried scalping, and found it too much of a drain just to make a few dollars per day. I studied Gann theory through Nick Flamboris, who had worked with Gann's partner. Nick knew the in's and out's of Gann theory, so I was very fortunate. I studied Gann for about 10 years and some Elliott Wave theory. But, these methods are too subjective for me, although I made some great calls in the market. I called the top of the big Dollar move in 1985. The problem I had was in trying to apply the techniques to good solid money management. Money management in the early 1980's was very elusive.

Finally in 1981, I put together a plan to do this trading not only from a money management standpoint, but also from a technical standpoint. It's been "on-the-job-training" ever since. My methodology changes based on what the markets are doing.

When did you feel that you were on your way as a money manager?
In 1981, the Bank of Rome gave me $100,000 to manage because they liked what I was doing. With this much money, I thought I had made it as a trader because it felt like I had been given a million dollars. In a way, that was the case because I began to develop more relationships

301

within the banking industry. The world had opened up in the international trading arena, and it felt good to be a part of it.

What happened to your seat?
I let my seat go after two years on the floor because I was trading foreign exchange through the bank. There was no point in handling futures contracts any more.

Were you using Gann and Elliott Wave theory when you were trading for the bank?
Yes. I was using a combination of moving averages with Gann and Elliot Wave. We were spending four or five hours after the close calculating averages because, in the early 1980's, everything had to be calculated by hand. We were also limited to the major currencies because they were the only currencies that were moving.

What criteria did you use for making trading decisions at that time?
We used support and resistance studies, and we looked for market oversold or overbought situations. If the market indicated an oversold condition, we would buy and if the market indicated in an overbought condition, we would sell. Based on Gann's work we would look at the balance points based on time and price, which was the major computation in all of Gann's work. Basically, his theory was balancing time and price yielding a greater occurrence of change in price. The dilemma in Gann studies is that time can be on an hourly basis, a daily basis, a weekly basis, or monthly basis. We recognized that the weekly and monthly scenarios would be best because of their long-range outlook. The drawback was that as markets correct themselves, the correction often goes quite far before the market actually turns. So, in an effort to solve this problem, we had a five-day balance point between long-term and short-term. As time went on, we settled on the intermediate term trading as best suited to us.

When did you finally get computers?
In the latter 1980's, we hooked up with people who were good at

writing programs on computers. It made life much simpler to have the millions of equations computed every day. Then, we used five computers to do the same job that two are doing today.

What was your money management strategy when you were using the Gann Method?
We were trading very subjectively. The money management rules we were using did not risk more than 1% to 3% on a given trade. If we thought the charts were telling us that we had a really great situation for a potential major turnaround, we would try to lay into the position slowly. Then, we would add to the position, or what the traders call "press the market," if it was going our way.

That strategy is very similar to what Richard Dennis used to do. He would test the market, and then press it if it was going his way. We would do the same thing. Initially, we would risk 1%, and if the market went our way, we would press it. The problem with pressing the market or adding on to a position all the time is that market momentum dries up and you end up buying highs and selling lows. When you are pyramiding a position, a relatively small market correction will eat away the initial position. We found that pyramiding did not fit our methodology very well, so we began to test and experiment with other possibilities.

What are some of the things you looked at?
Wells Wilder published a book some years ago, which was a pioneering book on technical analysis. There are probably 15 to 20 methodologies from that time that are still used today. Each methodology has had its heyday in the markets. Moving averages worked great until everybody started using them, and then they did not work as well. Moving average convergence/divergence systems were the same way, as were stochastic analysis, candle stick analysis, and the list goes on. We keep all of these methods of analysis running in the background on all currencies because, at some point, they will start to work again. It is important to keep your toolbox open because you never know when you may need one of those tools again.

How long did you work for the banks?
We always have been working for the banks with outside consulting agreements.

Now you are saying "we." When did you start working with your partner?
Dan Spitzer and I got together in 1987 with another guy named Jeff McKenzie. Jeff was trading bonds for Yamichi Bank. We used his name for our company until he left the partnership after six months. Then Dan and I changed the name from McKenzie to Kenzie because we had some name recognition. A public relations company recommended dropping the "Mc," but keeping the "Kenzie" name in place.

How did you and Dan meet?
Dan and I met at RB&H at the Chicago Mercantile Exchange where he was a broker at the time. Dan has an MBA and came into the partnership with a good business background. I knew I could not work alone if I was going to expand in any kind of business. One of the things that created a bond between us was that we each had debts to pay off. As we paid off our debts, we found that we worked together well as a team.

How did you make the banks happen?
We felt that currencies had great potential because they were not actively traded until the late 1970's. In 1973, the Brenton-Woods Agreement was adopted, which decoupled the dollar from the Gold Standard. This agreement let the dollar float freely against other world currencies.

What was the most difficult part of getting into currencies?
The most difficult part of getting into currency trading was developing a foundation of trust and building good relationships with banks' foreign exchange departments. Now, if you call the foreign exchange departments of City Bank, Chemical Bank, Chase Manhattan Bank, to name a few, they know who Kenzie Management is. It took many

years to develop the trust and rapport that we have with these companies. Our name recognition builds on itself now and because of it, we receive calls every week. Now, we are getting calls from stock firms for alternative forms of investment.

How does this work?

We have developed funds that are partnerships and are very inexpensive to run. They all require $100,000 minimum investments. The people who get involved with these funds are accredited investors, who have a minimum net worth of one million dollars. The trading we do for these clients is aggressive foreign exchange trading. The banks are different in that they tailor their own portfolios.

If a bank has fifty million dollars of risk capital in their foreign exchange department, they are going to give a certain amount of that money to their foreign exchange desk. If they decide to put together some outside managers, they divide the money up between a few of the foreign exchange managers. The way they structure their currency portfolio is based on the number of people trading for them. Most of the traders on their foreign exchange desk are short-term traders, which creates a lot of activity in their portfolio. The foreign exchange managers usually implement strategies that fall between long-term and short-term trading.

The trading that we do for the banks is customized to the individual banking institution. The funds that we do are much more conservative and for individual clients. This is a good business combination for us.

How have you done?

Our compounded rate of return over 18 years is around 45%. If you analyze the last 10-year period, our average rate of return is 39%. In the 1980's, our rates of return were higher because there was more volatility in the markets. The psychology of investors has changed over the years, too. The investors of the Eighties were looking for high risk with high returns. The investors of the Nineties want low risk and decent returns. Their first concern is loss of principal, and the second is consistent returns.

What system or systems do you use now?

We look at each individual currency and use one of the models that we have developed. For example, moving averages work very well with the British Pound. Stochastic analysis works well on the Swiss Franc. To trade the Japanese Yen, we use a momentum breakout system. Each currency has its own characteristics and diplomacy and the effectiveness of each system will be different for each currency. We monitor 45 different currencies on a consistent basis. At this time, there are about 200 world currencies. We cannot monitor all of the currencies at the same time, so we evaluate the strength of each signal on a scale of 1 to10. The signals between 7 and 10 get high priority and are the ones we look to trade. The portfolio is also structured to minimize drawdowns. If a market continues to trend, we will follow its movement with trailing stops. Our risk is minimal then.

Do you use the same risk across the board?

We do everything based on a portfolio basis and not on a currency basis. In other words, we keep our risk within a certain range on a daily basis. If we have a Black Monday or some sudden occurrence in world events causes a day when the markets flip-flop, we know what kind of loss to expect before it happens. We do not want to take a loss on any one day of more than 2% to 3%, and that is a worst case scenario.

Going back to your personal life, did you get married and have a family?

Yes, I got married when I was 23 years old. My wife, Shirley, comes from a family of seven children. She worked at Commerce Clearing House, which is more commonly known as CCH. They have the largest law publishing company in the United States. She was a paralegal by trade, and enjoys expressing herself through artistic endeavors. In this way, we had similar backgrounds and ways of thinking.

Do you have children?

We have four children. The eldest now is sixteen years old and the youngest is four years old. We have two boys and two girls. "Boys for bookends," Shirley likes to say. We have had a good marriage for 20 years with ups and downs like everyone else. A good thing about both of us is that we have learned to work things out. One of the reasons our marriage has worked so well is that Shirley has been very supportive in making my big dreams come true.

In becoming a successful money manager, what was the biggest influence to your success?
Of course, that would have to be the psychology of trading and developing an understanding of it. I used psychology in my trading when it was the last thing traders would consider.

What made you decide to use the psychology of trading when it was still in its infancy?
Trading was frustrating to me at that time because there were certain trades that were out of my grasp. I had taken some psychology classes in college and was a big believer in psychology. I knew that there was an element to trading that I just was not picking up. When I saw your company's advertisement, I contacted you, was evaluated, and signed up for private consulting.

Tell us about that experience?
It was a tremendous personal experience and was nothing like my expectations. I expected to become part of some think-tank and become involved with an elite group of so-called trader prodigies. In essence, I ended up working on many personal issues. The work that we did was very enlightening. My core level understanding was that I had to be happy with myself before I could bring out my best as a trader. Of all the realizations I had, that was my biggest one. I remember being asked what I wanted. My reply was that I wanted to be at peace with myself, which surprised you because most traders who come tell you that they want to make more money.

I knew that if I was not happy with myself, then there was no point in making money. At least, I had enough sense to realize that fact on my own. I still reflect on it as the seed to manifesting the dreams in my life.

One thing that has enhanced the psychological work that we did was filling out your workbook *Treasure Diary for Creating Affluence*. I still work with it today.

Why was it so valuable to you?
The *Treasure Diary* workbook is basically about bringing out and examining the best of yourself. The workbook gives you a place to write your resources, your hopes, dreams and desires. There are many things that can be your resources. They can be people you know, or experiences, or money, or talents, etc. I have discovered that the biggest resources I have are the people in my life and my experiences. These are my real treasures. The *Treasure Diary* provides a place to put your life plan. In one section of the book, you write down a wish list of things that you want to happen in your life. Of everything that I have written down on my wish list, 99% of those things have come true

I am still that deli clerk who needs to know that there is an added incentive of a brass ring out there to grab. That brass ring could span the range from being as materialistic as a new car, to the other extreme of developing myself spiritually.

I used to feel that I was not good enough to be a millionaire. I was not good enough to be successful, and that I was not good enough to have the things that I wanted. I had a problem with money. Sómewhere along the line, I felt that money was evil and that I would get criticized for possessing it. I have happily discovered that none of that is true.

The whole process of working with you has changed my trading, my business relationships, and the relationships with my family. I am not perfect, I still have little flair ups now and again. At least, I can look back at a negative issue and correct it before it becomes too much of an issue.

How do you like to recreate now?
My favorite sports passion is snowmobiling. I also enjoy water skiing, boating, biking, and long rides in the country. I work out with aerobic exercises and weight lifting daily. I work to maintain balance, supporting all areas of my life.

Where do you want to go from here?
We want to continue to do whatever it takes to maintain a quality, professional investment firm. We are looking forward to expanding and going with the flow of what is out there, like that old analogy, "You can't change the direction of the wind, but you can adjust your sails." We like to keep on top of things by designing new funds and developing new relationships with people who can do some of the things we cannot do.

We monitor what is going on with business in general, and keep ourselves informed on the domestic front, as well as international issues. Marketing is important. We work with people in New York who do a good job in marketing and handling our public relations. Our image is very good and because of that, we deal with Fortune 500 companies, which widens the product options for our clients, so they can diversify their investments with us.

Yen Weekly

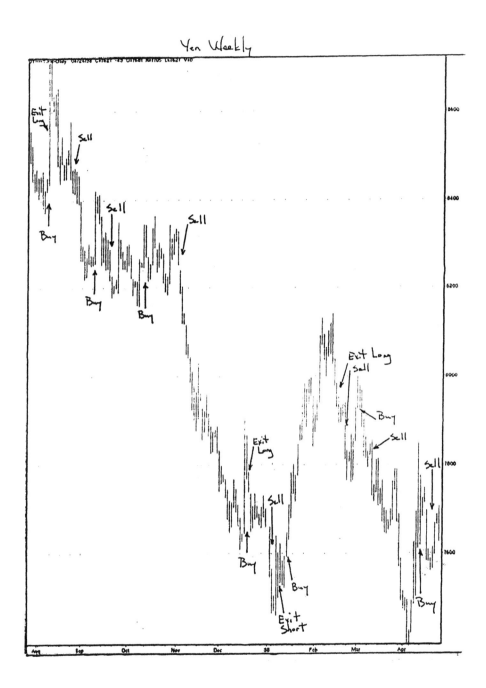

310

Yen Weekly

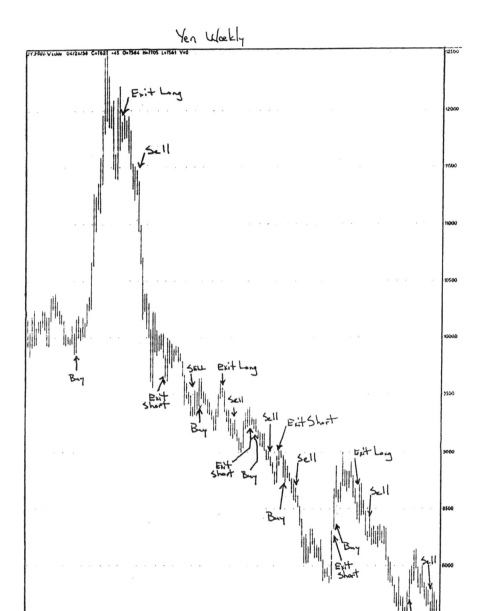

MODELING STUDY

CHILDHOOD FAMILY STATUS
- Al Gerebizza had a humble beginning to middle class Chicago

MENTORING - INFLUENCES
- Lost father in a tragic accident when he was young
- Little family support
- Teacher -- Mentored entrepreneurial skills
- Trader friend -- Mentored fundamentals of currency fluctuations
- Supportive wife
- Nick Flambouras -- Mentored Gann and Elliott Wave Theory
- Richard Dennis
- Adrienne Toghraie -- Psychology of trading

ENVIRONMENT
- No father and son activities
- Catholic boys' school

EDUCATION
- In grade school, low grades
- Bachelor of Arts Degree in Architecture with a minor in Business

INTERESTS -Skills - Abilities -Honors
Childhood
- Ice Skating
- Biking
- Baseball
- Action related sports
- Camp activities

Adult
- Wine collector

- Snowmobiling
- Water skiing
- Boating
- Biking
- Racquetball
- Long rides in the country

QUALITIES
- Artistic
- Relates well to people
- Likes putting together deals
- Motivated by material possessions
- Persistent
- Goal oriented

BUSINESS EXPERIENCE
- Sold vacuum cleaners
- Grocery stock boy
- Worked for delicatessen and local grocery chain
- Worked for car dealership in sales and finance departments

PHILOSOPHY - SUCCESS BELIEFS
- Maximize time and earn as much money as possible
- Consolidated efforts with incentives motivate hard work

PROSPERITY CONSCIOUSNESS
- Local parish

TRADING EXPERIENCE
- Held seat on Mid-America Exchange
- Licensed commodities broker handing client accounts
- Runner at Chicago Board of Trade
- Floor trader
- Currency trader at Chicago Mercantile Exchange
- Currency money manager

RECOMMENDATIONS
- Wells Wilder's products
- *Treasury Diary for Creating Wealth & Happiness* by Adrienne Toghraie
- *Market Wizards* by Jack Schwager

TRADER CONTRIBUTIONS
- Makes money for clients

FUTURE PLANS
- Continue to expand firm and design new funds
- Develop new relationships to expand diversification of our portfolios

TRADER GEMS - Fundamental - Intuitive - Psychological
- Methodology changes based upon what the markets are doing
- It is important to track all methods because they might wind up being useful in the current market
- Investors of the 90's want low risk and decent returns
- The effectiveness of systems is different for each currency
- Evaluate the strength of each currency and trade the strongest
- Keep risk consistent
- You must be happy inside before you can bring out the best in yourself as a trader. It is the seed to manifesting your dreams
- Al can always see his goals. He uses a *Treasure Diary* where he writes his goals and dreams with plans to make them happen

TRADER GEMS - Mechanical - Analytical - Technical
- Gann work on Time and Price Balancing is an important concept in trading and is a little understood technical area
- Moving averages work well in the British Pound, stochastic analysis in the Swiss-Franc, and momentum breakout in the Yen
- Al trades the world's major currencies and ranks the strength

of potential trades to select the ones to take positions in. This decision is made based upon a model developed to minimize drawdown

- Many classic indicator systems that worked on the currencies have degraded because too many people started to trade them. These include moving averages, Moving Average Convergence Divergence, stochastic analysis, etc. He monitors them because they might start to work again

Murray's Analytical Modeling Study

Trading Methodology Analysis

Mechanical--Objective: Use of price patterns and calculation of Gann levels of time and price.

Mechanical--Automatic: Charts indicators used in analysis

Discretionary: Combining the work of Gann with subjective price patterns and indicators to make trades

Analysis of Al's Methodology

Al uses Gann's time and price relationship analysis, but did not explain his method. For this reason, we will take a sidebar and look at some of this material as it was published in Gann's classic work, *How to Make Profits in Commodities*. In this book, he discusses analysis of the grain market using his concept of time and price. Let's discuss some of Gann's Gems.

- A 50% and 100% advance from any bottom in price are the most important points to look for resistance. Other levels of resistance are calculated by dividing the low price by 8. For example, 12.5%, 25%, 33.33%, 37.5% etc. In addition to this method, he used the size of moves and the same percentages to forecast more price levels. This develops 16 different price levels from a low. Prices where numbers are similar are more important levels.

- Gann studied time and divided the year into 8 which is about 45 days (1.5 months) or 6.5 weeks. This is why Gann often used seven weeks after a major bottom or top as an important point. Multiples of 1.5 months are also important for timing.

- Another important time element is identifying the months during the year in which major tops and bottoms occur.

Case Study of Gann Analysis

We will look at a case study and demonstrate how some of the Gann ideas work.

We will study a market that did not exist when Gann traded, the T-Bond market. First, we will record major lows on a monthly basis:

Month	Price
May, 1984	58.75
Oct, 1987	76.219
Nov, 1994	96.031

Next, Gann calculated Natural Resistance Levels from these prices. The following Table shows this analysis:

Analysis of Gann Natural Resistance Levels

Month	Year	Price	25%	37.5%	50%	62.5%	75%	100%
May	84	58.75	73.4375	80.78125	88.125	95.46875	102.8125	117.5
Oct	87	76.219	95.2737	104.8011	114.3285	123.8559	133.3833	152.438
Nov	94	96.031	120.0388	132.0426	144.0465	156.0504	168.0543	192.062

Some of the levels in this Table have been important to the T-Bond market. One example is the 95-00 price level, 95.27, which is at the 25% level from the 1987 bottom and 95.47, which is 62.5% from the 1984 bottom represented by the 95-00 price level. This level was important to the T-Bond market until the 1994 bottom. Bonds formed a minor top in 1990, just below this level and reached congestion just above it in 1991. This level was also less than one point above the major low in 1994. T-Bonds also topped in October of 1998 at 135.125. This is within three points of the 132.0426, which is at the 37.5% level above the November 1994 low, and 133.3833, which is 75% above the October 1987 low.

- Gann used the size of the move and the same multipliers to find these levels. Taking the 1995 high at 121.031 and subtracting the 1994 low of 96.031, gives a 25-point move. If we subtract 62.5% of this number from the high, we get 105.406, which is a few ticks from the actual low of October 1996 at 105.281.
- An example of the time element of major tops and bottoms is in the corn market where we would look for lows to occur in November, February, and April with tops occurring in June and July. If we combined this information with Gann price targets and assumed that both time and price targets overlap, the market should form a reaction near these points.
- If you want to trade based on a momentum trend, following the Yen is the best of the currencies. Let's look at a simple channel breakout system. Our simple rules are as follows:

Buy at Highest (high,N) stop;
Sell at Lowest (Low,N) stop;

Our research on the three major currencies, Yen, D-Mark, and Swiss Franc from 1/2/80 to 9/14/98 shows that the Yen produced the best overall results using an N of 12 days with no deduction made for slippage or commissions:

Net Profit	$169,638.75
Trades	189
Win%	45 %
Ave Trade	897.56
Drawdown	$ 12,787.50
Profit Factor	2.26

Using this system, the next best overall result on another currency was that of the Swiss Franc with a net profit of $143,436.25 and a drawdown of $14,511.25 for an N of 24 days over this same time period.

Al uses classic methods combined with his feel for the currency markets. He uses these technical tools to monitor them and then makes his trading decisions.

Adrienne's Psychological Modeling Study

The Toy Model

Acquiring toys can become a compelling motivation for a young boy born into a community of poor immigrants who came to this country expecting the streets to be paved with gold. Many of these immigrants saw hard work itself as the opportunity to achieve material success, having come from countries where the opportunity to work was not available.

When Al was five years old, he was given an additional reason to build his model for success when his father died and his mother had to work very hard to provide the necessities of life. For the rest of his life, Al would have the model of hard work from his mother. He learned that if he wanted to pave his own streets with gold, it would take his own initiative. In the midst of this bare-boned childhood, Al must have looked around at the people who had all of the things that he did not have and determined to do whatever it would take to fulfill those wants. This was the beginning of the "Toy Model."

The main goal for Al's family was to get away from the poor neighborhood in Chicago to a good neighborhood because they feared the temptations of gang life for young Al. At school and around him, boys were fighting, but Al stayed away from it. Then, one day, Al decided to pick a fight with a boy he thought he could best and got his running lights knocked out. He learned that if he were going to fight his way to success, it could not be as a bully or stepping over the people beneath you.

Another childhood experience that shaped Al's model was a traumatic experience for Al as a little leaguer when he dropped the ball. This experience shaped his determination to never drop the ball in life.

As Al grew up, he says, "I always tried to maximize my time and earn as much money as I could. I would do almost anything to earn money." Those things ran from selling vacuum cleaners door to door, to being a stock boy in local grocery store, to working in a delicatessen. From these experiences, Al gained extensive people skills, a sense of methodical order, and an appreciation for incentives. Then, in the process of studying to become an architect, he was challenged to put into practice what he was learning about business in one of the business courses he loved. The result was selling Christmas trees. Suddenly, Al was making money for himself. "I liked to have the incentive of having more money by consolidating my efforts." Also, in college, he worked for a car dealership. The incentive was getting his own car, his first major toy.

A broker with expensive toys was responsible for attracting Al to the world of finance. Young Al saw a tremendous opportunity in working at the Mid American Exchange. He worked himself up the ladder using what he describes as his "seat-of-the-pants method-ology." This analogy is not entirely accurate. People like Al that are motivated from childhood by the Toy Model have nearly unerring instincts for making the right decisions in order to reach their goals. Their intuition is often extremely well developed and provides them with an excellent guide in decision making that can stand alone or accompany an analytical methodology.

He went into the currency markets, studied Gann theory and Elliott wave for ten years, but traded intuitively, as usual. Then, when he went into partnership with Dan Spitzer, it was a match made in heaven. Dan was the perfect salesman and Al did the trading. Since Al is determined to succeed, he always works for what is best in the situation. He does this by trading many systems and applying the right system to the right situation.

One of Al's strategies is to be constantly looking for mentors. Perhaps this is an effort to fill the gap left by the loss of his father.

Nevertheless, it has helped him to reach his goals and acquire his toys. As a result of his Toy Model, I consider him to be one of my best clients because he has applied all of my recommendations and understands that balancing each part of his life is essential to his success. If this meant getting his next toy, Al was going to do whatever it took to obtain it. As a result, his company went from zero to ten million under management in six months.

The Toy Model has many benefits for a trader. Because it is a very palpable, tangible goal, it is very easy for the unconscious mind to visualize. As a result, it is a very powerful motivator. Secondly, the Toy Model provides immediate feedback and positive reinforcement. If you get the car, it proves that you have reached your goal, making you more likely to try for the next toy. And third, the Toy Model is an evolving model. As an individual acquires all of the toys on his wish list, then he is free to look around and ask himself the question: "Is this all there is?" The result for so many toy seekers is the gradual replacement of material toys with less tangible, adult ones. Some principle examples of these "adult toys" are overcoming personal limitations, advanced education, awareness, peace of mind, spiritual awakening, joyful relationships, giving to others, and goals for the betterment of world.

As a follower of the Toy Model, Al has shifted into this advanced, adult Toy Model. Yes, he still enjoys bringing home the expensive toys such as the second home, the new car, the snowmobiles, and the boats for himself and his family. But, he also enjoys the recognition that he has grown in his life, marking those milestones as he does the acquisition of his toys.

CHAPTER 12

Mike Battle

Sticking to his guns - How a young trader stands on his principles to live a balanced life and still manages to average 100-200% a year in returns.

Would you tell us about where you were born? About your family? Where you lived?. . . Generally about the first part of your life?

My parents were Irish immigrants into England. I was born in a suburb of London, and have lived all of my life within 15 miles of the city. I am the youngest of five children. My father, being an immigrant, made his way in the world, but he had to start near the low end of the spectrum to begin his life in a new country. As for family life, I have always had a very happy and supportive family. I have two elder brothers and two elder sisters and I consider them good friends. They live reasonably close to me, so there is a great support network.

What did your Dad do?

He started off as a decorator, drove buses, then ended up working his way up the ranks in a merchant bank. I suppose you would say to middle class income. We lived in a reasonably nice area of town. He was very aware of the responsibility of raising five children and wanted us to live in an environment which would support the ideals and aspirations he had for his children. We all benefited from going to reasonable schools with good peer groups with which to interact.

Tell us about how your parents met?

They met in Ireland, but they came to England independently. They lived about 50 miles apart on the western coast of Ireland. They met at a dance.

Your mother was basically a home keeper?
With five children to raise, she had a full-time job as a home keeper, but she also worked the night shift as a nurse.

Tell us about your young years.
I was always physically able because I was constantly wrestling with my older brothers. The physical side of things seemed very natural to me.

I was not that taken with formal education. To tell you the truth, it did not feel natural. Maybe I had a few stumps early on that spooked me into liking school, but it seemed more of a chore rather than something I enjoyed. I do not think I ever went into school skipping happily thinking about mathematics and English. I was more of a physical child, but I was fully able to get through school as well.

Tell us about when you went to high school. Was there anything that you really excelled in or enjoyed?
I am particularly artistic. I was a natural straight "A" student in anything that I have ever done relating to art.

What type of art did you like?
When I was in school, I liked fine art - still life paintings and so on. If I had not ended up becoming a trader, I would have chosen a profession where I could have been artistic. I seemed to be able to throw things together and people were amazed at the results. I seem to have a photographic memory for colors and patterns - things that go together and things that do not go together. My visual awareness started very early on.

Did you have any type of entrepreneurial spirit when you were a child?
Yes, I did. Have you ever heard of the Mini-Mouse car? In the 1960's, when they first came out, they were very successful rallying. When I was in my late teens, my friend and I organized a production

line painting them and fitting them inside and out with all of the extras that people wanted in them and sold them.

I had quite a lot to do with cars because I had a good friend whose father owned a garage. We both enjoyed cars and used to make a bit of money buying them, then fixing and selling them.

After high school did you go on to college or did you start working?
I did not go on to college, even though I did reasonably well in school. When I was at that crossroad in life, I did not see the path of my education moving towards a higher academic education. It did not seem that it was my destiny. I had a few different job interviews where I asked, "If I came back in two years time, with two more years of education, would I start at a better rate than I would now, and would it help me for future promotions?" They said, "Not really. If you are going to go right through and study at University, then that would make a difference, but otherwise it would not." I left school at sixteen.

Then what did you do?
I worked in the clerical back office of a brokerage firm. I seemed to do well because of my enthusiasm. I would settle the business that was done during the day. Once I showed a reasonable start in the back office, I was promoted to work down on the old stock exchange floor as a dealer for a couple of years.

Then we had what we called the "Big Bang" over here, where most of your American banks bought our brokers and stock-jobbers. These were people who were historically single capacity in that they were either brokers or market makers. After this, they became dual capacity. I worked for one of the brokerage companies that was taken over. As my position had to do with trading on the floor in a broker's capacity, I had the offer to become a market maker, which I took. Basically, you would type in the price that you were prepared to buy and sell stocks. Ideally, you would have a buyer and a seller come to you reasonably at the same time, match them and take a turn in the middle. My experiences were hit and miss. I felt like a target because insider traders would pick off market makers, who did not know what was going on in a stock. I was at the front end of the operation, trading the shares. The analysts were the back-end of the operation. Because the company was not particularly eminent in this area, it never really got that much business from it. I was very vulnerable to being taken out by someone who knew the correct stock price. This was a revolution in the industry, and the people in charge did not know how to manage this evolution of the business. Since no one wanted or knew how to take responsibility, I was pushed into having to make decisions in areas that I was not trained for.

How did you learn to trade?
I ended up teaching myself to trade and modeled other traders when I could. It seemed that no one really knew what he was doing. The guy in charge of the office was a broker. Even though he did not understand market making, he was put in the position. The trading company was actually owned by Midland Bank and they stopped trading because they were not making any money. In spite of this, I was making money. One of the reasons I was profitable was my defensive and reserved approach, even though I really did not know what I was doing. There were others who did not care about being reckless with money. There were 20 to 25 books of different sets or sections, i.e., construction companies and pharmaceutical companies. My book was the only one that made money, which pleased me.

What did you do specifically that was different?
I was attempting to learn the business by feeling my way into the job, as opposed to taking every trade because I was labeled a trader. The others took on rubbish positions that everyone was trying to get rid of within the market. Instead of charging in, I tried to sit back a bit and let the market tell me how it was.

So what happened after that?
I was making moves to leave the firm, but as it happens, they went bust. Since I had miraculously managed to make money against the odds, the guy who was in charge of the room gave me a few introductions. I narrowed my job options down to Security Pacific and Goldman-Sachs. Each company offered different benefits, but Security Pacific's position offered me a supervisor who would be my trader role model.

Goldman-Sachs was just beginning to operate in London, especially in the market-making area. I was interviewed by everyone in the company, and flown to New York to meet people at the main office. The company philosophy was to introduce the whole team and if no one blocks your path, then you get the job. The fact that I did not go to college spooked them. One of the head people asked me, "Why are you so good?" I said, "All I do is find out how much it is going to cost me if the trade does not work out, and what I will make if it goes in my direction."

If the probabilities are there to make money, you take the trade?
It was more innocent than that. I was not even thinking about probability or statistics. All I was thinking about was the next trade in front of me. Where is the buyer? Where is the seller? You sort of sticky tape a few ideas together. You think the market is going up, and you say that you can cut the trade 8 points below. That was my system. It was nothing that I had read in a book. From my earlier experiences of running a trading book, I had learned the Laws of the Jungle. The best way to protect myself was by realizing what a loss was going to cost me. If I thought the trade was worth the risk, I would give it a go.

Did you work with them?
No, they offered me the job, but I knocked them back.

Why did you do that?

I kept saying the word "spooked" to myself. New York was a new experience for me. Being introduced to it first class with all of the razzmataz at 21 years old was very exciting. After my all day interview, I went to a 7:00 P.M. dinner with a few of the traders on the desk. In the course of conversation, I found out that many of the people working there had not taken a week's vacation in the last 17 years. One of the guys who worked the Australian market was going back to the office to take calls at 9:30 P.M. He also said that he had to be back in the office at 6:30 A.M.

Is that why you chose Security Pacific?

I went with Security Pacific mainly because I thought I would learn more from them. I wanted to go somewhere where I could learn market making. When you are a broker, you are like a bit of meat in a sandwich. I used to get complaints from the salesmen in the office asking why I did not get them more for their stock. Then, you would get complaints from the jobber on the floor asking for more takedown on the stock. I hated being in the middle of that, having to put up with complaints from the two sides of the coin. I wanted to be responsible so that when I said buy or sell, it was from me.

Is that what you got when you went with Security Pacific?

I started at Security Pacific, but again, there was no training. They gave me a book of stocks and said, "You are now a paper market trader." With the equivalent of 10 million quid to balance my books, I was told to go trade. That was it. I had to make my way from there. Again, I miraculously managed money, but this was after lots of ups and downs. I was not that much of a shooting star, just consistent.

Tell us about your experience at Security Pacific?

Within two years, I had moved up the greasy pole to an Assistant Director position. I was in charge of about ten people while continuing to do market making. This was the late 1980's and the industry was exploding. People were asked if they could say the

330

word "trader" and given a job with a "yes" response. I was taken on at 22, just before the big rally that led to the Crash.

How did you do during the Crash?
To start with, I was like a stunned animal. I could not believe the size of the moves that the market was making. Toward the end of the week, I started to have some fun. Early in the week, I lost a lot of money. I tried to fight the pain of realizing the loss. Every time the market rallied, I was as quick as anyone trying to move the prices back up. But then as soon as the market went down, I went all the way down again.

In general, do you now have a bias toward being long or short?
Short. I do not know if that is something that I learned in the Crash. It might be. When you are aggressive in a down market, you can have much more control because you are trading off of people's fears. People get very erratic then. When the market is going up, apart from the day traders, you do not get that sort of raw panic where people will just take anything. You get very fierce rallies, but from my experience, I invariably make more money in the down market.

How long did you stay with Security Pacific?
I was at Security Pacific for about two years.

So, after you became a manager, you did not stay very long?
No. I had an offer from an ex-colleague who was setting up a futures brokerage firm. He had some clients that did a bit of volume in futures. He was to do the brokering and I was to do the trading. The carrot for me was that he was going to give me half the commission that he made and half the money I made trading. The theory was that if we had a bad day, the commissions would bail us out. If he had a good day on commissions, and I had a good day trading, we would be rich. That was the trigger that got me out of Security Pacific.

331

Was it still in the same area of London?
Yes, it was. One of the reasons that I was happy to leave Security Pacific was that my role model had made a few moves in Security Pacific and gotten into a position where he had to resign. This other guy took over a year after I joined. He was erratic, aggressive, and his management style was very hostile. Often the people that were succeeding in the company were his close friends, and it came to the point where you had to drink in a certain bar to get your career going. That was not my style, so I was quite happy when this offer came along for me to move on to other things.

I went into the partnership with this other chap. While we were setting the firm up, we were sitting next to each other in a bucket shop, which is a very low-key brokerage. It picks up all of the hot business, all of the wrong traders, and is not a professional outfit. It was very much on the borderline.

It gives you a desk to trade at and allows you to trade and keep some of the commissions because they are underwriting the tickets. For example, they are charging you $10 U.S. for a ticket and you are charging $20 U.S. for it.
Yes, that is right. They were doing all sorts of things that I would not want to put my name to. I was going to be there for a month or two while setting up the operation with my new partner. But while we were setting up the new operation, my new partner could not leave trading alone. He was trading markets night and day, losing money and half of it was my money. Not only could he not leave trading alone, but he also started to neglect his clients. At that point, we decided to part company rather than continue on.

The guy who was in charge of the trading room at Security Pacific rang me to offer my old job back. I was faced with the choice of carrying on in what some people might consider an easy life working in a big bank with the fringe benefits, or I could start on my own. I figured that if it did not work at age 23, I had no real costs.

Were you in a serious personal relationship?
Yes, I was seeing the lady who now is my wife. We were not going to get married for at least a good two years. I have been with the same lady since I was 18. I am now 32.

What did you decide to do?
I decided to give it a crack on my own and trade the futures market. I did not know one end of a price quote from the other. I had this intuitive talent for trading, but I did not understand why, or how it worked.

How much were you trading with?
I began trading with 30,000 Sterling.

What was that worth in U.S. dollars back then?
That would have been worth about $53,000 U.S. I traded in a room full of people where there were a lot of desk kickers. By this time, I was reasonably confident in my ability to trade stocks, so I traded large positions. But this was a whole new arena for me where I did not know exactly what I was doing, so I decided to learn. I tried many different things.

Back in those days, did you have the computer power to test an idea before you traded it?
No, I was even hungrier than that. I was quite prepared to look at a few examples of an idea and give it a go. If somebody would tell me and show me a few charts that I had never seen before saying this happens and the market goes up, this happens, and this happens, and the market goes down, I would give it a go.

When did you "get religion?"
Ultimately, you have to learn that trading is incredibly difficult, and then, eventually realize that trading is simple. That is sort of where I am now.

Let's go step by step to how you got to now.
I came to the book *Mind Over Markets* by Jim Dalton. It dissects the basics of the Market Profile system developed in the early 1980's by Peter Steidlmayer. It also takes you through quite gently as well. Some of the technical books get a bit heavy too quickly. You really do not understand the information that you have been given, and then they say now use what you have been given and you get completely confused. I went through the basics of what I was actually attempting to do and what the market was trying to do. I learned that if I align myself with those things then I would make money. And I did.

When I first started trading as a market maker, I felt my way into it. It was like a jungle and you stepped into it slowly. Instead of the idea of taking one or two examples and thinking you understand the meaning of life, I started working from the other way. I would take three examples and give it the benefit of the doubt, but I was quite skeptical. I also became intolerant of things that I did not understand. People always want to teach you their religion and they are not happy when you tell them that you are happy with your system. They try to sell you on Gann, Elliott Wave, or stochastic analysis, or anything else that is out there.

This profile approach seemed very logical, graphically based, visual and simple. I believed in the main tenants, the foundation, the philosophy of how the markets worked, and how it is reflected through the profile system. I never liked it when there were some absolute rules given to me. For example, every time you have a reversal day and the market makes a new high, and then it does not make a new high, then two tics on the low and then makes a high, then it is going to go up 400 points. I never liked those absolutes. I would read three quarters of a book, and then it would get into all of the complicated stuff, and I would get turned off.

Do you take a trading system and then trade around it?
Yes.

What happened from there?

Every time I made a mistake, I could rationalize it into the technical analysis. I actually never made a mistake, which was really good.

It sounds like you had the system of the week club, but how did you manage to make money with that type of attitude?

I made money because I was fairly street wise. I basically took a system and traded around it using intuition.

So you were trading intuitively, but you were explaining the trades that you did not get right on a technical basis?

No, I always said that the technical analysis worked. The reason that a trade did not work was because of me. I did not remember to do this or that. One thing that I found with technical analysis was that it was always quite easy to give myself a break. Let's say with stochastic analysis - I would lose money on a trade and think it was because I forgot to look at the stochastic, or to look at the retracement levels. I would always say there is a catch-22 because you have got to look at the charts to improve, to find out if there is anything to learn, if there was anything genuinely that you should have done.

I was not really aware that trading involved probabilities. I was looking at technical systems to give me the answers. I wanted a "yes" or "no" that worked, and not a probability. I had no concept of that.

Were you able to live off of your earnings?

Yes.

What percentage were you making at that time?

I was always making 100-200%.

And you were making 100% to 200% by using this system that was sort of intuitive, based on some technical analysis?

Let's say, if I pick up a market now in the beginning of June, so all of the dates were available for me to click on. Even though it was

July, I would pick up a chart as if it were June and start it at June. I would look at the technicals and say if I sold it here, I would cut it here, and I would buy it back there. Invariably when I did that I made a lot more money theoretically than I was actually making.

How much were you actually making in cash terms?
I started with $30,000, so I was probably making between $30,000 to $60,000 a year.

So you are telling me that if you traded perfectly the way you were supposed to you would have made 300%?
Yes, I would.

How much of your account was exposed to risk?
The stop would have been about 200 to 400 quid on a trade. I would look to be making four hundred, five hundred, maybe a thousand pounds on it.

You took trades that you had better than a two to one ratio?
Yes, probably, but it was not that controlled or studious.

What was your biggest loss of capital?
About 2,000 I would more likely bleed to death than go in one big hit.

Basically, what you would do is you would get into a trade and if it did not fit what you thought it was going to do, you would get out even with sometimes a one-tick profit?
Yes. If it did not do what I hoped it would do fairly immediately, I would give it a bit of time, but I would be very twitchy.

Did you have a scenario on what the markets should do from the point that you bought it?
Yes.

So you traded scenarios. Even if the trade went in your direction the wrong way you might bail?
Correct.

Suppose you expected the market to breakout and hold above some support level, and once it hit the next level, it had to continue to move and not see the open of the day. You would get out of the trade if it went back through the open even though you still had a profit in it?
Yes, and often I would grab profits as well. I seemed to develop my risk aversion game fairly well. I am struggling with it today. I can get into the trade quite well and I can control the profit/loss on a trade if it does not work. Usually, when I get out of a trade it does not work anyway so it was a good trade to get out of. What usually happens is the trade bounces into profit, and I am between the evolution of the moment and falling in love with a position. Often you run it up and run it to nothing again or you grab a profit by mixing your time frames.

I align different time frames in my head, look to get a buy signal in the short-term which leads into a medium-term time frame, and then trade at medium-term. This is a challenge because when medium-term does not work, you say to yourself that you should have just let the market do the work.

Let's catch up on the personal side. Tell us about your wife.
She's wonderful. She is the same age as me, and is a primary school teacher.

Do you have children?
Yes, we both love children. Our oldest boy is 4½, and our second came about two years after. We went for a third hoping for a girl and got ambushed by two little boys. So, we have twin boys that are about 6 months old. My wife works one day a week at the school, and her mother looks after the children. She is pleased to have that balance in her life.

How do you like to recreate together?

We go out as a couple as much as we can. Obviously, with very small children, we are fairly limited as to the amount of time that we can get away. We are committed parents and are aware of where we are in the story of our family. These times are when you are in the trenches, and you have to dig in and not get too manic about where you are at the moment. You just have to keep looking at the horizon and enjoy the time that you have. At this point, we do not think we will have any more children. We are blessed with very good boys. The two older boys are not really threatened by the twins, partly because I have been at home and partly because they have each other.

Let's get back to the trading. You were about 25 years old.

Just before I got married, I came home to trade on my own. I was in mental turbulence trying to evaluate myself through my performance in the markets.

I did not really enjoy the trading room atmosphere because there were too many people trying to tell you how to trade. At that point, I was vulnerable and insecure about my knowledge of the markets. Everyone would offer their opinion and cause you to get completely confused about your position. Everyone was ego driven, and there was a lot of politics involved in the room.

Now you came home and you set up your trading. Tell us about that.

Economically, it worked out about the same. I became much better at technical analysis and had a clearer view of what I was actually trying to do.

Was getting better at technical analysis messing up the intuitive side of trading for you?

Yes. But to be fair, technical analysis got me into all kinds of messes as well. Intuition is great as long as you know when you are not intuitive.

What were you looking at?
Market Profile.

What made you decide to play Market Profile?
It seemed logical to me. It seemed fairly methodical. I liked that it worked in the short time frame, and it also worked in the massive time frame. You could look at a chart and say there is a breakout and there is a retracement. You have a greater chance of Market Profile being authentically linked with how the market actually is rather than overlaying something on it.

You were pretty much exclusively studying Market Profile and dropped everything else?
Yes, I studied a few nuts and bolts indicators like RSI, stochastic, and things like that, but predominantly Market Profile. I was making a living at trading, nothing amazing.

What were your returns?
My returns were probably similar to what they were before.

100% returns? That puts you in the elite in the world.
Yes, but that is not fair to the elite of the world because me chucking around 30,000 quid is nothing compared to attempting to double 90 or 100 million pounds.

Where do we go from there?
I am in my padded cell at home. Looking back now I have been on my own now in my own office for the last 7 or 8 years.

Have you ever lost money in those 8 years?
Oh, yes. I had a year when I did not make any money.

What year was that?
It was halfway through 1997, and the half-year before that.

Why do you think that happened?

I was making a lot of money selling the market and then the market stopped going down. I had to learn how to make money on the bull market. I was fortunate to be able to make money by nipping and tucking a little money here and there. I was able to make a living even though my trading was not holistic in itself.

Did you ever decide to go into money management in any way?

I went into money management briefly, and I do harbor the ambition to manage money. One of the things that kept me from going into money management is dealing with customer problems. I want to control my environment. I do not like the idea of other people interfering with my decision making process. Markets come to a blunt end and within that blunt end is a probability. If you buy the market here, it is going up. You might get that probability up to 90%, but it is never going to be 100%. On that basis, if you have a probability, you have got to play that probability out.

The problem with fund management is consistency. Funds do not want fantastic gains; they just want consistency. As these funds seem to be judged monthly, it is difficult to run through all trades of a system without a drawdown that will set their money management alarms off.

Are you trading with more money now, or are you still trading with the same amount?

I am still more or less trading with the same amount. I am considering being sponsored by someone who is aware of how markets work, but is not a fund.

How would that work? Would that be similar to exempt people in the United States that can trade up to 15 accounts and take a percentage of the profits?

Yes. I seem to make good money, but I am not getting ahead. I want to try something else.

How much are you trading with now?
I can trade up to $80,000.

What have you averaged?
This year I am back on 100% already.

So, you are prepared to do 180% if the year continued?
Probably, yes.

Have you had any breakthroughs in your trading?
I sort of grew up metaphorically in the stock market. When I traded futures, I traded stock market futures. My trading evolved when I suddenly realized that I could trade other things. What is the point in chasing around for small amounts of money when it is not really there to be made? When I let go of the idea that I could only trade one market, I seemed to benefit and to be more balanced in my whole view.

I view markets as growing fruit trees with each tree growing something different. That is the technical analysis part, which depicts the way that the markets set up where you get the short, medium, and long-term reference. Various technical combinations are like where the tree comes into leaves, blossoms, and then bears fruit. When the technical parameters are all in place, that is when you pick the fruit off of the tree. What I mean is that the trade is highly probable and it is going to do something from the analysis. When you are trying to trade one market, you are just growing one harvest, one fruit all through the year, and the money is just not there.

What happens is that you start reaching and taking less than ideal trades?
Yes, exactly right. You are cobbling together a few things, you take the trade, you do not make money, and you do not really understand the reasons why. Everything has been done correctly and you keep bashing your head against the wall.

You like to harvest more than one crop?

Yes, if I am looking at the English stock market and there is not much going on, like it is in the budding phase, I cannot sit there and wait for it to fruit. I will leave it and go off and look at a pear tree, which might be the German stock market. It still might not work, but the point is that you are going to the right place. You are in the place where you should be. You are trying to trade at harvest as opposed to trying to trade when the buds are growing.

When you see these markets, are you looking at a trade and saying, "You have got to be kidding this is like stealing candy from a baby?"

Yes, but in actual fact, that is the error of my game. I have colleagues who are reasonably large floor traders and we have a term that we call "code red." I will ring them up on the floor and say "code red" on the English stock market. They will buy a big lump of stock for themselves and invariably make a lot of money. "Code red" is when everything lines up. The market is not only going to move, but will have a very dynamic move as well.

If I were to ask you to teach me how to trade and teach me your method, how would you do it?

First of all, I would not want to teach you my method. I would say that my method suits me, but it does not necessarily suit you. If someone came to me and said, "I want to trade Market Profile," I would introduce it to them, but would encourage them to read the book to see if it makes sense. If they do not like the feel of it, then they should look at some other form of analysis.

What sort of trading principles would you teach them?

A big principle would be that trading is based on probability. That is something that I would keep telling them over and over. You almost do not need to tell them anything more as the other stuff is all fairly logical. You do not realize that you are in a probability environment until quite far along in your career.

342

What do you do as far as money management is concerned?

My philosophy is that I am trying to let the market tell me the trade, and allow myself to manage the risk. If a trade has a breakout to the upside and I know if I buy the bull market then the cut is 5 or 10 tics below that. I absolutely know that is my risk and that is my money management. If the risk is larger than that, then that is my money management and it is up to me to make a call on whether I am prepared to accept that risk.

If you had a bond trade where you were risking 10 ticks and you were wrong, you will just buy 3 or 4 contracts versus maybe more?

Yes, if I accepted the risk.

Do you ever not take a trade because your stop would be too far?

Yes, I do. Sometimes, I take a trade where the stop is so close that the market should move immediately and if it does not, then I get out. If the stop is too far for me, then I should not do the trade because I am not prepared to accept the risk involved in the trade. Sometimes, if I have a short-term set up, it is highly probable that the market will move in my direction even though the stop is right down where I will buy the market.

What would happen if the trade fell off the swing set?

I would not put the trade in, because I am fairly hands-on.

So, you watch the market constantly?

Yes, pretty much. It depends on if I am loading to a medium term trade, then I'll detach myself from it.

Do you ever find yourself micromanaging trades a little too much?

Yes. That is a big challenge going from short-term to long-term trading. Let's say that you are long and the market drops down again into what you had in profit in the trade. If you interpret that as being threatening, your instinct is to get out. After the fact, you say to yourself, "Why did I get out?" The short-term fear overrides the trade. You become threatened by losing profit that you have in a trade.

When I get an emotional charge in my head, my reaction is to do nothing because my mindset is not appropriate.

When my mind settles down, if I can settle it fairly quickly, then I will get back in if I can still control the risk.

Where do you go from here?
I'm going to join the real world again. I am setting up an office with three good friends who have been traders as long as I have.

Does it scare you to change your environment?
No, I have gone past that. I have been looking forward to doing something like this for the past year because I am bored with my existence. Everything has been on my own. It is not that I necessarily want to lean on anyone. I am quite whole in myself. I just like the idea of being more human.

I obviously have traded on my own for some reason. Probably to control my environment, so that I can restructure it; now I feel that I can go out again. I actually feel that I will gain a lot from the others, not necessarily to do trades, but just the discipline and the professionalism. These guys are all positive spirits. They are all up for it and are confident. I like that. If someone is having a bad day, you can say, "Come on, you are a good trader, keep going," and vice versa. I think the whole will be greater than the individual parts. Not only that, it will be fun and we will enjoy it as well because making money should be fun. It should not be all this discipline where you study for years and eventually make a few quid. Trading should be fun.

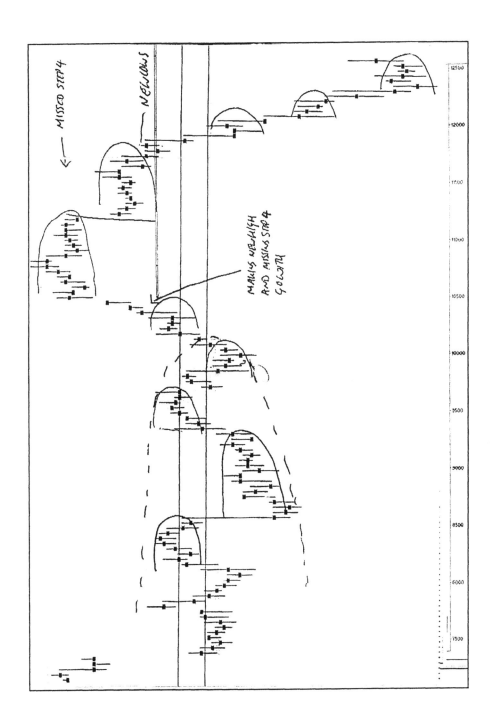

MISSCO STEP 4

NELSONS

MARLIS NELSNIGH
AND MISSIAS STEP 4
GOLGITH

345

MODELING STUDY

CHILDHOOD FAMILY STATUS
- Mike experienced going from poor to middle class in London

MENTORING - INFLUENCES
- Parents Irish immigrants
- *Mind Over Markets* by Jim Dalton
- *Market Profile Course by J. Peter Steidlmayer*

ENVIRONMENT
- Youngest of five children
- Brought up outside of London
- Father and mother both had strong work ethic
- Supportive family and happy childhood
- Supportive stable relationship with wife and four children

EDUCATION
- Youth - schooling was of little interest, but did well
- Self taught trader

INTERESTS - Skills - Abilities -Honors
Childhood
- Physically able - loved wrestling with brothers
- Artistic

Adult
- Plays with his children
- Basketball
- Running

QUALITIES
- Optimistic
- Team player

- Tenacious
- Ambitious
- Compassionate
- Humbled by the markets

BUSINESS EXPERIENCE
- Assembled cars at a young age and sold them
- Bought, fixed, and sold cars
- Back office brokerage experience

PROSPERITY CONSCIOUSNESS
- Children's charities

TRADING EXPERIENCE
- Stock exchange floor as dealer
- Initially, an intuitive trader, then became both technical and intuitive
- Market maker
- Money manager
- Traded from office at home for 8 years
- Consistently averages between 100% and 200% in returns

RECOMMENDATIONS
- *Mind Over Markets* by Jim Dalton on Market Profile System
- Peter Steidlmayer's works on Market Profile
- *Reminiscences of a Stock Operator* by Edwin Lefevre
- *Market Wizards* by Jack Schwager

FUTURE PLANS
- Joining three friends and trading in the same office as a support team
- The market tells me the trade and I manage the risk
- Refine my profit/risk strategy

TRADER GEMS - Fundamental - Intuitive - Psychological

- Intuition is great as long as you know when you are not intuitive
- When you manage money, investors do not want fantastic gains they want consistency
- Trading is a probability
- When you get emotionally charged, do nothing because the mindset is not appropriate
- The market tells me the trade and I manage the risk
- If you act from choice rather then fear you will see the other side of the coin

TRADER GEMS - Mechanical - Analytical - Technical

- One problem during Mike's early trading career was that he tried to trade too many systems and used his intuition to trade around them. This leads you to not being able to follow your systems.
- Mike, like Glen Ring, trades using scenarios and when the market does not do what he thinks it will, he exits the trade even if it marginally profitable.
- Mike Battle currently trades using a methodology called Market Profile. This method was developed by J. Peter Steidlmayer and is a measure of a price frequency distribution using time, rather than volume as its key element.
- Mike, like many other successful traders, uses multiple timeframes in his market analysis
- Mike trades more markets so he can pick his trades and not force trades in any one market
- Mike does not take a trade if risk is too high.

Murray's Analytical Modeling Study

Trade Methodology Analysis
Mechanical--Objective: Market Profile Analysis

Mechanical--Automatic: Charts market indicators

Discretionary: Interpretation of Market Profile and risk analysis of a given trade

Analysis of Mike's Methodology
Mike Battle bases most of his trading decisions on the concept of Market Profile. This methodology, developed by J. Peter Steidlmayer, develops intra-day distributions of price based on time, not volume. This work was viewed to be unique enough that it was copyrighted as Market Profile and Liquidity Data Bank. When Market Profile is understood, the analyst can separate market internals by timeframe and trading pattern. The original method used three different types of customer trades:

CT1 the local floor traders
CT2 the commercial clearing members
CT3 clearing member who fill other members
CT4 clearing member with public orders

CT1 and CT2 accounted for 65% of the total volume and both of these groups have different trading styles than groups CT3 and CT4.

Market Profit combines CT1 with CT2, and CT3 with CT4 to simplify the analysis. Market Profile charts are plotted on intra-day data by listing the prices on the left hand side and then plotting in a series of right hand columns a combination of time and price. The trader assigns time by using the letter A for the first half-hour of the day, B for the next half-hour, and so forth.

351

Let's assume that a market trades from 10:00 A.M. to 3:00 P.M. An example of an intra-day market profile chart is as follows: A=10:00 to 10:30, B=10:30 to 11:00, ect.

```
1100.00
1099.00
1098.00   H      (Buyers stop buying)
1097.00   G  I
1096.00  D F  J
1095.00  B C E
1094.00  A      (Sellers stop selling)
1093.00
1092.00
1091.00
1090.00
```

This chart shows that the market tested 1098 on the high side and 1094 on the low side and showed a tendency to fluctuate between 1096 to 1095. The area in which the market shows a tendency to trade is called the value area. When charts contain enough data, the value area is plus or minus one standard deviation unit from the mean. Market Profile can be charted over several days or using daily data. Market Profile is an interesting area of market research and deserves attention as a method for trading decisions.

References on Market Profile
Steidlmayer on the Markets by J. Peter Steidlmayer, John Wiley and Sons, 1989
Market Logic School--Original Course by J. Peter Steidlmayer
Mind Over Markets by Jim Dalton

Adrienne's Psychological Modeling Study

The Support Model

Mike's success as a trader is largely based upon a psychological Model Support. From the time that Mike was a small child, he has benefited from the presence of his older brothers and sisters, who have supported him like emotional bookends. His family's wealth could be measured in their sharing of love. Mike parents were hard working people to whom nothing was given; his father worked his way up the ranks of a large bank while his mother worked nights as a nurse. They were committed to doing whatever it took to raise their children in a decent neighborhood with a peer group that was also supportive.

For highly creative right-brained children like Mike, the structure and regimentation of English schools can make their educational experience a very difficult one. Mike perceived his schooling as feeling somehow "unnatural" except his art studies, where he excelled. Understandably, Mike left school at sixteen and did not return.

Without the support of his family, Mike could have drifted into all manner of trouble. But, with his creative juices flowing, Mike was able to create a Mini-Mouse car business. He had the support of another adult figure during this venture, the father of one of his friends. The result was that Mike had his first taste of being an entre-preneur - an excellent first step for a trader-to-be. Entrepreneurial experience at an early age tends to develop "street smarts" in an individual that is never consciously analyzed, but is of tremendous value to an intuitive trader.

The support of his family provided Mike with a wealth of energy, enthusiasm, self-confidence, and a sense of responsibility from which to draw. This model allowed him to try things without the fear of failing and without the self-doubts that prevent others from trying something new. A sense of being supported also allowed Mike to attempt challenging activities without the emotional immaturity that makes other individuals sabotage their efforts by taking excessive risks. Mike is willing to take reasonable risks for himself, but not with other people's money.

The tremendous enthusiasm for life, which was derived from his supportive environment, allowed him to feel that he could do anything. He was also attractive to others who wanted to be associated with him. So, Mike was able to lead others at a very young age.

The Support Model brings out the very best in people by giving them the opportunity to express their own nature in a very positive way. People who have been supported know how to support themselves and they know how to teach themselves when they do not have models. They know how to find the resources to succeed because they are self-confident and believe they can make things happen. With this level of self-confidence, Mike plowed into trading without having a clue as to what he was doing. However, he used his instincts as a guide and made money when no one else was. In fact, according to his figures, he has consistently made annual returns of 100% to 200% for years. A supported person makes choices in life based not upon the material needs alone, but on the need to create a continually supportive environment. He will automatically attempt to forge a family structure that will provide balance and support. When Mike was offered the position at Goldman-Sachs, he was turned away by the lack of trading support. He felt that he would get support at Security Pacific, as well as a mentor, and left when the environment became too unsupportive for him. Mike already knew the importance of mentors from his own family.

People with a Support Model also tend to make better choices in their relationships with their spouses. They are programmed to make lifetime commitments. Mike has been with the same woman since they were eighteen and they have four young children, to whom he is devoted. Analytical, left-brained, mechanical traders would have great difficulty trading in the chaos created by four small children. Mike does not.

What kind of a trader develops from the Support Model? Mike, being right-brained and artistic, was comfortable utilizing his own strengths and applying them to his unique approach to developing systems and trading. He has never been a technically based trader, but has gravitated to the market profile approach because it is logical, visual, and simple. Coming from hard-working parents, Mike is not afraid to do what has to be done to succeed, but he can do it his way, which is the simple way: "Ultimately, you have to learn that it is tremendously difficult, and then you realize it is simple." Then, he feels comfortable applying his intuition to the process. He does not like absolute rules which do not flow with his intuitive understanding of the world. Because he comes from the Support Model, he has the confidence to be a free spirit and make money from his street smarts, intuition, and hard-earned experience. "These are the trenches and you have to dig in and not get too manic about where you are at the moment. You have got to keep looking at the horizon and enjoy the time that you have."

CHAPTER 13

Scott A. Krieger

West meets East - How he used his business savvy,
world travel experience and spiritual insight
to become an exceptional trader.

What was it like when you were a child?
Good and not so good -- like most of us, right? My father was somewhat emotionally distant, or that is how it seemed to me. I think it is almost in spite of my upbringing that I am the kind of person I am today. I wanted to explode out into the world and discover everything, but felt repressed at times. Traveling much of my life overseas, especially in the Orient, gave me many fascinating experiences and opened me up to life. I must say that my father did always have an intuitive appreciation of nature, and that fact affected me positively.

What did your father do?
They called him "Designer to the Stars." My parents each had interior decorating businesses for people in the film and entertainment industry of their generation. This was in Manhattan, and their client list included Otto Preminger, Steve and Edie Gorme, Kenny Rogers and others. My father also loved gardening; getting his hands deep in that black loam.

What kind of things were you interested in when you were in school?
Besides reading and more reading, one of my interests was being an amateur radio operator. I got the highest license available in that field and enjoyed communicating with people from all over the world. I also became a pretty good acoustic guitar player.

While I was in junior high and high school, I was more focused on the sciences than English. As I grew and moved onto college, I became more interested in English literature and then Eastern thought and philosophy. This progression expanded my thinking dramatically.

What positive influence did you get from your family?
Two positive elements that were instilled in me by my parents were the desire to succeed and determination. Determination is one personality trait that is necessary to be successful in trading.

My grandfather came to the United States from somewhere in Western Russia. I grew up in a Jewish household where my parents followed a basic pattern of tradition. Aschkanazi Jewish - you know, "the smart ones." It's certainly my only connection to Einstein, Speilberg and Bob Dylan! I do appreciate the intelligent and humorous aspects of the tradition. My own fundamental beliefs, however, came later and are mostly drawn from Eastern philosophy.

Tell us about your education?
I went through the normal kindergarten through high school schedule and then went through undergraduate school and got my degree. That is what I consider my formal education. I did not go beyond a Bachelor of Science Degree in Biology. At that point, I was interested in India and spiritualism, in addition to science. For some time, I thought I wanted to become a medical missionary.

I got a degree with honors in Biology from the University of Buffalo in New York and thought about combining this knowledge with my interest in Eastern philosophy and medicine. I wanted to go to India and become an Ayurvedic doctor studying under a famous Calcutta physician whose fame came from the fact that he had worked with the president of India and other illustrious people. Instead of becoming a doctor, however, I started working with a large publisher of books on Indology and Oriental philosophy. There was a lot of spiritualism running around in that atmosphere, which captivated me into studying deep issues. I feel that my experiences in that atmosphere shaped the most important aspects of my life and education.

Whose writings inspired you?
Early in college, I enjoyed Norman Mailer's brand of eloquent grit. Books by Alan Watts, Aldous Huxley, and Laird inspired me. From these I moved into some profound Eastern texts, *Patanjali* and *Srimad Bhagavatam*. I was gradually drawn to metaphysics, and then philosophical and ancient spiritual texts. I became very interested in translations of the ancient Vedas. One of the most remarkable books I have ever read is the *Bhagavad-Gita As It Is* by A.C. Bhaktivedanta.

How did you see yourself?
I had a strong bent toward every imaginable definition of independence and freedom of thought. I am very intuitive and when I felt something had little depth to it or was just some type of ritualistic concept, I cringed and ran from it. As a child you cannot run from teachings that have no depth; that is why I felt a great liberation in college.

What teachings impressed you the most?
I learned Sanskrit when I was in India and I studied the ancient Vedas. "Veda" means "knowledge" in Sanskrit and these writings are the oldest books on earth. There is so much value one can attain from reading them. There are many different fields in the Vedic teachings, such as math, architecture, medicine and in many other areas of science and art. Of course, the higher teachings include deeper philosophical issues.

There are three types of personalities, Vata, Pitta and Kapha, and an understanding of your personality type will give you great insight into choices you should make for your life. My personality is a vata type. Vatas are very active people and I think I am one of the more hyper-vata types. Einstein writes about a unifying force or unifying principle beneath everything. The Vedic texts write about a unifying principle in a philosophical sense, but they go much deeper so you can have a better understanding of the concepts they are describing, which includes the very nature of the self. In this regard, the written works of A.C. Bhaktivedanta seem to provide a perfect blend of scholarship and devotion.

How has your experience in India influenced some of your daily habits?

I meditate daily. I have been a vegetarian for about twenty-nine years, which means no meat, fish or eggs of any kind. If you spent nine years in India, you might become a vegetarian, too. It does something to you by making you become more aware of, conscious of, your actions. What you are really doing. Like what you are actually eating! I think that living in an enriched spiritual atmosphere helps one to develop compassion. Not just for other people, but ultimately for every living thing.

What would you say are your best qualities?

My best qualities are my intuitive and analytical abilities. I look for what is behind the facade, I am extremely determined, and I think that I am also very resourceful. I can enjoy deep friendships.

How do you define your intuitive ability?

Intuition for me goes toward my spiritual realizations. I am also a quick study on people and I know when I am being taken in or someone is not being truthful. At one time, I was more tolerant, or perhaps naive, of these behaviors, but now I will only open up to people, activities and situations that I think are serving the highest good for all concerned. Intuitively, I know when to get away from things that are not good for me or are just not going to go anywhere. This comes as the result of a lot of experience.

Do you believe in intuitive trading?

The intuitive element in trading is undeniable. Successful traders may not talk much about it, but it exists. Any statistician will tell you that a large enough population of anything can be graphed to illustrate its inherent natural order, Natural intuition is a part of this order.

What in your personality have others found difficult to deal with?

I am definitely a perfectionist. I recently employed a secretary. It has been educational for me to learn to be a little more tolerant. People are not robots like I've sometimes been! To get to my level of knowledge of the markets I have been obsessed at times. Looking at a screen all day and half the night can lead to compulsive behavior, but I am trying to balance my life now. That is why I am going back to India, periodically to visit, and generally to travel more. To get out more, so to speak. I have finally gotten to a position where I feel that I can do that.

Tell us about your work history and your travels?

I did not have that many jobs as a teenager, except for a short stint in a restaurant and behind the wheel of a taxi. After college, I went to India and got involved with a large Oriental publishing company. That job took me to university, college and public libraries, where I met with professors in Australia, Japan, the entirety of India, and other countries as well. Fourteen in all. I became fascinated with the ancient culture pervading the whole of the Orient. India, Thailand and Indonesia have clear vestiges of this profound culture, and even Tagolog, the local language of the Philippines, has Sanskrit roots. It was a pretty remarkable, unifying, inspiring feeling working over there. I felt at home.

Before returning to the United States, I lived in Hong Kong for a year. I did voice-overs for a large English television station. In fact, my TV ads are still used there. No royalties unfortunately. I also owned a little pre-press company where I did color separation work. I also exported Kalagas, which are wall hangings, and woodcarvings from Thailand and Burma. I had a company called SourceLink

International in the States that imported these items and sold them in Manhattan and Beverly Hills.

So what did you do when you came back to the States?
When I came back to the States, I worked in a number of different types of businesses. I was a legal editor for the 3rd largest law firm in New York. We had the Trump and Eastern Airlines accounts. I worked for R.R. Donnally and Sons, which is a large printing company, in their financial printing division in Manhattan. We put together the stock and investment proposals for the Security Exchange Commission. After we would finish a proposal, they would throw it in a Lear jet and fly it to Washington for the meetings to be held the next morning. I was even a distributor for No-Run panty hose outfit. I tried to be the connection between the Canadian manufacturer and a distributor in Australia and New Zealand, but of course, they jumped over my head and went right to the manufacturer. Obviously, none of these endeavors did much to satisfy me.

I bet there were many lessons along the way.
Oh yes. My very last job, before becoming a trader, was being part-owner with the co-creator of a world-famous cartoon character (four characters, actually), in a pre-press film operation. That was a tremendous learning experience. Believe it or not, it became a real inside close look at the ugly underbelly of corporate America. Through that experience I finally understood that if I need to develop psychosis in life, I can do that on my own, thank you. I don't need a psychotic partner to help me! I finally realized that I had all the intelligence I needed -- without bosses or crazy partners -- to make it on my own.

The feedback from all of these experiences I brought to futures trading. This has been the culmination of a long evolutionary path with lots and lots of feedback. Remember, there is no failure in life, only feedback. This path has lead me to the financial freedom and freedom of thought which I wanted all of my life.

Trading is all about life. If you treat trading like a business and put in your stops and manage your resources properly, it is like any other business. One remarkable attribute that I love about trading is that the more detached you are, the more successful you become. This refers back to the Vedas and the *Bhagavad-Gita*. There is an ancient verse there that states, "Perform your duty equipoised. Abandon all attachment to success or failure. Such equanimity is called yoga". This detachment from the fruits of action represents the real Vedic view, and it is perfectly applicable to futures trading. Successful traders know that you shouldn't be thinking of the money while you are trading, just the trading process itself. The work, the duty, of trading. Trading like this, in an emotionally detached way, is the formula for great success.

What got you interested in the markets initially.
It was after my last "partnered" experience that I realized I was intelligent enough and analytical enough to find something where I did not need to rely on anyone. So, I decided to go where the money was, and what better place than the six trillion-dollar financial markets. I had to ask myself, "What kind of minimum action can provide maximum result." - and the futures market was the answer. From that start, I tried to find out more about it.

Can you relate any of your studies to trading?
The ideas of the 13th Century mathematician Fibonacci described a natural order behind nature, and they also apply to market behavior. If you go deep enough, you can find a connection in a pattern of numbers as it relates to the markets. And, of course, as I described before, I found that the Vedas point to both successful action in life and life's natural order. This relates to trading and everything else I do.

How did you try to find out more about it?
I dug through libraries and went through *Books in Print* to try to find information. This was around 1989 to 1991, when there was only highly technical material available, and not even much of that. It

seemed that for a beginning trader, there was very little information. In fact, this is one of the main reasons I wrote my own book; just to get everything clear in my own head. I really wish I would have had something like it back then. Anyway, I stumbled along for a long time. Finally, I bought a QuoteTrek machine advertised in *Investor's Business Daily*. I also read a book about momentum indicators or something. Armed with this "wealth" of information, I started trading lots of Swiss Franc contracts. I built up quickly to a ten-lot, then borrowed $10,000. I was pyramiding, which means that I was increasing the amount of money I was trading as soon as I made a profit. In the beginning, I did real well. Basically, I was just looking at a QuoteTrek and doing what Toppel talks about, "if the price now is greater than the price of the last tic, buy." In other words, if the market was moving up, I bought it. At the time, this meant momentum to me.

One day, when Boris Yeltsin decided to start firing on the Russian Parliament with tank shells, the QuoteTrek quotes started to drop. I thought, "Oh, I've seen this before. It's retracing and will bounce right up again." But it didn't. In fact, it just kept going down and down with me long 12 contracts. I finally got out and lost over $5,000, which was a lot of money to me then.

So, what lesson did you learn from this experience?
The lesson I learned was that I needed more knowledge about the markets. I finally started paying close attention to these things called "charts!" Then, I went all the way with my trading. I was one of the first people to get TradeStation and bought many systems. They didn't work well at all, so I started developing my own.

During this time did you have enough money to live on or were you earning a living from trading?
I was living on some savings and credit cards.

Whatever you have now, did you make it from trading?
That is correct. I had invested it all.

How did you become more of a technical trader?
I originally got interested in moving averages. Parabolic analysis had also interested me for a long time. I ultimately spent hundreds and thousands of hours in front of the screen, using various general charting packages until I settled on TradeStation.

Were any of the books you read useful?
I do have a pretty large library. The books were good in a general sense; not specifically. Nothing I could *really* use. I would research every indicator I read about in *Futures Magazine*. It seemed that I was always up until 2 o'clock in the morning working on the markets. One time, I thought that I had discovered the Holy Grail. But, to my dismay, I found that the system worked well going backwards, but would not work going forward. That is when I started studying the markets using natural principles. Like the weather, the market seems to be a random phenomenon, but it is not. It is just an utterly complex movement of orderly principles. Computer programmers are trying to apply super computers to analyze weather patterns and they are starting to have some success in following these remarkably complex patterns. In the same way, the markets do have a natural order to them. My fascination with these patterns led me to more success by just doing my own research. I put that research into my own trading software, the KC Collection.

How did you discover the existence of Keltner channels?
I read about them in an old book and talked with someone from the Midwest about them. The version that I use is a distant cousin of the old version. If you used the default version of the Keltner channel, you could put maybe three of them inside of mine. I have a proprietary Keltner channel formula that I have developed that is much wider than the default Keltner channel with a much slower response. Default Keltner channels tend to be much too price responsive. Some people might find that helpful, but I do not. The outer bands of my channels are so wide that sometimes they work near the edge of the charts. I find this to be extremely useful as the

wide bands become a very effective price target to the trader. The price tends to bounce off or kiss one of these outer bands and retrace. Over and over again. The market takes off from the middle of the band and then, if it is extremely powerful, it can also break through the outer bands. Action can occur from the other bands as well. I find that the channel moves organically with the markets in a gentle wave-like motion, providing for both entry points into long trends and a then clear price targets for exits. I think they're fantastic.

*Keltner channels are a series of moving averages that vary according to a type of average movement and a type of standard deviation measure. They are somewhat similar to Bollinger bands, but use some percentage of an average range and a true range off the moving average rather than standard deviation measures.

How do you use this to enter the market?
Because the Keltner channel is so wide, and has so many good attributes, it tends to act as a template over which I lay the other system and discretionary elements of the KC Collection. The mechanical elements are comprised of a special pivot system that signals at the beginning of profitable wave-like patterns that I have seen occur again and again.

The discretionary elements are used to strongly confirm the good signals and filter out most of the losers.

Is the pivot-based indicator anything similar to the Commodity Boot Camp Numbers?
No, my pivot system is dynamic and it issues signals according to the wave-like motion of the markets. But I have another indicator included in the Collection that is a bit similar. It is a support-resistance auto calculator that produces static numbers that are applicable throughout the day. It automatically calculates the five most powerful areas for the next day's trading. The pivot system, however, provides an audible and visible signal that occurs just near

the bottom of a retracement. It often happens at a very pivotal moment within the Keltner channel itself. In other words, the real power and length of the trade often depends upon where on the three Keltner bands the signal or original event occurs. I am looking at two-minute, three-minute or five-minute charts for the signals, and then I glance at the longer time frames for multiple-time frame confirmation. I have indicators on all of these time frames and it only takes a glance to see if there is a profitable pattern or not. However, even without using any of the discretionary elements of the KC Collection, the pivot system does very well by itself, often approaching 70% wins:losses, or greater.

Have you done statistical analysis or is this an intuitive feel on how these indicators interact?
Yes I have, and as mentioned before, the pivot system is generally around 70% profitable.

I receive a visual and an audible signal from TradeStation and the positioning on the Keltner determines if the signal is a go or not. This action alone can help to filter out a good amount of the losers, thus making the overall method even more profitable. I think there is a powerful synergy when you use discretion in addition to a mechanical signal. At that point, you have everything. Another element included is a peak and valley oscillator, which is the counter trending element to the trending elements. The different indicators and the system complement each other.

How do you know that you know?
As far as discretion is concerned, you see a pattern that you have seen a thousand times and you know. A discretionary trader will not be successful unless he checks across multiple time frames. I compare the lack of multiple time frame analysis to being lost in a forest. A helicopter view of the forest shows the shape of the forest, but if you are stuck in the forest, trying to get out, you can see the pathways, but you cannot see the whole forest. You don't know

which one to take. What you need is both perspectives. You need to be seeing both the short-term direction and the long-term trend.

I will get one of these pivot signals and simply see where it is happening relative to the Keltner channel and what the other indicators are doing. For example, if the signal is happening just above the middle Keltner, I have a higher high on my oscillator and the long term chart shows a profitable pattern also developing off the middle or the top Keltner channel, that is a point I should definitely enter the market. I have seen it happen a thousand times.

How do you know that it is time to take a signal?
You cannot separate the intellectual recognition of the pattern from the feeling that it is right. I think it is both. The feeling is always in the chest.

When markets start to change, how do you know when a pattern is no longer working and how quickly do you adjust your methodology to that?
If you look at indicators long enough you can see the exhaustion patterns and changes, as well as the countertrending indications. For example, something happens when a certain moving average is midway between the middle and upper bands of my Keltner channel or the middle and lower bands. If it is just floating, it is definitely a counter-trending time. The market will eventually explode one way or another out of the range. It is a matter of looking far enough in multiple time frames that you start to get a strong sense of the direction the market is going to take. I think the information is clearly there in the technicals. One advantage to day trading is that you are able to look at a micro view of what is happening in the market. Position traders would say that it is a changing event when you are looking at a minute chart. You can actually see the changes that precede the so-called "sudden change." It is in terms of the time frames you are looking at. If you look long enough at the different time frames, especially in the micro versus the macro view, you can get a much clearer sense of those changes. A lot of change can occur

over a day in the market, and if you are looking at shorter time frames, the picture can get clearer. Of course, if you are only looking at a minute chart, that is insane, because things happen too fast. That is why I am saying that a trader should be looking in multiple time frames.

If you are trading on a minute chart and the hourly trend is down, will you go long?
Yes, but I keep very tight stops. I would actually be experiencing the upward rise of a retracement on the hourly chart, so I am catching some of that upward movement, which is simply a retracement in a downward trend.

So you realize that it is a retracement and you would trade it accordingly. What if the market is in an uptrend in the hourly chart...?
Going long on a good short-term signal within a clear long-term upward trend is exactly what we are looking for.

Do you ever look at daily bar charts?
Yes, I have a long-term page where I have daily, hourly, and half-hourly information. I do glance at this page at the beginning of the day and occasionally during the day, but only for a few seconds to get valuable information. I look at candlesticks, too. If I clearly see that the market has retraced, it is in an upward trend, and it retraces to the top Keltner or so on a daily chart. If I have a bullish engulfment the previous day, for example, I am really going to look at some buys short-term. It is all in the multiple time frame analysis.

How do you manage your money?
I want to keep the equity to risk number correct, as far as the maximum risk I am taking in relationship to the equity in my account. I like to keep very tight stops.

How tight is very tight?
It can be pretty damn tight in a one-minute chart situation.

Especially now that the S & P contract size is reduced by half. In a situation where I am getting a buy signal on the one or two minute timeframe on the middle Keltner channel, which is also supported by a 20 bar moving average, I can put a stop on the other side of that technical barrier with confidence and feel protected. This is especially true when the long-term indicator is telling me it is a go. Generally, we are talking half a point. If there is a trade on the one minute, I have no problem placing a $100 stop because the Keltner band is very powerful technical protection. Again, I would never do this if I did not see that it also looked good in the 5-minute and 30-minute timeframes, for example.

When your stops are so tight, what percentage of your trades do you expect to be winners?
Approximately sixty-five to seventy percent.

How many trades do you take in a day?
If it is a strongly trending day with many retracements and it is clear to me that the market is going to continue with similar action, there can be five or six trades a day.

So, you're buying on a retracement on the uptrend?
Yes. Then again, I am constantly looking at the different time frames.

Do you ever look at anything else? Do you look at what Treasury bonds are doing or do you care?
I don't care.

How do you deal with drawdowns?
I have done the drawdown discomfort, and now I am okay with it. I typically do not have more then two drawdowns in a row. I try to get in on a beautiful pattern with everything lined up in each of the time frames. Then, it becomes a matter of intelligently moving up the stops. A key to my trading is to take what the markets will give me. I have learned to listen to the market.

Do you have a way to judge how much the market is going to give you before you enter a trade?
Yes, there are times when everything will be in agreement on all the indicators in the different time frames. By viewing in multiple timeframes, I can see what is going to happen to an extent. If I see the same pattern on the one or two minute chart as I do on the sixty-minute chart, I know that it is going to be one remarkable week.

Back to your personal side. Have you gotten married and had children?
I have never been married and people just do not understand that. I am looking now however.

The whole India experience made me look at life in a different way. Then, when I came back here, I became so absorbed in my work that there was no time to devote to a relationship. Now I feel secure so I can spend a lot of time and effort developing that side of me, and really integrating the many experiences of my life.

What activities have you pursued other than your work and your spiritual path?
Besides my current and previous books, I am currently working on a novel about India. Also, I am traveling more and meeting some very interesting people.

What do you want to do with your profits besides living a good life? What charges you up to earn money in the first place?
There are many projects that I am currently funding in India and elsewhere. Some are spiritually oriented and some have to do with food relief funds. I want to do more work, which has to do with philanthropy. As far as inspiration is concerned, India is one big temple, you can feel it when you get off the plane and you can smell it in the air. It is an ancient experience. Devotion is thick in the air. That mood inspires me. It just gives me realization of what life is all about. And what money is for. After all, there is a purpose to all of this, to life, you know. Real purpose inspires.

371

What is your feeling about money?

I do not get a rush out of just having money any more. Money is called "Lakshmi" in India. Sri Lakshmi is the name of the Goddess of Fortune. We get the word "lucky" from the Sanskrit word "Lakshmi." The understanding is that money is innocent, but it is how you use it that determines its morality for you. It is not bad or good. It is a divine power. Money is a divine gift of power. How you use this power determines your karma (cause and effect) and ultimately your destiny. The proper use of money is what excites me.

There has to be a balance. Personally, I am looking to perhaps buy a home on the Bay of Bengal when I go back to India and Thailand. I want to be comfortable, but there is a balance in the use of this money to both give me a good life and to benefit others. I am not Mother Teresa and I am not Donald Trump. I am someplace in the middle. Hopefully I can make some kind of difference and do some lasting good before I disappear.

The KC (Keltner Confirmation) Collection

A profitable synergy occurs in technical analysis when mechanical system signals can be strongly confirmed (or filtered out) by complementary discretionary indicators. This type of system/discretion blending can offer a unique trading perspective and a greater net profitability than that realized through either system trading or discretionary trading alone.

The **KC Collection** was developed to take full advantage of this unique blending effect. It is comprised of a profitable stand-alone mechanical system (from 65% - 75% daytrading wins:losses) plus six other discretionary elements which act in concert to either strongly confirm or filter out those mechanical signals. In addition, the discretionary elements of the methodology offer further synergy through their special balance of trending and countertrending (oscillating) indicators. This tends to both amplify the strengths and nullify the weaknesses of using one approach in exclusion of the other.

The following charts illustrate recent examples of how the system and discretionary elements of the **KC Collection** work separately and together:

CHART A: 10/12/98 and 10/15/98 — 15 minute Dec. S&P 500

This chart shows profitable KC Collection system entries and exits without the benefit of using any of the discretionary elements of the software for confirmation or filtering.

373

The KC (Keltner Confirmation) Collection

A profitable synergy occurs in technical analysis when mechanical system signals can be strongly confirmed (or filtered out) by complementary discretionary indicators. This type of system/discretion blending can offer a unique trading perspective and a greater net profitability than that realized through either system trading or discretionary trading alone.

The **KC Collection** was developed to take full advantage of this unique blending effect. It is comprised of a profitable stand-alone mechanical system (from 65% - 75% daytrading wins:losses) plus six other discretionary elements which act in concert to either strongly confirm or filter out those mechanical signals. In addition, the discretionary elements of the methodology offer further synergy through their special balance of trending and countertrending (oscillating) indicators. This tends to both amplify the strengths and nullify the weaknesses of using one approach in exclusion of the other.

The following charts illustrate recent examples of how the system and discretionary elements of the **KC Collection** work separately and together:

CHART A: 10/12/98 and 10/15/98 — 15 minute Dec. S&P 500

This chart shows profitable KC Collection system entries and exits without the benefit of using any of the discretionary elements of the software for confirmation or filtering.

374

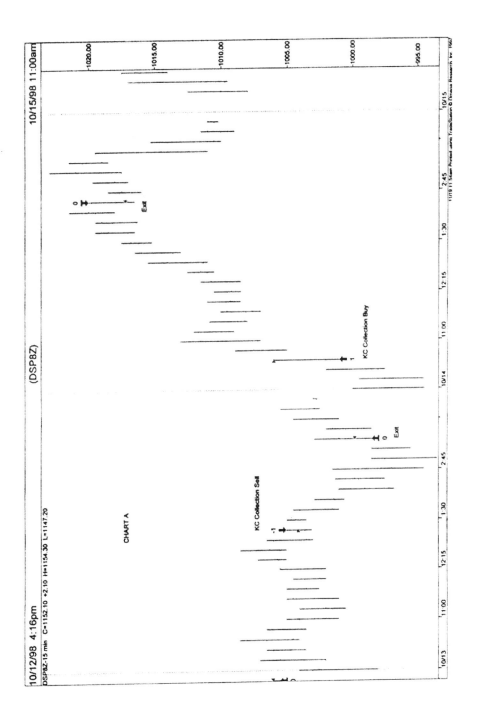

375

CHART B: Same market and time period as CHART A

The KC Collection discretionary elements confirm the mechanical signals:

Sell Signal:

1) The Peak/Valley Oscillator: This indicator confirms sell signals when the valley just preceding the signal is lower than the previous valley. Since Valley B is lower than Valley A, the sell signal and continuation of the downward trend is confirmed.

2) XMA Set: The signaled bar closes just under this exponential moving average indicator confirming the signal and trend (the XMA set includes three indicators that are designed to work in concert with the Keltner bands to form a "profit fan"; just one is shown here).

Buy Signal:

1) The Peak/Valley Oscillator: This indicator confirms buy signals when the peak just preceding the signal is higher than the previous peak. Since Peak B is higher than Peak A, the buy signal and continuation of the upward trend is confirmed.

2) Middle Keltner band and XMA set: Signaled bar closed just above both of these strongly supporting indicators: Perfect positioning for a longer move.

3) Gann Time Alert: This profitable buy signal was confirmed in a third way as both the entry and the exit occurred during Gann time. These are critical times during the market day that are signaled by a KC Collection alert on a 5 minute bar chart.

Note on Osc. Divergence: Another effective leading indication of the P/V Oscillator is illustrated here as its divergence from price predicted the end of the upward move and the upcoming reversal. Immediately following the lower divergence peak on the oscillator, the price dropped nearly 10 points.

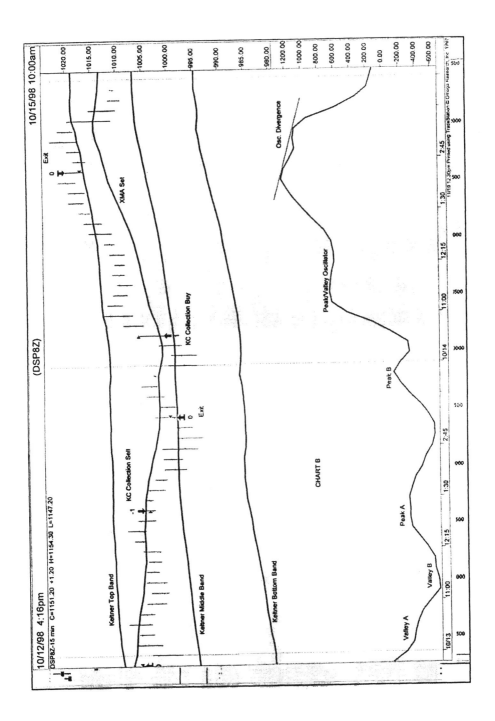

377

CHART C: 11/18/98 — 3 minute Dec. 30 Year T-Bonds

The KC Collection discretionary elements both confirm and filter out the mechanical signals:

Sell Signal:

1) The Peak/Valley Oscillator: This indicator confirms sell signals when the valley just preceding the signal is lower than the previous valley. Since Valley B is *higher* than Valley A, the sell signal and continuation of the downward trend is *not* confirmed.
2) The Bottom Keltner band: We avoid selling into the strong support of any Keltner band. Since the price of the signaled bar is poorly positioned on the Keltner channel for continuance of the trend (the low is so close to the bottom), the sell signal is again *not* confirmed. These two discretionary elements have effectively filtered out this losing sell signal, thus increasing the overall profitability of the system.

Buy Signal:

1) The Peak/Valley Oscillator: Again we are confirming buy signals with this indicator when the peak just preceding the signal is higher than the previous peak. Since Peak B is higher than Peak A, the buy signal and continuation of the upward trend is confirmed.
2) Middle Keltner band and XMA set: Signaled bar closed just above both of these powerful trending indicators: Perfect positioning for a longer move. Buy signal is confirmed.

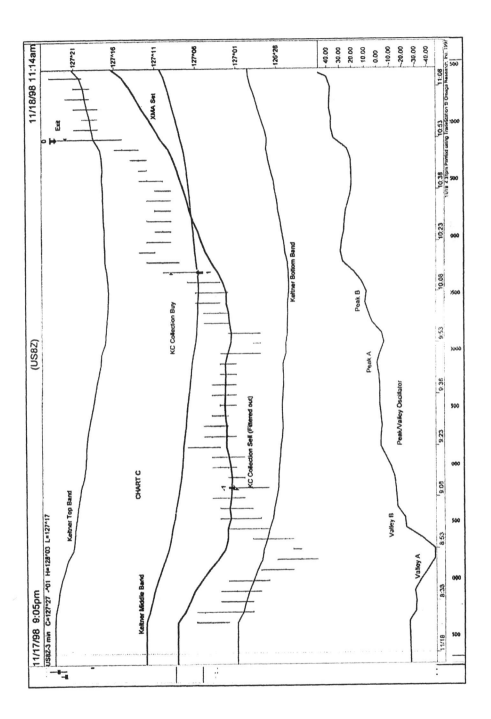

379

CHART D: 11/5/98 — 3 minute Dec. S&P 500

The KC Collection discretionary elements both confirm and filter out the mechanical signals:

Buy 1:

1) The Peak/Valley Oscillator: This indicator confirms buy signals when the peak just preceding the signal is higher than the previous peak. Since Peak C is higher than Peak B (which is higher than Peak A: This is a triple confirmation), the buy signal and continuation of the upward trend is confirmed.

2) Middle Keltner band and XMA set: Signaled bar closed just above both of these powerful trending indicators: Perfect positioning for a longer move.

Buy 2:

Everything is set up for a longer confirmed move, just as in Buy 1. This time we have quadruple upward confirmation at Peak D, with excellent positioning again on both the Middle Keltner band and the XMA Set.

Buy 3:

A very strongly *unconfirmed* buy signal with three things going against it: (1) Very bad positioning for a buy, with the close of the signaled bar just below the Top Keltner band (we don't like buying into the strong resistance of a Keltner band) (2) Peak G is lower than Peak F when it supposed to be higher (3) Strong divergence on the oscillator predicting a reversal to the "north" trend. Again, immediately following the bar corresponding to Peak G, the market began its strong reversal. The discretionary elements have again filtered out a losing signal, thus increasing the overall profitability of the KC Collection.

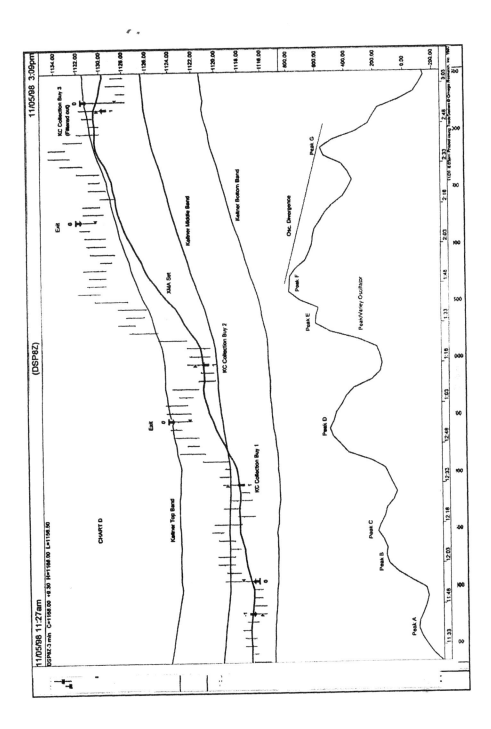

381

MODELING STUDY

CHILDHOOD FAMILY STATUS
- Scott experienced middle class living while growing up in New Jersey

MENTORING - INFLUENCES
- Parents were entrepreneurial and creative
- Desire to succeed and determination were attributes he got from parents
- Books - Norman Mailer - Alan Watts, the philosopher - Aldous Huxley and R.D. Laird
- *Patanjali*, *The Bhagavad-Gita*, ancient Vedas
- Influenced by Fibonacci - natural order behind nature applies to market behavior

ENVIRONMENT
- Traditional Aschkanazi Jewish - considered to be the "smart ones"
- Wanted to be the opposite of his father's distant nature, so it pointed him in the opposite direction
- Enriched spiritual atmosphere

EDUCATION
- Bachelor of Science Degree in Biology with honors

INTERESTS - Skills - Abilities - Honors
Childhood
- Reading
- Amateur radio operator
- Acoustic guitar player

Adult
- Interest in Eastern Philosophy and Medicine

- Traveled through Orient
- Interested in Sciences - then English - then Eastern Thought and Philosophies
- Learned Sanskrit while in India
- Studied ancient Vedas - meaning knowledge - science and art
- Meditation
- Vegetarian - makes you conscious of your actions
- Non fiction author

QUALITIES
- Intuitive (spiritual realizations)
- Analytical
- Determined
- Resourceful
- Enjoys deep friendships
- Perfectionist
- Obsessive/Compulsive

BUSINESS EXPERIENCE
- Worked for a publishing company while in India
- Advertising voice-over work in Hong Kong
- Owned pre-press company
- Import company
- Legal editor
- R.R. Donnally & Sons - put together stock and investment proposals for the SEC
- Distributor of consumer products
- Worked with co-creator of famous cartoon character

PHILOSOPHY - SUCCESS BELIEFS
- Bent toward independence and freedom of thought
- No failure--only feedback
- Culmination of long evolutionary path
- Money is innocent, but its use determines its morality for you

384

- Attributes emotional detachment in trading to his success

PROSPERITY CONSCIOUSNESS
- Funds food relief and spiritual causes

TRADING EXPERIENCE
- Currency trader
- Independent day trader of S&P Index

RECOMMENDATIONS
- Steve Nison's class on Japanese Candlestick charting techniques
- *The Bhagavad-Gita*

TRADING CONTRIBUTIONS
- Author of *How to Become a Real-Time Commodity Futures Trader from Home*
- Author of KC (Keltner Confirmation)-Collection of trading software

FUTURE PLANS
- Novel about India
- Plans to build several homes one of which will be in India
- Have a significant relationship in his life

TRADER GEMS   Fundamental - Intuitive - Psychological
- Trading is all about life - the more detached you are the more successful you become
- When you use intelligent discretion, in addition to a mechanical signal you have everything
- You must check across multiple timeframes in order to get a reliable prospective on the true market direction
- Intuition for trading is a part of the natural order
- Learn to recognize the most important reversal patterns

TRADER GEMS **Mechanical - Analytical - Technical**

- Keltner Channels are a little discussed technical indicator that creates a price envelope similar to Bollinger Bands. It is a moving average plus or minus a given percentage of the average true range.
- Scott's variation of this indicator produces much wider bands than the standard version. He views the standard indicator as too price sensitive
- Keltner channels are best used as a template to overlay other technical systems and discretionary elements. By doing this, you will see patterns that set up over and over again.
- How a trade sets up in the Keltner channel is often indicative of the trade's potential
- A discretionary trader will not be successful unless his analysis covers multiple time frames

Murray's Analytical Modeling Study

Trading Methodology Analysis
Mechanical--Objective: Uses pattern between indicators and Keltner channels to make trades.

Mechanical--Automatic: Charting of indicators used in analysis including his proprietary Keltner channels. Uses charts produced by TradeStation in real time combined with pattern recognition based upon his experience

Discretionary: human expertise for pattern recognition and weighting factors for making the trades.

Analysis of Scott's Methodology
Scott's trading methodology is based upon a proprietary version of Keltner channels. The formula that he calculates creates a price envelope that is much wider and smoother than the standard formula. Scott believes that the calculation of the standard formula is too price sensitive. The outer bands of his Keltner channels are so wide that they become very effective price targets. Prices tend to bounce off of these outer bands and then retrace. Prices often take off from the middle price band. Price action can occur off of the other bands as well. He looks for price patterns and wave-like action relating to the bands which he combines with his special pivot point studies and discretionary elements. Scott trades using multiple timeframes and indicators, which produces a synergy.

One pattern that Scott sees repeatedly is prices crossing the center Keltner band and an oscillator making a higher high, which is often a good entry. Scott believes that studying indicators and prices long enough will enable a trader to discover reliable trading patterns.

Scott did not give us the proprietary formula for his Keltner channel, but we can study the standard Keltner channels. They are like

Bollinger bands except the bands are based on range or TrueRange with the center band being based on a moving average. For example, we can use a five bar moving average plus or minus 2 times the five bar average true range. This combination for standard Keltner channels works fairly well in containing price data on an intraday time frame.

If we combine Keltner studies with other indicators, we can see patterns that are tradable as mechanical objective patterns combined with discretionary elements. The best way to trade this methodology is in the direction of the longer-term trend upon reconfirmation after a retracement. The topic of combining Keltner channels with other technical methods is a good area of research that traders wanting to intraday trade the S&P500 or T-Bond markets should spend time studying.

Adrienne's Psychological Model Study

The Seeker Model

Scott Krieger is a true seeker, and as such, brings to trading the determination to uncover the natural order of the way things work. Scott's "seeker model" developed as a result of his early determination to succeed and to break free from his family and their narrow point of view. Although he wanted desperately to be far from his father's emotional distance, it is this model of emotional distance which has also allowed Scott to be a truly effective seeker and to develop an expanded point of view of the way the world works. His readings also shaped this model and expanded his thinking as he read Norman Mailer, Aldous Huxley and Alan Watts, all independent thinkers who were searching to understand the nature of man and of life. Then, because he is a real seeker, he went outside the lines of Western thinking and began to read the great philosophical and spiritual works of the East. These included the ancient Vedas, which mean "knowledge" in Sanskrit. Synthesizing these readings, he then studied Fibonacci who wrote about the natural order that applies to the market.

Another factor in the development of the "seeker model" for Scott was the fact that he came from the traditional Aschkanazi Jewish order in which you were considered one of the "smart ones." If a child is told that he is part of the intellectual elite, he will either reject the entire notion or spend his life in intellectual pursuit, which is what Scott has done. Not only was he an intellectual seeker, he also became a worldly explorer. He traveled to India and other countries in the Far East, learning first hand about their cultures and ways of thinking. He learned ancient Sanskrit, learned to meditate, and undertook the discipline of vegetarianism. When he returned to the West, he undertook a long list of different assignments, as though he were seeking for the one place to apply his talents: He worked with a printer, made voice-overs, owned a company, imported, did editing work, wrote a book which got him media recognition, etc. None of these efforts seem related as some are creative while others are mechanical. This is much like the activities that he was involved in while in high school - music (creative) and amateur radio (mechanical.) This odd combination of the creative and mechanical, the right brain and the left brain, the analytical and the spiritual, is a perfect reflection of Scott's urge to understand and to seek out the order in things. If Scott were totally wed to one side or the other, he would only be seeing half of the picture. For a true seeker, this imitating response to reality would be anathema.

Scott has successfully applied his seeker model to trading by balancing the intuitive with the mechanical: "When you use intelligent discretion in addition to a mechanical signal, you have everything." This balanced view of trading allows him to view trading as a whole, helps him to discern patterns and to be open to signals from multiple sources. While using the mechanics of his system, his model allows him to be open to his intuition - a winning combination.

CHAPTER 14

Tom Bierovic

On the road again - How a schoolteacher
became an internationally recognized trading teacher
and prolific systems developer.

Can you tell us about where you grew up and some of your early history?

I grew up in Markham, Illinois, a small town southwest of Chicago. My dad owned a hardware store, and our family lived in the back of the store. My folks started with nothing, worked very hard, and created a successful business. Soon after I was born, my dad built us a little house a few blocks from the store.

How about your mom?

My mother came to America as a young girl from a small town in Scotland. Her family settled in Harvey, Illinois, where there was a large Scottish community.

Do you have any siblings?

I have two younger brothers, Brian and Mark. They work together, running the hardware business and another store of their own.

What were you like as a kid?

I had a happy and active childhood. I played little league baseball and football, and went to a YMCA camp in Wisconsin for two weeks every summer. I was in Cub Scouts and my school's band. In all respects, it was a normal and fun childhood in the '50s. Also, from a very young age, I enjoyed reading. My parents and aunts and uncles provided me with all the books I could read.

Can you remember some of the books you enjoyed at the time?
I liked the series of novels about Bronco Burnett, a high-school sports star, and the Hardy Boys mysteries. I also remember reading books about the American Revolution, the Texas Rangers, the FBI, and the French Foreign Legion. I also liked the Sherlock Holmes stories. *Treasure Island* became my favorite book when I was a little older.

Did you work at the hardware store?
I helped out a little at the store, putting price tags on new merchandise and sweeping the floor. When I was twelve, my dad offered me the choice of working at the store or keeping his commodity charts up to date to earn my allowance. I chose commodities. In those days, we would get commodity prices from the newspaper, draw our charts by hand, and calculate a few simple moving averages.

Did your father influence you in that direction?
My dad had a severe stroke when I was in junior high. The doctor told us that it would have killed ninety-nine percent of the people who experienced it. My dad is a very strong man physically and spiritually. He survived the stroke, but his recuperation took months. He made good use of the time by studying Edwards and Magee's *Technical Analysis of Stock Trends*. Eventually, he bought a seat on the old Chicago Open Board of Trade, which is now the Mid America Exchange. When my dad could get away from the hardware store, he traded corn, wheat, and soybean futures in the pits.

Why did he get involved in futures trading in the first place?
He started his trading career by buying stock in companies that reinvested a significant percentage of their profits in research and development. After a short time in stocks, he became more interested in commodities because of the increased leverage.

What were you like as a teenager?
I was a fairly good student in high school. I was a member of the National Honor Society, and I won a scholarship to travel and study in South America after my junior year. My main extracurricular activities were band and tennis. Of course, I was also charting the futures markets and paper trading.

Which subjects were your favorites?
My favorite subjects were English and history. I enjoyed *MacBeth* and *King Lear*. My favorite novels in high school were *The Old Man and the Sea*, *The Pearl*, *The Red Badge of Courage*, and *Catcher in the Rye*.

Tell us about your college experience, where did you go, and why did you make the choices?
I went to Central College, a small liberal arts school in Pella, Iowa. The main reason I chose Central was that they offered me an academic scholarship called the President's Award. Also, Central had very good departments of philosophy and religion, and I was interested in those fields.

Were there any subjects in college that captivated you?
Sure. I especially liked English, history, theology, and philosophy. Philosophy has been the most useful subject I studied. Philosophy taught me how to think, how to learn, how to ask questions, and how to make rational decisions.

Hardware, commodities, religion -- that is a complicated mix. What did you finally choose?
I chose to become a teacher. After college, I taught language arts while completing a masters degree in education. Over the years in my teaching career, I taught at every level from elementary school to high school, college, and adult education.

393

How did you meet your wife?
I took a year off from college to go to Denver to run an activity center for teenagers. The job didn't pay much, so I was living in a VW camper. The parents of the girl who eventually became my wife invited me to live in their basement apartment for a year. Laurie and I got to know each other very well since we were living in the same house, and we got married when we both finished school. We've had 26 very good years together so far.

After you were married where did you live?
After we were married, we moved to Chicago. I taught school and continued to study technical analysis and the financial markets. Laurie began a very successful career in banking. We saved $3,000, and I opened my first commodity account.

Was there something significant about this phase of your trading career?
There was one significant difference between my first trade and the first trades of most new speculators. The difference was that I had studied the markets and paper traded for eight years before I made my first trade.

Tell us about the beginnings of your trading?
For my first trade, I bought 5,000 bushels of soybeans on a breakout of a triple top after a rising bottom on an intraday point-and-figure chart. About fifteen minutes later, I exited the trade with a profit of $950 and actually began calculating how much money I'd be making at $950 every fifteen minutes. It hasn't always been that easy.

What commodity contracts and methodology were you using when you began trading with your $3,000 account?
As you might suspect, the only way I could have survived trading with a $3,000 account was to trade commodities with low margins and to trade one-lots. I traded one contract of corn, wheat or soybeans at a time. My methodology came from the summers I

spent on the floor of the MidAm while my dad traded in the pits. I kept point-and-figure-charts and bar charts with moving averages and trendlines for him. My dad would always find time to trade at the MidAm during the spring and summer when the agricultural markets were active. Basically, I maintained a five-bar simple moving average and a 20-bar simple moving average on 15-minute bars for my dad. We were also using an oscillator -- the spread between the five-bar and 20-bar moving averages.

I continued to use this strategy when I began my own trading. When the five-day moving average was above the twenty-day average, I would be long the market. As long as the oscillator (the difference between the two averages) was making new highs along with prices, I would remain long with a loose trailing stop. However, when there was a bearish divergence, I would tighten the stop to lock in most of the open profit. I used trendlines and pivot points as trailing stops. The five-day average crossing below the twenty-day average would signal an exit from a long position. I tried to anticipate the end of the trend when there was divergence and to move the stop closer to the market in case the loss of momentum was a precursor to a change in the trend.

Did charting by hand help you as a trader?
Yes, although having a computer and TradeStation from the beginning would have helped me more. It's true that maintaining your charts with a pencil, a straight edge, and a piece of graph paper will force you to slow down and take a good look at the market. However, the beginning trader can accomplish this goal without spending countless hours getting prices from a newspaper, drawing charts by hand, and calculating indicators on an adding machine or a slide rule. The important thing is to learn the basics of technical analysis, to become a competent chart analyst, rather than plunging headlong into artificial intelligence, neural networks, fuzzy logic, genetic algorithms, etc. Those fields have a place in the analysis of financial markets, but they are not a good starting point for the

beginning trader. Learn your ABCs before you try to write the great American novel.

How did your trading develop from this starting point?
In 1980, I bought my first computer and technical-analysis software. This made the daily task of maintaining charts and calculating indicators fast and effortless. I was still teaching school, so my free time was limited. Becoming computerized enabled me to devote more time to studying the markets and testing my ideas and less time to updating my charts and indicators.

When was the next major turning point?
I spent several years studying divergences between prices and oscillators. As I mentioned earlier, I had been using divergence as a component of my exit strategy, tightening my stops when there was a divergence against the position. I expanded my use of oscillators and divergences to include entries as well as exits. If a market was oversold but losing bearish momentum, I would buy; if a market was overbought but losing bullish momentum, I would sell short. Guess what? It didn't work very well.

What did you learn from doing this?
I found that using divergence alone as an entry technique is not profitable. By this time, I had several years of trading experience, a computer, state-of-the-art software, and an impressive library of books about trading. Ironically, my trading results were not as good as they had been years earlier. In the "good old days," I was entering long positions on strength, buying high and selling higher. I was selling short low and covering my shorts lower. Then I thought I could make more money by using divergence to pick tops and bottoms. That kind of trading was very appealing to me because when it worked it was spectacular. I was buying just after a market had fallen to a new low and selling short just after a market had risen to a new high. Unfortunately, only about one third of my trades were profitable. As I look back, that shouldn't have been surprising. All my trades were against the direction of the trend.

How did you solve that problem?

I knew that 33% winning trades was not accurate enough without a much greater reward-to-risk ratio than I was getting. For example, if I had two losses of $300 each, my one winner would have to exceed $600 for me to see any profit. My next idea was to find a way to filter out just one of the two losses in an average series of three trades. In other words, I wanted a typical series of three trades to result in one small loss, one win that was bigger than the loss, and -- this is the important part -- one divergence signal that I passed on because subsequent price action did not confirm the signal. Don't misunderstand this -- I did not expect the trades to always or even usually occur in a series of loss, win, pass. I did expect, however, to be able to average 50% winners with a reward-to-risk ratio of at least two-to-one by being more selective in my trades. I had a reasonable goal: lose $300 (for example) on an average loss, make $600 on an average win, and filter out a divergence setup that was not accompanied by trend-following confirmation.

What was the next major turning point of your trading?

I read Buckminster Fuller's book, *Synergetics: Explorations in the Geometry of Thinking*. Fuller taught that synergy represents the integrated behaviors of nature's systems, and that the whole is greater than the sum of its parts.

Can you give us an example?

Sure. An example from Fuller's book is the creation of the first jet engine. The aerospace engineers knew exactly how the jet engine was supposed to work, but they didn't have a metal that was strong enough to withstand the heat and pressure of jet combustion. The prototype engines were always cracking or deteriorating too fast. Eventually, metallurgists came up with an alloy of chrome, nickel, and steel. The alloy was six times stronger than its strongest component and ten times stronger than its weakest component.

How did you apply synergy to your trading?

I realized that by synergizing oscillator-divergence signals and trend-following indicators I could design trading systems that were more accurate, more powerful, and more profitable than the sum of their parts. For trend-following confirmation of oscillator signals, I used trendlines, a moving-average channel of highs and lows, key reversals, the parabolic, true-range expansion, and the spread between a moving average of closes and a moving average of opens. I also created several indicators of my own, including the Pentagon Reversal Pattern, Micro-M Tops / Micro-W Bottoms, and On-Balance True Range.

Will you share one of your indicators with us?
Of course. One of my best indicators is the Micro-M Top / Micro-W Bottom. Here are the rules for trading with Micro-M Tops:

1. When you identify a bearish-divergence high (a new high in price that is accompanied by a lower high in an oscillator), watch for a day that closes below the previous day's close, followed immediately by a day that closes higher.
2. After the down-day / up-day sequence, sell short when prices fall below the low of the down / up pattern. In other words, sell short a tick below the lower of the two days in the down-day / up-day combination. The day of entry does not have to be the day immediately after the down / up pattern. The only days in a Micro-M Top that must be consecutive are the down-close / up-close days. To determine the number of days the set-up is in effect, count the bars from the price high that the oscillator confirmed to the divergent high. Then add that number of days to the up-day of the Micro-M pattern. If prices do not trigger an entry by then, the set-up is canceled.
3. Risk to a tick above the bearish-divergence high or to a tick above the high of the down-day / up-day sequence. Exit when prices decline to your profit objective or rise to your trailing stop.

The rules for trading with Micro-W Bottoms are analogous: you're looking for a bullish-divergence bottom, an up-day / down-day sequence, and a rally above the high of that two-day pattern.

Here's why I think Micro-Ms and Ws work so well: let's take Micro-W Bottoms as an example. After a market forms a bullish divergence, prices will usually rally for at least a few days because new buyers, recognizing the divergence, enter long positions. More often than not, the downtrend reasserts itself, and the weak longs are forced out. However, when the resumption of the downtrend fails, and prices penetrate the high of the up-day / down-day sequence, the rally frequently represents more than just bullish-divergence buying. You see a reversal to an uptrend rather than a short-term rally in a downtrend.

Do you view trading as a form of gambling or as a form of investment?
The kind of trading I do -- carrying a position for a relatively short time (from a few days to several weeks) -- isn't generally considered investing, which implies a much longer holding period. Trading has a lot in common with *skillful* gambling: knowing the odds, varying the bet size, applying sound money management, understanding the psychology of the game, and practicing nearly perfect self discipline. However, there are two important differences between trading and gambling:

1. In gambling, the odds are fixed against you. There are unbeatable, unalterable odds against you in every casino game except blackjack and poker. (For an expert card counter, blackjack is a game of skill; for a professional poker player, poker is an very challenging profession requiring physical stamina, a killer instinct, an expertise in mathematics and probability, and a world-class understanding of applied psychology).

2. The other difference between gambling and trading is the fact that there are real economic reasons for the stock and futures markets to exist apart from providing an opportunity for speculators to make bets on price fluctuations. There are fundamental and technical reasons that the stock and futures markets move in a certain direction. If you understand the

reasons, it will give you an edge that doesn't exist in pure gambling. However, there is no real reason for the existence of a roulette wheel or a craps table, except to make it possible for gamblers to bet on where the ball is going to land or what number is going to come up on the dice.

Were you ever interested in gambling or playing games?
Many years ago, I spent some time in Las Vegas trying to learn to play poker. Although I had studied several books and could win a little money consistently in low-limit games, I usually ended up losing against tougher competition. In a 48-hour marathon of Texas Hold 'Em, I was one of the losers, and Doyle Brunson (a repeat champion of the annual World Series of Poker) was the big winner. Over coffee, I asked Brunson if he knew why I hadn't been able to win in the big games. I'll always remember his answer. He said, "You don't win because you think poker's a card game. Great players could play without any cards." I caught the next flight back to Chicago and my commodity charts. Although I travel to Las Vegas once or twice a year to speak at trading conferences, I've never played high-stakes poker again.

I remember that you have a defined risk and a defined profit objective on every trade before entering. Why do you feel that's important?
The most important requirement for a trader's success is that he trades in a way that is consistent with his own personality and belief system. "To thine own self be true," Shakespeare said. I've always needed simplicity, structure, and a clear vision of the path ahead. My trading method has to reflect those values. I need to know why I'm getting into a trade, where I'll get out if the market moves against me, and how I'll exit with a profit if the market trends in my favor. I have to be careful not to overcomplicate my trading method, not to make up new rules as I go along, and not to lose sight of my goals. These are not necessarily the same values that other traders need to focus on, but they are important to me.

So, how do you determine the entry, the risk, and your profit objective?

One of my best systems is called Momentum Retracement. In Momentum Retracement, the entry, the risk, and the profit objective are well-defined.

Can you share some details? What makes your system unique?

In Momentum Retracement, I first determine the trend. I use exponential moving averages of highs and lows with a faster EMA of closes. I confirm that trend indicator with the signal line of a sensitive MACD. Second, I check to see if the trend has good momentum and consistent directional movement. I use an RSI to evaluate the momentum and the DMI spread to evaluate the market's current "trendiness." (The DMI spread is the difference between the + Directional Index and the − Directional Index of Welles Wilder's Directional Movement Index.)

If you determine that the market's in a good uptrend, what do you do next?

Next I look for a retracement. At least three of these four conditions must be met: prices decline into a moving-average channel, the MACD line crosses below the signal line, the RSI declines below its midpoint, and the countertrend decline is at least a 38.2% but not more than a 61.8% retracement of the previous trend wave.

What's next after you identify a retracement?

In an uptrend with RSI declining at yesterday's close, I buy at a one-third retracement of the countertrend decline; in other words, one third of the way back up. If RSI was rising at yesterday's close, I buy at one-third of the way back up or at a return to yesterday's high, whichever is lower.

Once you're long the market, how do you determine your protective stop in case you're wrong?

I set a protective stop at the low of the countertrend decline or at one ten-day average true range below my entry point, whichever is lower.

What's your strategy when the trade goes your way?
I trail a stop at the highest high since entry minus one tick more than the size of the previous corrective wave. Let's review a little. I look for an impulse wave and a corrective wave. I buy if the market starts back up, and I set a reasonable protective stop. Then I trail a stop at the highest high since entry minus one tick more than the number of ticks in the corrective wave.

Do you always continue to trail such a loose stop until the market stops you out?
No. There's a time to trail a loose stop and a time to trail a tight stop. On the day that the market reaches my profit target, I raise the trailing stop to the intraday low.

How do you decide on the profit target?
I rely on a measured-move objective. It's a little complicated to explain, but here goes: After my entry into a long position, I look back on the chart and find the most recent pivot-point low (a low with higher lows to its left and right) that would make the recent countertrend decline a 38.2% to a 68.1% retracement of the uptrend. Then I subtract that pivot-point low from the high of the uptrend and add the difference to the low of the countertrend decline. That's the measured-move objective.

What?
Sorry. I'm hoping that the new upswing will go up as many points as the previous upswing did. When it does, I'll tighten my stop.

How important to you is trading psychology?
Psychology is the most important aspect of trading. There are hundreds of profitable trading systems, but not many traders who

can follow them. Very few traders of stocks and commodities have ever followed the rules of a system for ten consecutive trades. To become a successful trader, however, you must learn to follow the rules of your system for hundreds and thousands of trades. Of course, you need to acquire a basic knowledge of the financial markets, and you must learn or create a profitable trading system, but that's just the beginning. The real challenge is to develop mental toughness and self-discipline

How do you adapt to a changing market?
I think that the best way to deal with changing markets is to design trading systems based on market truths that do not change. For example, a system that makes money buying Orange Juice futures on alternate Thursday mornings at 11:35 if the Dow is down by at least 15 points may test well but might not be likely to maintain its profitability into the future. I prefer systems that attempt to capitalize on a more general kind of market tendency. Micro-Ms, for example, make money because they accurately depict the battle between bulls and bears at a certain type of market top. An overbought, divergent market attracts new sellers. When the bearish-divergence selling is exhausted, the uptrend reasserts itself. If the resumption of the uptrend fails, and prices fall below the low of the previous decline, the market is more likely to continue lower than to rally to a new high. In my opinion, that's the kind of market truth that is unlikely to change in our lifetime or beyond.

So, you are mapping crowd psychology that is rooted in human nature and that will probably endure for the foreseeable future?
All the classical chart patterns that have been studied and traded for many years are really applied social psychology. Head-and-shoulders patterns, triangles, flags, rectangles, and so forth, graphically describe the behavior of crowds under the intense strain of hope, disappointment, fear, and greed. Basic human nature does not change quickly or easily. Trading methods based on these truths will probably continue to perform well.

403

Where do you want to go from here in your trading or in your life? Is there something else that you want to do?

I've been very fortunate my whole life. No complaints at all. I've enjoyed studying the markets, trading, and teaching people how to trade better. One thing I'd like to do in the future is to become more adept at programming and testing my trading ideas. Although it's been a long time since I relied on colored pencils, graph paper, a straight edge, and a slide rule, I still need to work on my computer skills to stay competitive.

[Editors' Note: We interviewed Tom in May, 1998, at the Omega World trading conference in Orlando, Florida. Tom told us he wanted to find a way to improve his computer and programming skills so that he could write and test his own trading systems. On June 1st, Tom accepted a newly created position at Omega Research, Inc., the company that produces SuperCharts, OptionStation, and TradeStation software for systems traders. In addition to trading for his own account every day, Tom is now Manager of System Trading & Development Education at Omega. His main responsibilities are to become an expert user of Omega's software so that he can offer suggestions to Omega from a trader's point of view, to increase his knowledge of EasyLanguage (the language Omega invented for designing and testing trading systems), and to share his trading ideas with Omega's customers by creating educational programs. Be careful what you wish for, Tom; you might get it!]

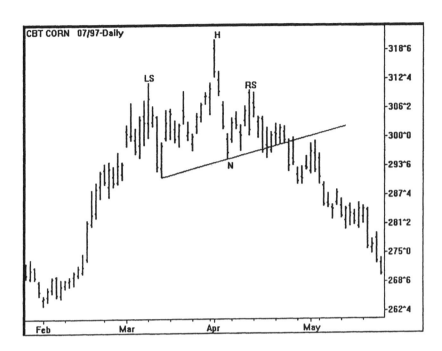

CBT CORN 07/97-Daily

Head-and-shoulders tops and bottoms are among Bierovic's favorite reversal patterns. LS is the left shoulder, H is the head, RS is the right shoulder, and N is the neckline. Sell short when the market penetrates the neckline. Risk to a tick above the right shoulder. To determine the minimum profit objective, calculate the distance from the top of the head to the neckline and subtract that distance from the point at which prices decline below the neckline.

Created with TradeStation by OmegaResearch © 1996

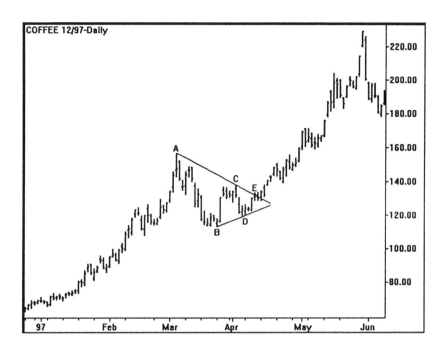

Symmetrical triangles are usually continuation patterns. After the upthrust from January to March, prices formed a symmetrical triangle. Draw the triangle by connecting points A and C and points B and D. Buy at E when prices rally above line A – C. The minimum price objective is determined by measuring the height of the triangle (the high of A minus the low of B) and adding that distance to the breakout point at E. As was true in this case, a market frequently exceeds the minimum price objective.

Created with TradeStation by OmegaResearch © 1996

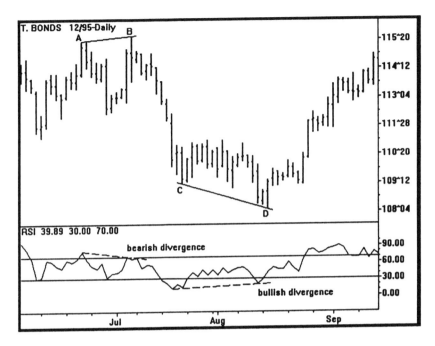

Bearish divergence occurs when prices rally to a higher high, but an oscillator (e.g. RSI) fails to make a new high. (See line A – B) Bullish divergence occurs when prices decline to a lower low, but an oscillator fails to make a new low. (See line C – D)

Created with TradeStation by OmegaResearch © 1996

407

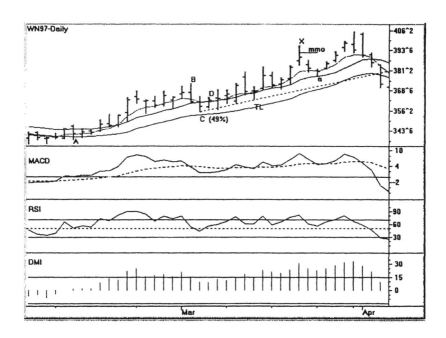

Here is an example of a Momentum Retracement trade in the wheat market.

A (low) = 338 1/2
B (high) = 373
C (low) = 356
D (entry price) = 361 3/4

B-A = 34 1/2
B-C = 17
17 ÷ 34 1/2 = .49, so the corrective wave was a 49% retracement of the impulse wave.

17 ÷ 3 = 5.7; 5.7 + 356 = 361.7
Bought at 361 3/4 on day D; risked to 356 (361 3/4 − 356 = 5 3/4, $287.50)
Exited at 390 1/2, the measured-move objective (356 + 34 1/2) for a gain of $1,437.50 per contract. The reward-to-risk ratio was 5 to 1.

Created with TradeStation by OmegaResearch © 1996

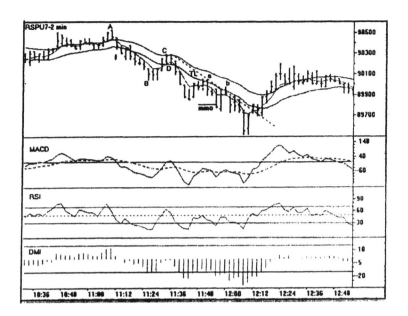

This is an example of a Momentum Retracement trade on a 2-minute chart of the S&P.
A (high) = 90525
B (low) = 90050
C (high) = 90290
D (entry price) = 90210

A-B = 475
C-B = 240
240 ÷ 475 = .51, so the corrective wave was a 50% retracement of the impulse wave.

240 ÷ 3 = 80; 90290 − 80 = 90210
Sold short at 90210 on bar D; risked to 90290 (90290 − 90210 = 80, $400)
Exited at 89815, the measured-move objective (A-B = 475. 90290 (C) − 475 = 89815)
The gain was 395 points, which is $1,975 per contract. The reward-to-risk ratio was 4.9 to 1.

Created with TradeStation by OmegaResearch © 1996

MODELING STUDY

CHILDHOOD FAMILY STATUS
- Tom experienced going from poor to comfortable in Illinois

MENTORING - INFLUENCES
- Dad was an entrepreneur with spiritually and physically strong survival mechanisms
- Father owned a seat on the Mid-American Exchange trading corn, wheat, and soybeans
- Tom kept commodities charts up for his father
- Mother was an immigrant from Scotland

ENVIRONMENT
- Supportive immediate family
- Good supportive marriage

EDUCATION
- Master Degree in Education

INTERESTS - Skills - Abilities - Honors
Childhood
- Little League football
- Camp
- Cub Scouts
- School band
- Loved reading - solving mysteries - sports and high risk heroes
- Interested in religion

Adult
- Enjoyed English and History - favorites *Macbeth & King Lear* (self awareness of flaw and books about individual courage)
- Member of National Honor Society
- Won scholarship to travel and study in South America

QUALITIES
- Flexible
- Clever
- Dedicated
- People person
- Good communication skills
- Optimistic

BUSINESS EXPERIENCE
- Taught language arts - at all levels of education
- International speaker for the financial field
- Entrepreneur

PHILOSOPHY - SUCCESS BELIEFS
- Think, learn, ask questions, and make rational decisions
- When he commits to any new venture, he approaches it as if it were already successful.

PROSPERITY CONSCIOUSNESS
- Mentor for traders

TRADING EXPERIENCE
- Studied the market 8 years before entering his first trade
- Spent summers on the floor of the Mid-American Exchange while his father traded in the pits
- Learned charting by hand, which forces you to slow down and take a good look at the market

RECOMMENDATIONS
- *Flow: The Psychology of Optimal Experience*, by Mihaly Csikszentmihalyi
- *Market Wizards* and *The New Market Wizards*, by Jack Schwager
- *Schwager on Futures: Technical Analysis*, by Jack Schwager

- *Technical Analysis of Stock Trends*, by Edwards and Magee
- *Trading As a Business,* by Charlie Wright
- *Synergetics*: *Explorations in the Geometry of Thinking*, by Buckminster Fuller

TRADER CONTRIBUTIONS
- Teacher and mentor to new traders
- Writer of articles for trading newspapers and magazines
- Has spoken in 35 countries teaching technical analysis and trading
- Wrote a book called *Playing for Keeps, Ten Trading Systems that Really Work*

FUTURE PLANS
- Continue to teach, research, trade, and write
- Improve computer skills

TRADER GEMS Fundamental - Intuitive - Psychological
- To be a good trader you must:
    Know the odds
    Vary the bet size
    Apply sound money management practices
    Understand the psychology of the game
    Practice nearly perfect self-discipline
    Be consistent with your own personality and belief system
    Not complicate your trading method
    Not make up new rules as you go along
    Not lose sight of goals
    Remember that psychology is the most important part of keeping discipline
- All of the classic chart patterns that have been studied and traded over the years are applied studies of social psychology
- It is important to learn technical analysis and become a competent chart analyst before going into anything else

413

TRADER GEMS   Mechanical - Analytical - Technical

- Tom learned to trade with a very small account and has never had to add to that account, which shows that he learned to be a defensive trader
- He learned to be one with the markets by hand charting the markets
- Tom uses oscillator/price divergence to help him set stops He trades with the trend and uses a loose stop until he sees a divergence against the trend. When he sees a bearish divergence in an uptrend and bullish divergence in a downtrend, he tightens his stops
- He learned the basics of market analysis before learning more advanced methods of analysis
- The concept of synergy is important in trading and is the heart of Bierovic's trading methodology. Tom learned that he could combine indicators to work better than the individual indicators themselves. Divergence alone does not work well as an entry method because as a stand-alone trading method, you only win about 33% of your trades
- Tom confirms trend following oscillator signals using:
    1. moving average channel of highs and lows
    2. key reversal patterns
    3. trend lines
    4. parabolic analysis
    5. TrueRange expansion
    6. spread relationship between moving average of the close and the open.
- Before entering a trade, you need to define the risk and potential expectation for the trade
- The concept of momentum retracement, which is entering a position in the direction of the long-term trend after a counter trend move, is the heart of Tom's trading methodology. See charts at end of chapter for an explanation of how he trades.

Murray's Analytical Modeling Study

Tom's Patterns and Indicators

1. Micro-M tops
2. Micro-W Bottoms
3. On Balance TrueRange

In the interview Tom explains the concept of Micro Tops and Bottoms and is a trading gem by itself.

Trading Analysis
Tom has shared many of his trading methods with us. Some of these methods are unique to him, while others are variations and different implementations of methodologies which are at the heart of many successful traders' methods.

Trade Methodology Analysis
Mechanical--Objective: Combining systematic approaches which cannot be mechanized to measure price targets and entries. An example of this is Fibonacci retracement analysis.

Mechanical--Automatic: Charting of indicators used in analysis.

Discretionary--Weighting the factors used to decide if a trade should be taken.

Analysis of Tom's Methodology
Starting with how Tom uses oscillator/price divergence to help him set stops, he trades with the trend and uses a loose, trailing stop until he sees a divergence against the trend. When he sees a bearish divergence in an uptrend or a bullish divergence in a downtrend, he tightens his stops.

Let's analyze how and why this works. In a classic sense, momentum precedes price. If the market is losing momentum, then you should expect the market to turn. If we view this in terms of Elliott wave analysis, we often get divergence at the end of waves 1, 3, and 5. In Waves 1 and 3, corrections often lead to retracements of nearly 50%. The question is "why give up that much profit?" Since divergence occurs when the market is moving in the direction of the trend, it will often happen near an extreme point. When the market turns back in the direction of the trend after a retracement, we will reenter the trade. If the market makes a deeper correction than anticipated, we will still protect most of the profits. Waves 3 and 5 rarely end without divergence. Wider stops are used before a divergence appears because subdivisions of waves 3 and 5 can result in explosive moves which would stop a trade out of a trend and not allow a low-risk reentry.

The Problem with Trade Entries Based on Divergence
Tom discussed divergence not working well as an entry method because it only wins about 33% of its trades and the win/loss ratio will give only break even results. This is because a move can continue in the direction of the trend long after a divergence occurs. Tom found that by combining different technical elements with divergence, he could obtain better results than individual elements. This concept called synergy is important in trading and is the heart of Bierovic's trading methodology. This concept of combining technical elements is very effective and has been proven to be successful for many methodologies.

One example of this concept of synergy is the Cambridge hook. Analyzing Tom's work and the work James T. Kneafsey, Ph.D. illustrates of how similar methods can be developed by starting with different approaches. In Tom's case, he started with divergence and added other patterns and indicators. In the case of the Cambridge hook, Kneafsey started with key reversal days and added divergence and other filters to develop his hook indicator. The hook pattern is based on RSI levels as well as divergence with price. Kneafsey also

416

incorporated volume and open interest patterns as well as price patterns to form the Cambridge hook. Tom's work uses a more advanced and reliable pattern, the Micro M Top and Micro W Bottom, as a trigger instead of the key reversal days.

Momentum Retracement: Another Classic Concept

The concept of momentum retracement is another classic concept that still works today. Tom has researched this concept and developed a very reliable version of it. Let's discuss some of the elements that make Tom's work unique.

First, he confirms the direction of the trend by:

1. Taking an exponential moving average of the highs and lows
2. Calculating a faster exponential moving average of the closes
3. Determining if the faster moving average of the closes is above the slower moving average of the highs. If it is, then the trend is up. If the faster average is below the slower moving average of the lows then the trend is down.
4. Confirm the trend using MACD, RSI, and the spread between DMI+ and DMI-. The DMI spread is the raw indicator which creates ADX.

Once the trend has been confirmed, Tom looks for a retracement which meets at least three of these four conditions:

1. Prices decline into a moving average channel in an uptrend and rally into one during a downtrend.
2. MACD line crosses the signal line.
3. RSI crosses though the midpoint.
4. The countertrend move is at least 38.2%, but less than retracement of the previous move in the direction of the trend.

417

Rules for Entering a Long Position in an Uptrend
In an uptrend, with an RSI decline based on yesterday's close, Tom enters on a one-third retracement of the counter-trend decline. In other words, he buys as the market is on the way back up. If RSI was rising yesterday in an uptrend, he buys at the one-third point or yesterday's high, whichever is lower.

Rules for Entering a Short Position in a DownTrend
Tom did not give us his rules for entry in a downtrend, but let's use the inverse of the buy rules listed above.

If we are in a downtrend, and RSI is rising at yesterday's close, we would sell after the market has declined one-third of the counter-trend rally. If RSI was falling, we would sell at this point, or yesterday's low, whichever is higher.

In both cases, the predictive stop is placed at the swing point formed by the counter-trend move or at least one ten-day average true range from the entry price, whichever is further away from the entry.

If the trade is profitable, the trailing stop is the highest high since entry minus one tick more than the size of the previous corrective wave for long trades. For a short trade, it is the lowest low since entry plus the size of the previous corrective wave plus one tick. Once the market reaches Tom's target price, he tightens his stops. The targets assume the next market move will go as far as the previous move in the same direction. When the market reaches this price level, Tom tightens his stops.

The concept of momentum retracement is deeply rooted in many trading methodologies. One example of this is the work of Richard Dunnigan, *New Blueprints for Gains in Stocks and Grain & One Way Formula for Trading in Stocks and Commodities* reprinted by Pitman Press in 1997, and originally published in 1957. I discussed this book in my November 1998 article in *Futures Magazine*. This method works because trend-following methodologies typically require very wide stops. Trading these retracement levels accompanied by a continuation of the original pattern, offers lower risk trade entry opportunities combined with the possibility of large winning trades.

Adrienne's Psychological Modeling Study

The Independent Thinker Model

Tom Bierovic was helping out in his father's hardware store and charting commodities when his schoolmates were playing football and watching television after school. In addition, he was an avid reader. His favorite books were about brave and clever individuals who fought wars or villains, solved mysteries, and found buried treasure. In the midst of his happy, normal childhood, his father had a stroke. What did Tom learn from these early experiences? First, he learned from his reading that the individual, pitted against the forces around him, could win. And from his own father, he learned that utter determination could pull you out of a potential tragedy. Finally, he learned very early that the markets required disciplined observation and that you could make money in them.

By charting commodities in such a formative period of his life, Tom learned lessons about how the world operated. Then, in college, he studied philosophy and religion. These disciplines, when taught well, train young minds to think about the most important questions in life. All of these experiences freed Tom to make choices that were off of the beaten path; he chose teaching as a profession and ran a center for teenagers. You would think that after having spent his youth charting commodities that he would bide his time in college just waiting to get onto the floor of an exchange to trade on his own. However, Tom's early lessons in life led him to do what he wanted to do. When he was in the midst of his teaching, Tom was spending his days demonstrating to others ways to think and question. By that time, Tom had also developed a model of independent thinking and action.

This model has served Tom very well in his systems development and trading, while his teaching experience has also shown him that you have to "learn your ABC's before you to try to write the great American novel."

Tom further expanded his universe and his thinking by traveling the world as a speaker for the Dow-Jones Telerate tours to over thirty countries. He has done this for many years, up to the present time. While speaking is a tremendously expanding experience, it is also a very physically and mentally demanding one. Each culture has its own requirements that must be met for individual acceptance. One day, you have six people at your seminar, and the next day, there will be several hundred in attendance.

In addition to adapting to a different weather environment each day, you also have to adapt to the legal and political environment, which is sometimes very threatening. The result for Tom was an expanded awareness and independent thinking. People with a safe world and a limited safe environment to live in know what to expect from each day. This limited daily experience has the effect of reducing the arena in which a person can think and operate.

Having completed one of these tours myself and having traveled in six different countries and nine different cities in two weeks, I can personally attest to the tremendous pressure you are under to adapt and think creatively in order to function. How has this model affected Tom's success as a trader? The model has given Tom the unique ability to develop ten new trading systems every eight weeks in his new position at Omega World as Manager of System Trading and Development. I know few traders who could handle the demands of this position. It is one thing to be able to develop one unique system and hone it until it produces results. It is quite another thing to be able to think in such a way as to visualize dozens of unique possibilities.

MODELING STUDY
Overview

- The success of traders has nothing to do with their family status when they grew up.
- Most traders had mentoring influences of entrepreneurial parents and others that influenced them to attain the qualities of a good trader.
- Another general theme is an enterprising spirit at a young age.
- Many traders were not "whiz kids" in primary school, but they did show exceptional ability in some talent or skill.
- While most of our traders did attend college, education for trading was ultimately self-taught.
- Achieving the discipline that comes with team sports, artistic skills, and competitive games is something that we see in all of these traders.
- All are copious readers when it comes to trading.
- Even when working for others, they were entrepreneurial in their thinking.
- All but two use discretion as an indicator to make trading decisions and one believes that is the next level he wants to reach.
- Intuition for most of them is as important or even more important than technical skills.
- They all believe that self-growth and psychology are important to developing as a trader.
- They are generous in time and/or money to family, charities, the financial world, and society.
- All of the traders have a supportive environment.
- Religion or spirituality is an important part of their lives.
- All of them enjoy trading, challenges, and continued growth in all areas of their lives.

423

Where do you go from here?

If you want to shorten your path to success, make the decision to use any or all of the models presented in this book. Before you proceed, I would like to pass on to you the most important modeling lessons of successful trading that I have distilled from the hundreds of traders with whom I have worked.

Before you start out, you must know where you are going and which route you are going to take. So, develop a business plan including your system or methodology.

Second, in reference to your system, if you do not have a system, buy one and make it your own, have someone develop one for you and make it your own, or develop a system or methodology for yourself.

Third, once your system is in place, test it until you believe that it is going to give you a positive outcome. If you do not believe in your system, do not trade it. If you have a system that cannot be tested because it is discretionary or for some other reason, choose a company to track your system while you test trade it without risking your capital.

Fourth, if you discover patterns of sabotage in your trading which keep you from following your system, seek psychological coaching before you lose your capital.

And finally, when you are consistent in following your rules for trading, a new and improved version will emerge because you will see patterns within your system that can be improved.

We wish you profitable trading!

Trading on Target
Resources and Services

Resources

The Winning Edge 1	Psychology of trading
The Winning Edge 2	A coach in a book
Dear Coach **book**	Questions & Answers
Get a Life: Treasure Diary	Building self-confidence
Traders's Evaluation	Pinpoint psychological issues
Six Steps to Great Success **Video**	A model for reaching success
Trading on Target 2, 3, 4 **tapes**	Interviews of top traders
Discipline Workshops 1, 2, 3 **tapes**	Models for discipline
Heebie-Jeebie/At-a-Boy **tape**	Overcoming stress
The Commitment **tape**	For starting the day right
Trading on Target Newsletter	Discipline perspective

Services

Workshops	On psychological issues
Seminars	For transformations
Private Consultation	For major life changes

For additional information contact:

Trading on Target
100 Lavewood Lane
Cary, North Carolina 27511
Call   (919) 851-8288
Fax   (919) 851-9979
E-Mail Adtoghraie@aol.com

Ruggiero Associates
Resources and Services

1. **Time Tested Trading Methods for Profit Home Study Course**
   This course contains six hours of video, software, course book and work-book which will teach you many of the classical trading methodology which have withstood the test of time. TradeStation and Supercharts users will actually be able to test all of the methods in this course historical and allow them to use them in their future trading. Finally, you get three hours of consulting .

2. **Inside Advantage System Trading Newsletter and Disk Service**
   This newsletter contains fully disclosed mechanical trading systems. Many of these systems have outperformed $3,000 systems that are on the market. The disk service included the systems from this newsletter as well as other utilities for TradeStation and Super-Charts, for example a NextOpen command which allows back-testing of system which requires knowing tomorrow's open when using a multi-data chart.

3. **TradeCycle**
   MEM based cycle tool for TradeStation and SuperCharts. Cycle trading software with user functions for developing adaptive system and indicator based on the MEM algorithms.

4. **Intermarket HomeStudy Course**
   This Course will first overview how markets interrelate and how these relationships can be used to predict future market direction for various markets, bonds, stocks, crude oil, gold etc. Next it will show you how to use these relationships to develop mechanical trading systems. This course comes with 7.5 hours of video, plus software and three hours of one-on-one consultation.

5. **Universal Seasonal**
   Automatically find and test seasonal patterns in any market using TradeStation or Supercharts.

6. **TSEvolve**
   Use Genetic Algorithms in TradeStation to automatically discover trading systems

7. **Report Day Database**
   This is a database of government report released dates and dates of the 2,5,10 and 30 year auctions. We then show you how to develop mechanical trading systems using this information.

If you have any questions or would like more information contact:

Ruggiero Associates
1-800-211-9785 or 203-469-0880.